ARE JEWS REALLY NO GOOD AT SPORT?

MICHAEL MEYERSON

Copyright © Michael Meyerson 2021

All rights reserved.

No part of this publication may be altered, reproduced, distributed, or transmitted in any form, by any means, including, but not limited to, scanning, duplicating, uploading, hosting, distributing, or reselling, without the express prior written permission of the publisher, except in the case of reasonable quotations in features such as reviews, interviews, and certain other non-commercial uses currently permitted by copyright law.

CONTENTS

FOREWORD VII

INTRODUCTION 1

CHAPTER 1   ATHLETICS...9

CHAPTER 2   SWIMMING 65

CHAPTER 3   GYMNASTICS 106

CHAPTER 4   MARTIAL ARTS 123

CHAPTER 5   WEIGHTLIFTING 189

CHAPTER 6   WATERSPORTS..198

CHAPTER 7   WATER POLO...230

CHAPTER 8   SOCCER..239

CHAPTER 9   TABLE TENNIS..265

CHAPTER 10 BASKETBALL 280

CHAPTER 11 TENNIS..290

CHAPTER 12 FIELD HOCKEY..300

CHAPTER 13 OTHER SPORTS...306

CONCLUSION...317

APPENDICES 319

ABOUT THE AUTHOR 331

ACKNOWLEDGEMENTS 333

REFERENCES..335

TO SOPHIE

FOREWORD

Mike Meyerson has an encyclopaedic knowledge of Jewish sporting achievement. This is a subject on which he has been gathering information for more than thirty years, as I discovered when I was researching a book on the subject myself fifteen years ago. Meyerson's archive, to which he generously gave me access, was invaluable. His interest in Jewish sport, I soon realised, was far wider than merely a concern with sporting statistics, results and records. He is just as interested in the people and wider social contexts behind the games and contests in which Jews have prominently competed. What readers of this book will find is not only a comprehensive account of Jewish sporting achievements but also a wealth of information about the people and personalities behind them. They will hear fascinating stories—some of them moving, some heroic, some humorous, and some tragic.

Many of these stories illustrate the bigotry faced by Jews in the first half of Twentieth Century Europe, and the courage and resilience with which Jewish athletes responded. Readers will hear the stories of several Jewish athletes who survived Nazi concentration camps to go on to compete at the Olympics, and how three of them set world records and one of them won a gold medal. Irony is another recurrent theme of the book. Meyerson tells of how Leni Riefenstahl's Nazi propaganda film 'Olympia' unintentionally celebrated the achievements of a Jewish athlete, and he relates the story of a German scientist in charge of Germany's nuclear weapons program during World War Two who came to owe his life to a Jewish athlete.

Meyerson finds an ingenious way of rating Jewish sporting achievements against a standard, by comparing them systematically with those of a country whose sporting excellence is beyond dispute—namely, Australia. With this device he decisively disproves the still prevalent misconception that Jews lack sporting talent, and indeed shows that, if anything, they have far more than their fair share!

Paul Taylor

INTRODUCTION

Among the many myths spread about Jews, one that is relatively benign, but is nevertheless annoying, is the old story that Jews are no good at sport. It is reflected in the words of bigots such as the American representative to the International Olympic Committee in 1936, General Charles H. Sherrill, who once said: 'There never was a prominent Jewish athlete in history'.[1]

The influential Australian journalist, Philip Adams, known for his generally sceptical outlook on things, writes in *The Weekend Australian* that he 'can't think of too many Jewish sporting heroes, if you leave out David's gold-medal skills with the sling-shot', and adds, by way of example, that it's 'hard to think of a Jewish golfer on the US circuit'.[2] I briefly rebutted Adams's claim in *The Skeptic*.[3] A fuller repudiation seems worthwhile, hence the chapters that follow.

While Adams cannot think of a single Jewish golfer on the US PGA circuit, a quick internet search brings to light ten of them. They are: Amy Alcott (29 LPGA wins), Corey Pavin (15 wins), Herman Barron (4 wins), Jonathan Kaye (3 wins), Morgan Pressel (2 wins), Bruce Fleischer (1 win), Monte Scheinblum, Skip Kendall, Rob Oppenheim, and Laetitia Beck. (Pavin subsequently converted to 'Born Again' Christianity!)

The claim that Jews are no good at sport is disproved by books such as Paul Taylor's *Jews and the Olympic Games*. One reviewer described this as a book that 'finally and forever puts to rest the myth that Jews aren't sportspeople'. Myths, however, are not easily put to rest. It took Philip Adams just a few taps of the keyboard to revitalise the one about Jews and sport.

There are accurate records of the results at the modern Olympic Games since its inception in 1896 to the present day. At the Summer Olympic Games Jewish athletes have won at least 510 medals, of which 222 are gold. One would think that this medal tally alone would be sufficient to bury the myth that Jews are no good at sport. Perhaps the most conclusive method for refuting this myth is, however, by a comparison. Australia is surely one of the great sporting nations. Let's therefore compare the success of Jewish Olympians against Australian Olympians. This is a fair comparison because the current world Jewish population is about 14 million while the population of Australia is about 25 million, whereas from 1896 until 2018 the average population of the two groups has been similar—approximately 12 million.

Michael Meyerson

An internet search provides a list of athletes considered to be Australia's ten most successful Olympic athletes. I have compared the Olympic records of these Australians—legends all—with my choice of the ten most successful Jewish Olympic athletes.

The Australian athletes won the following medals:

	Gold	Silver	Bronze	Total
Ian Thorpe—swimming	5	3	1	9
Dawn Fraser—swimming	4	4	0	8
Libby Trickett—swimming	4	1	2	7
Murray Rose—swimming	4	1	1	6
Betty Cuthbert—athletics	4	0	0	4
Liesel Jones—swimming	3	5	1	9
Petria Thomas—swimming	3	4	1	8
Grant Hackett—swimming	3	3	1	7
Shirley Strickland—athletics	3	1	3	7
Shane Gould—swimming	3	1	1	5
TOTALS	36	23	11	70

Are Jews Really No Good at Sport?

My chosen Jewish athletes won the following medals:

	Gold	Silver	Bronze	Total
Mark Spitz—swimming	9	1	1	11
Ágnes Kéleti—gymnastics	5	4	2	11
Morris Fisher—shooting	5	0	0	5
Dara Torres—swimming	4	4	4	12
Jason Lezak—swimming	4	2	2	8
Myer Prinstein—athletics	4	1	0	5
Lenny Krayzelburg—swimming	4	0	0	4
Jenö Fuchs—fencing	4	0	0	4
Irena Kirszenstein—athletics	3	2	2	7
Aly Raisman—gymnastics	3	2	1	6
TOTALS	45	15	13	73

The Jewish athletes won a total of 73 medals, whereas the Australians won 70, but more striking is the discrepancy in the gold medal count. Jewish athletes won 45 golds compared to 36 won by the Australians.

Moreover, amongst these sports heroes there is one athlete who is surely the hero of heroes. That is Mark Spitz, who in 1972 won seven gold medals—all in world record times.[4]

While myths will forever be perpetuated, official records cannot be disputed. Analysis of the Olympic records reveals a multitude of Jewish athletes who qualify as sporting heroes. If the biblical David—almost certainly mythological—is the only 'Jewish sporting hero' that Adams can recall, then the record books show that his knowledge is massively defective. Adams's biblical David may have been the first Jewish sporting legend, but he was certainly not the last.

In this book I propose to present a comprehensive argument in defense of Jewish sporting prowess. I will do this using the Summer Olympic Games as my reference point because there are many sports that make up the Olympics and, as mentioned, records of the Games have been kept since their inception. Books listing successful Jewish athletes, of which there are several, all have a common flaw—a list of athletes (and their accomplishments) does not allow us to gauge the relative ability of Jewish athletes—hence my plan to address this issue by comparing the achievements of Jewish athletes with those of Australian athletes. Not only are the two groups similar in number but, if a correction is made for current population, then Australia tops the world in the number of Olympic medals won. Taking current population numbers as the standard, Australia has won one medal per 50,000 people.[5] Compare that figure with the USA 1/136,000, Great Britain 1/87,000, France 1/102,000 and China 1/3.4 million.

We need, however, also to consider that Australia has competed unhindered in all the Olympic Games. Jewish athletes have been hampered by genocide, terrorism, bannings, boycotts, sanctions and selection bigotry. Obstacles with which Jewish athletes have had to contend include the following (1) Hungary, Austria, Turkey and Germany, with their large Jewish populations, were excluded from competing in the 1920 Games as punishment for their part in World War One. (Germany also remained excluded from the 1924 Games.) Jewish athletes from these countries were therefore unable to compete at those Olympics. (2) Germany barred its Jewish athletes from Hitler's 1936 Games. (3) Several Jewish athletes from other countries self-boycotted Hitler's Games. (4) The Holocaust devastated Europe's Jewish athletes. (5) Jewish Olympians were subject to a terrorist attack at the 1972 Munich Games. (6) Many Jewish athletes did not compete for the USA in 1980 due to the USA boycott of the Games (7) Israel boycotted the 1980 Games in support of the USA (8) Jewish athletes from Russia could not compete in the 1984 Games due to Russia's boycott of those Games. (9) South African Jewish athletes were unable to compete from 1964 until 1992 due to sporting sanctions against that country's apartheid policy.

There is perennial debate as to what defines someone as Jewish. For the purposes of this book, I have included as Jewish anyone who has at least one Jewish parent (of either sex). I consider this to be acceptable because having a single Jewish grandparent meant that one fell foul of Hitler's racist Nuremberg laws. That the person concerned may not have regarded themselves as Jewish was of no relevance to Nazi thinking.

Disturbingly, Jews themselves subscribe to the myth that Jews are no good at sport. In 1996 the comedian Jackie Mason gave a show in Israel. Here are some excerpts: 'Jews want to think they're athletes but there's no Jewish athletes. Jews don't go in for athletic activities. In the U.S. I never in my life saw a Jewish athlete. A Jew can't swim'. Yet again, the old falsehood was reinforced—this time by a comedian.

Or consider this exchange in the movie *Airport*, written and directed by David and Jerry Zucker and Jim Abrahams.

Air Stewardess: Would you like something to read?

Passenger: Do you have anything light?

Air Stewardess: How about this leaflet, 'Famous

Jewish Sports Legends?'

Do Jews who hold to the myth that Jews are no good at sport realise that they are parroting Nazi propaganda? A Nazi handbook issued a year before the Berlin Games said: 'Among the inferior races, the Jews have done nothing in the athletic sphere. They are surpassed even by the lowest of the negro tribes'. Yet Hitler knew that both Jews and those of colour were as good at sport as anyone else. He saw to the banning of several of Germany's most successful Jewish athletes—many of them ranked number one amongst Germans. There is an obvious irony in Nazi thinking, because if the Nazis truly believed they were superior to another group, then instead of barring the 'inferior' group from sporting competition, they should have encouraged these people to compete. In this way the 'superior group' would prove their superiority while humiliating the inferior people. Why was this not done? You may find the answer between the covers of this book.

Finally, a myth cannot be destroyed when the victims of the myth collaborate in its propagation. It is Jews who are therefore most in need of changing their minds. This is what this book hopes to achieve.

CHAPTER 1

ATHLETICS
CITIUS, ALTIUS, FORTIUS
(Faster, Higher, Stronger…)

'Among the inferior races, the Jews have done nothing in the athletic sphere. They are surpassed even by the lowest of the negro tribes'.

Nazi handbook by Kurt Munch, published in 1935.[1]

CITIUS

Who takes gold in the 100m dash is decided in about 10 seconds in a spectacular show of speed and strength. Little equipment, no team—just man against man, woman against woman. It is pure speed—the zenith of the Olympic Games.

Black athletes, mainly from the USA, have dominated the 100m sprint for several decades. Only three British athletes have won this race at the Olympics. The first was **Harold Abrahams**, at the Paris Games in 1924. It took until 1980 for Allan Wells to become the second British athlete to take gold. Wells was also the last white athlete to win the Olympic 100m title. His 1980 Moscow triumph was, however, clouded by the fact that the USA boycotted the Moscow Games. The third British athlete to take gold was Jamaican-born Linford Christie in 1992. Australia is yet to win the event.

Harold Abrahams (1899-1978) served as a lieutenant in the British army prior to studying at Cambridge.[2] He competed in the 1920 Olympics in the 100m, 200m and 4x100m events as well as the long jump, but failed to win a medal. A month before the 1924 Olympics Abrahams set a new English long jump record (24ft 2½in)—a record that stood until 1956.[3] At 7pm on 7 July 1924 Abrahams wrote himself into the history books by winning the 100m sprint at the Paris Olympics. He beat the American favourites—who included the 1920 gold medal winner Charley Paddock—and equalled the world record set by Paddock in 1921. In third place was Arthur Porritt, who later became the Governor-General of New Zealand and the Queen's Surgeon. Abraham's world record time of 10.6s stood until 1929 when Eddie Tolan of Sweden clipped off a further 0.2s. Abrahams' also won silver at the 1924 Games as the opening runner in the 4x100m relay.

Abrahams and Porritt dined together at 7pm on the 7 July every year following the 1924 Games, until Abrahams died in 1978.[4]

Abrahams' athletics career ended prematurely after he fractured a leg in the long jump in 1925. He subsequently became a sports journalist and commentator. He reported on Hitler's Games in 1936 for the BBC. During the Second World War Abrahams and his wife fostered two Jewish refugees— a German boy and an Austrian girl. Later in life he served as President of the Jewish Athletic Association and chaired the Amateur Athletic Association.[5] He wrote several books including *The Olympic Games 1896—1952* and *The Rome Olympiad, 1960.*

In 1957 Abrahams was made Commander of the Order of the British Empire (CBE). He established the Sybil Abrahams Memorial Trophy in memory of his wife. The award has been presented by the Duke of Edinburgh yearly since 1964 at Buckingham Palace to the best British woman athlete.[6]

This is what Philip Noel-Baker, captain of Great Britain's Olympic team in 1912 and a Nobel Prize winner said about Abrahams: 'I have always believed that Harold Abrahams was the only European sprinter who could have run with Jesse Owens, Ralph Metcalfe and the other great sprinters from the USA. He was in their class, not only because of natural gifts—his magnificent physique, his splendid racing temperament, his flair for the big occasion—but because he understood athletics and had given more brainpower and more willpower to the subject than any other runner of his day'.[7]

Abrahams was immortalised in the 1981 award-winning film *Chariots of Fire*.

Abrahams' eldest brother, Adolphe, founded British sports medicine, while another brother, Sidney, was an Olympic long jumper. Sidney was Chief Justice of Ceylon from 1936 to 1939. He was the first Jew to be President of the London Athletic Club.[8] Adolphe and Sidney both received knighthoods.

Two other Jewish runners to star at the 1924 Games were **Elias Katz** (1901-1947) and **Louis Clarke** (1901-1977). Katz was born in Turku, Finland, but his heritage was Russian. His grandfather, **Meir Lipmanof Katzeff**, was born in Vilna in 1840. In those days Canton law forced Jewish boys into the Russian army from the age of eight. Most of those drafted served 25 years in the military—the equivalent of a death sentence. Katzeff was caught up in this merciless conscription of Jewish children. During his time in the military he was sent to Turku in Finland. Here he abbreviated his name to Katz and was subsequently given a special permit to stay on in Finland, where he married and started a family.

It was serendipity that started Meir Katz's grandson, Elias Katz, on the road to Olympic glory. Katz was 18 when he was invited to take part in a 1,500m race. It was his first competitive race. Running in long trousers and regular shoes, he ran the first lap in a world class time of 58s. He won the race in 4mins 19s, defeating the reigning champion.[9] It was suggested to Katz that he train and become an athlete. He joined the main athletic club in Turku, Turun Urheilulitto.

Here he met Paavo Nurmi—the 'flying Finn'. Nurmi won nine gold and three silver medals at the Olympics held in 1920, 1924 and 1928. He set 22 world records[10] and is the only runner ever to hold the world records for the 1,500m, 5,000m and 10,000m simultaneously. Nurmi is still regarded as one of the greatest ever distance runners, as is his fellow Finn, Ville Ritola.

Nurmi, however, remains forever a mystery. He was described as a deeply committed runner, yet appeared to run without passion or pleasure. He loved winning but never smiled. He studied the science of running but would not impart his knowledge.[11] Yet Nurmi bonded with Katz and shared his tightly-held knowledge with the four-years-younger man.

Under Nurmi's tutelage Katz's technique improved. In 1924, along with Nurmi and Ritola, he took part in the 1924 Games. He set an Olympic record in the semi-finals of the 3,000m steeplechase. In the finals, with only two laps to go, Katz tripped and fell on a hurdle, but recovered sufficiently to take silver behind Ritola. Katz's most cherished memory from these Games must, however, have been the 3,000m team event in which he won gold alongside Nurmi and Ritola. In 1926 his time for the 3,000m steeplechase was the fastest in the world. On 12 July 1926 he, Nurmi, Frej Liewendahl and Niilo Koivunalho set a new world record for the 4x1,500m relay. Katz ran the fastest leg. Five days later the same four men broke their own world record. The new record stood for five years.[12]

In 1925 Katz went to Germany and joined the Jewish Club, Bar Kochba, in Berlin. Katz ran his best ever times for the 3,000m and 5,000m in 1926 and 1927 in Berlin. By 1930 the Bar Kochba club had 5,000 members. Times were, however, changing for Jews in Germany. Once the Nazi regime came to power, the Bar Kochba club was disbanded and Jews were barred from sporting competition. Katz left for Palestine. Here he was killed by an Arab sniper on 26 December 1947.[13]

A year later the State of Israel was founded and a team of six Israelis was selected to compete in the 1948

Games. The hopes of Olympic competition for the first Israeli Olympic athletes were, however, dashed by the International Olympic Committee (IOC), which barred the new country from the Games. The reason given was that the Committee feared an Arab boycott should Israel be allowed to participate.[14]

Louis Clarke ran the second leg for the USA 4x100m relay team that won gold while setting a world record (41s) at the Paris Games. In the same year Clarke held the 100y indoor world record of 9.8s.[15]

While Harold Abrahams is the best known of Jewish Olympic track athletes, he was not the first Jewish athlete to win a medal at the Olympics, nor is he the most distinguished of Jewish track athletes. The first Jewish athlete to win an Olympic medal did so at the first modern Games in 1896 in Athens. **Gyula Kellner** of Hungary came third in the marathon.[16] It was not until 2004 that another Jewish athlete won a medal in the marathon—again in Athens. **Deena Kastor** (1973-) took bronze, making her the first American to win an Olympic medal in this event in 20 years. Kastor went on to win the Chicago marathon in 2005 and the London marathon in 2006. In 2006 she was ranked first in the world. Kastor held 12 American records over various distances.

The most distinguished of Jewish track athletes must be **Irena Kirszenstein-Szewińska** (1946-2018) although, as will become evident, there are multiple Jewish athletes whose successes exceeded those of Abrahams.

Irena Kirszenstein's parents fled to Russia in the same month that Germany invaded Poland—September 1939. Had they stayed in Poland they would almost certainly have been amongst the 90% of Polish Jews killed by the Nazis. The occupation ended in 1945. In 1946 Irena Kirszenstein was born in a refugee camp in Leningrad.[17] The Kirszensteins returned to Warsaw shortly thereafter. Here, Kirszenstein evolved into one of the greatest female track and field athletes ever. She was a reedy 5ft 9in in height with the perfect physique for a track athlete. Making use of a devastating kick, she often snatched victory from harrowed rivals in the final strides of a race.

Kirszenstein won seven Olympic medals. In Tokyo in 1964 she won gold as part of Poland's 4x100m relay team. She collected silver in the 200m sprint and the long jump.

In 1968 in Mexico City she competed under her married name, Szewińska, taking bronze in the 100m and gold in the 200m sprint.

In 1972 she won bronze in the 200m sprint. In 1976 in Montreal she won gold in the 400m.

Szewińska broke the 100m world record on two occasions—July 1965 and October 1968. She set new world records for the 200m on four occasions between 8 August 1965 and 13 June 1974. On 22 June 1974 Szewińska became the first woman to break the 50s barrier for the 400m, in a time of 49.9s. She broke the world record for the 400m for a second time in June 1976 and yet again lowered her time, to 49.28s, while taking gold at the Olympics in July 1976.[18] Forty four years on and her time of 49.28s for the 400m remains the Polish national record.

In 1965 Szewińska was Poland's athlete of the year and was named 'The Outstanding Woman Athlete in the World' by the official Soviet Press Agency TASS. In 1974 she was named 'The United Press International Female Athlete of the Year' and *Track and Field's* 'News Woman Athlete of the Year'. In April 2020 Szewińska was named as the greatest female athlete of all time by America's Track and field News magazine.[19] She became a member of the International Olympic Committee and was President of the Polish Athletic Association from 1997 to 2009. In 1992 she was inducted into the International Women's Sports Hall of Fame.[20]

The most distinguished Australian track athlete is Shirley Strickland. Strickland competed in the 1948, 1952 and 1956 Olympics and, like Szewińska, won a total of seven medals—3 gold (in 1952 - 80m hurdles and 1956 - 80m hurdles and 4x100m relay), 1 silver (in 1948 - 4x100m relay), and 3 bronze (in 1948 - 100m sprint, 80m hurdles and 1952 - 100m hurdles). Szewińska's spread of medals is slightly better than Strickland's (3 gold, 2 silver and 2 bronze as against 3 gold, 1 silver and 3 bronze), but what really sets these two athletes apart is the number of individual world records each set. Szewińska set nine individual world records whereas Strickland set three.[21] Moreover, Szewińska remains the only athlete, male or female, to have held the world record for the 100m, 200m and 400m sprints[22]—something that even the legendary Usain Bolt has not achieved.

Szewińska's achievements need to be put in context from a Jewish perspective. Ninety percent of Poland's three million Jews perished in the Holocaust. The population of Poland today numbers about 38 million, of which about 10,000 (0.03%) are Jewish. Szewińska, one of the virtually-destroyed Polish Jewish population, has won more Olympic medals than any other Polish Olympian. Szewińska is not only Poland's most distinguished Olympian, but is one of the greatest female track and field athletes of all time.

Another Jewish Polish athlete, **Jadwiga Wajsówna** (1912-1990), won bronze and silver medals for the discus in the 1932 and 1936 Games, making the number of medals won by Polish Jewish athletes nine out of a total of 57 Polish medals (or 16%).[23]

On 26 May 1912 an American, **Abel Kiviat** (1892-1991), set a world record of 3min 59.2s for the 1500m. Six days later on 1 June 1912 Kiviat bettered his own world record in a time of 3min 56.8s. On 8 June 1912 a crowd of fifteen thousand filled a sold-out Harvard stadium to see if Kiviat could do it yet again. He did not disappoint, finishing in 3min 55.8s—almost 4 secs faster than his first world record set 14 days earlier. The race is remembered in the book, *The Milers*, by Cordner Nelson. Kiviat set 14 world records over various distances during his career.[24]

Kiviat and two other Americans, Paul Jones, the world record holder for the mile, and Mel Sheppard, the defending Olympic 1500m champion, were the favourites to win the 1500m Olympic final on 12 July 1912 in Stockholm. In sport, however, there is no such thing as certainty. In a race acclaimed at the time as the greatest ever, Kiviat led into the final lap.[25] He was 30 metres from the tape and seemingly assured of gold when Great Britain's Arnold Jackson suddenly broke away on the outside, snatching victory from Kiviat by 0.1s. Jackson's time set a new Olympic record but was a second slower than Kiviat's world record. After the race a reflective Kiviat said: 'That race was the biggest disappointment of my life. I never saw Jackson. It was my own fault. What was I waiting for?'[26]

Kiviat received some consolation as one of the USA gold medal-winning team in the 3000m relay. His consolation would have been greater had he known that his 1500m world record was to last another five years. It was not until 5 August 1917 that John Zander shaved 1.1s from Kiviat's world record time.

Kiviat saw active service during World War One fighting on the frontline in France.[27] After his discharge he continued his running career until 1925. He was the track coach at Wagner College from 1924 to 1925.

Long after his death and more than a century later, Kiviat remains the only athlete to have broken the world record for the 1500m three times in 15 days—a record that's unlikely to be broken.

In 1985 Kiviat was inducted into the USA Track and Field Hall of Fame.

Another Jewish athlete missed out on gold at the Stockholm Games, by 0.1s. In the 100m sprint **Alvah Meyer** (1888-1939), also of the USA, finished 0.1s behind his compatriot Ralph Craig, who took gold in 10.8s. Meyer held world records over 60y and 330y, achieved in 1914 and 1915 respectively.[28]

It was at a softball competition at a sporting carnival in Beaverton, Ontario in 1923 that **Fanny 'Bobby' Rosenfeld** (1904-1969) found her talent for sprinting. There happened to be a track meeting at the carnival.

Spurred on by teammates, Rosenfeld entered the 100y dash organised by the Canadian National Exhibition (CNE). Although she had to run in her big softball tent bloomers, Rosenfeld won the race.[29] Unbeknown to her she had beaten the Canadian champion, Rosa Grosse.[30] The daughter of immigrants who had fled the Russian pogroms, she was now set on a path to Olympic glory. She and Grosse began a sporting rivalry on the track. Grosse won the 100y sprint in the annual CNE Athletic Day in 1924. Rosenfeld took the title the following year while setting a new world record. In the same year she also set a new world record in the 220y dash.

In the 1928 Olympics Rosenfeld was one of the gold-winning, world-record-breaking Canadian team in the 4x100m relay. At the same Games she won silver in the 100y dash.[31] Rosenfeld was, however, much more than a champion sprinter. She excelled at the discus, javelin, shot, running and standing long jumps, ice hockey, field hockey, baseball, basketball, tennis, and softball.

After arthritis ended Rosenfeld's athletics career in 1933, she turned to coaching and sports journalism. She coached the Canadian women's 1934 track and field team for the London Commonwealth Games and wrote a column titled *Feminine Sports Reel* for the *Toronto Globe and Mail*.[32] Decades ahead of her time, Rosenfeld wrote with wit and insight, championing women in sport and challenging the unflattering stereotype of the female athlete.

In 1950 the Canadian press voted Bobbie Rosenfeld the top Canadian female athlete of the first half of the 20th Century. In 1987 Rosenfeld and three male athletes were acknowledged as the most important figures in Canadian sporting history by the Historic Sites and Monuments Board of Canada. There can be few greater sporting honours for a Canadian.[33]

Edward Ralph 'Teddy' Smouha (1908-1992) also competed in the 1928 Games. Smouha ran for Great Britain, winning bronze in the 4x100m relay. In the 1940s he served as Wing Commander with the Royal Air Force. He was awarded the Order of the British Empire for services to the British community in Geneva.[34]

Smouha's son, **Brian Smouha**, also a sprinter, represented Great Britain in the 1960s. Smouha's grandson, **James Espir**, competed for Great Britain in the late 1970s and early 1980s as a middle-distance runner.

Maria Itkina (1932-) of the Soviet Union broke the 400m women's world record even more times than Szewińska. Itkina lowered the record on four occasions between 1957 and 1962.

She also set new world records for the 220y sprint in 1956 and in 1963. In September 1959 Itkina set a world record (53.7s) for the 440y, beating Betty Cuthbert of Australia.[35] In 1963 Itkina ran the third leg for the world-record-breaking Soviet 800m relay team.

Itkina was, however, unlucky at the Olympics. She competed in three Olympic Games, never winning a medal but finishing in the dreaded fourth place on four occasions—the 100m and 200m sprints in 1960, and the 4x100m relays in 1956 and 1960. She was nevertheless awarded the Soviet Union's highest honour for athletes—the Merited Master of Sports.[36]

While Itkina's series of fourth places at the Olympics must have been agonising, **Marty Glickman** (1917-2001) and **Sam Stoller** (1915-1985) had a worse experience. They were Jewish runners chosen to compete for the USA 4x100m relay at the 1936 Olympics. After practising with their team-mates for two weeks prior to their event, and knowing that they were almost certain to go home with a gold medal, they were dropped from the team the day before the race. It is extremely rare that uninjured athletes chosen to compete in the Olympics are excluded at the last minute. The American officials who saw to their exclusion were the IOC President Avery Brundage and the American track coach Dean Cromwell, both Nazi sympathisers. It has been suggested that Glickman and

Stoller were replaced by Jesse Owens and Ralph Metcalfe in order not to humiliate Hitler by having two Jewish athletes take gold. Owens and Metcalfe were also 'non-Aryans', but at this stage their participation could hardly have caused the Nazis further embarrassment because their successes were by now an accomplished fact. It would, however, have caused further humiliation for the Nazis if two Jewish athletes had taken gold in the high-profile relay event.

Brundage denied the accusation that he was pandering to Hitler. He continued as the President of the USA Olympic Committee until 1955. From 1952 until 1972 Brundage served as President of the International Olympic Committee.

Ironically, a week after the Olympics, Glickman ran in a 4x100y relay in London. The race was between an American and a British Commonwealth team. The American side broke the world record in the event.[37] This achievement did not ease Glickman's pain. He lived the rest of his life haunted by the injustice meted out to him as a 17-year-old at the 1936 Games.

Hitler rewarded Brundage in 1938 by giving him the contract to build the German Embassy in Washington DC.[38] After stepping down as President of the IOC following the 1972 Games, Brundage married a German woman 45 years his junior. He lived the last years of his life in Germany, dying in Garmisch-

Partenkirchen on 7 May 1975.[39]

In 1998 William J. Hybl, President of the USA Olympic Committee, honoured Glickman and Stoller (the latter died in 1985) with the first General Douglas MacArthur awards 'in lieu of the gold medals they didn't win in Berlin'.[40] The award honours lifetime achievement and adherence to Olympic ideals. Hybl said that it was clearly the case that Glickman and Stoller were left out of the team in order to appease the Nazi regime although written proof was lacking. Hybl added: 'We regret this injustice and we feel it was an injustice. We're not only atoning for this but recognising two great individuals.'[41] Hybl, who had been a prosecutor in law, concluded: 'I'm used to looking at evidence. The evidence [that the USA team officials dropped Glickman and Stoller to appease the Nazis] was there'.[42]

The 1940 and 1944 Games were cancelled due to World War Two, finally ending Glickman's and Stoller's hopes of competing in the Olympics. Glickman served with the USA marines during the war.

In the 1950s the head of NBC Sports, Tom Gallery, wanted to hire Glickman to host the weekly broadcast of an NBA game on national television. Gallery told Glickman that his only reservation was his name—it sounded 'too Jewish'. Glickman replied that was no problem he would change his name. 'And what would that be?' enquired Gallery. 'Lipshitz' Glickman replied, 'Marty Lipshitz'. On that note the meeting ended, as well as any intention Glickman had to work for NBC. Even without the NBC, Glickman became such a successful sports commentator that after the introduction of television, viewers would turn off the sound and listen to Glickman's radio commentary. Between 1948 and 1957 he narrated the sports reels for Paramount Pictures. After that he covered a wide variety of sports, including: the New York Knicks (basketball), the New York Giants and New York Jets (football), and The Yankees (baseball). He also broadcast for roller derbies, rodeos and even a marbles competition. Glickman worked until the age of 74. He died in 2001.[43]

Jewish athletes had a difficult decision to make with respect to Hitler's Games. Were Jewish athletes to compete and prove Hitler's notions of racial supremacy wrong or were they to boycott the Games in protest against Nazi anti-Semitism?

Milton Green, **Norman Cahners**, **Sid Koff**, **Nat Jaeger** and **Herman Neugass** were among the many American Jews who boycotted Hitler's games. Green and Cahners were persuaded to boycott by a well-respected Rabbi who told the two athletes about the terrible things occurring in Germany. German Jews were being attacked, they were losing their legal rights, their businesses were boycotted and synagogues were being vandalised. Worse was to follow. This is what Green said: 'Of course that was my hope, to be in the Olympics. I had held the world's record in the high hurdles and also the Harvard-Yale record in the broad jump... I knew that I'd qualify because I won the preliminary events. I think back on making that decision [to boycott] and whether I would have won silver or gold or some sort of a medal, and every time I go to the Olympics—I've been to three of them—I particularly watch the high hurdles and the long jump, and I picture myself as maybe having won a medal in it'.[44]

Sid Koff, born Sybil Tabachnikoff in 1912, qualified for the USA team in both the high and broad jumps for the 1936 Games[45] but chose to boycott, as did **Nat Jaeger**, who qualified for the Games as a race walker.[46]

Herman Neugass equalled the world record for the 100y dash in 1935 with a time of 9.4s. Neugass was coached by Fritz Oakes, who told Neugass that if he improved on his start 'Jesse [Owens] might be following you'. On three occasions Neugass came second to Owens by just half a yard. He may well have taken gold in 1936.

Neugass was not one to mince words. He wrote to *The Times-Picayune*: 'I would not participate in games in any country in which the fundamental principle of religious liberty is violated as flagrantly and as inhumanely as it has been in Germany…I feel it to be my duty to express my unequivocal opinion that this country should not participate in the Olympic contests if they are held in Germany'.

Neugass was, however, up against Avery Brundage, president of the USA Olympic Committee, and General Charles Sherrill, a member of both the USA and International Olympic Committees. According to Brundage, 'The persecution of peoples is as old as history' and 'the customs of other nations are not our business'. Sherrill was even more cold-hearted: 'It does not concern me one bit the way Jews in Germany are being treated,' he said, 'any more than the lynchings in the South of our own country'.

Neither Brundage nor Sherrill deserved to hold positions on Olympic Committees. Both betrayed the Olympic ideals. The Olympic rules state that no athlete can be denied the right to compete because of race, ethnicity or religion.[47]

Moreover, Brundage had revealed his true colours long before he was elected to any Olympic Committee. He competed in the decathlon at the 1912 Stockholm Olympics. With the event almost completed, Brundage was well behind, and at this stage he chose to drop out—in effect he took his bat and ball and went home. Could there have been an explanation other than puerile petulance for this unsporting behaviour, which was in direct conflict with the Olympic charter? As it happens, the winner of both the pentathlon and decathlon at the Stockholm Games was the brilliant Jim Thorpe—an American Indian. Thorpe was later disqualified when it was discovered that he had previously played semi-professional baseball, receiving $5 per game, thereby violating the amateur code. It later emerged that the disqualification of Thorpe was illegal, because complaints against a competitor had to be received by the Swedish Olympic Committee within 30 days following the distribution of prizes. The letter from the American Athletic Union disqualifying Thorpe arrived long after the deadline. With Thorpe expelled from amateur competition, Brundage became the national all-around champion.

Brundage subsequently conceded that his newly elevated status as an athlete helped open doors in his new construction business. Thorpe supporters lobbied for his medals to be restored throughout Brundage's term as president of the IOC. Brundage mean-spiritedly refused to petition the IOC to restore Thorpe's medals. In 1982, seven years after Brundage's death and 30 years after Thorpe's death, the IOC restored the medals to Thorpe.[48]

On the other side of the globe, the South African 100m high hurdles champion, **Sid Kiel** (1916-2007), also said 'No' to Hitler's Games. In the 1930s Kiel was considered one of the best track athletes South Africa had ever produced.

Still at school, Kiel became the South African 120y (110m) high hurdles national champion. He was chosen to represent South Africa against the touring Oxford-Cambridge team in 1935. Kiel ran brilliantly to beat the Englishman Pilbrow into second place. The previous South African champion, Snaar Viljoen, came third. Kiel's performance was acclaimed by Jack Morgan, the South African half-mile champion. 'If there is such a thing as a certainty in selecting international teams, then Sid Kiel, the 18-year-old hurdler, must be a certainty for the South African Olympic team. [In this race] Kiel gave the most brilliant exhibition of hurdling ever seen in this country, and I consider his 14.5 seconds was a true reflection of his abilities'.

Viljoen, gracious in defeat, wrote in one of the daily papers: 'South Africa has always been fortunate in producing world class high hurdlers, and Sid Atkinson, Weightman-Smith, H.Q. Davies and others must be highly delighted to see that their old hurdling standard has been maintained this year, and that by a schoolboy 18 years of age. Kiel the Western province "timber topper" is a potential world champion. I doubt if I would have believed the time possible if I had not seen it—or, more, competed in the same race. People in Europe and the USA are bound to discredit the time;

all I can say is that it was as genuine a race I have ever competed in. South Africa can rest assured that she will have another worthy representative at the Games in Berlin next year'.

Viljoen's words were not hyperbole. Sid Atkinson came second in the 1924 Olympics in a time of 15s and in the 1928 Games Atkinson won gold in 14.8s. In the same event Weightman-Smith came fifth in 15s. At the 1932 Games in Los Angeles George Saling won the 120y hurdles in 14.6s. Kiel's time (14.5s) would have won him gold at the 1932 Games! Of South African track athletes, Kiel was considered the most likely to bring home a medal from Berlin in 1936. Kiel, however, made himself unavailable for Hitler's Games. In personal correspondence he told me that he would have been unable to live with himself had he attended the Games. His place was taken by Tom Lavery.

South Africa failed to win a medal in track or field events at Hitler's Games. Following the Games, Kiel defeated Lavery in the 120y high hurdles at a meet in Johannesburg, equalling the Transvaal record. In October 1937, at a meet in Cape Town, Kiel ran a personal best of 14.4s for the 110m hurdles. This time would probably have earned him a medal at the 1936 Games. The athletes who came second, third and fourth at the Games all shared the time of 14.4s! (The 120y hurdles changed to 110m at the 1936 Olympics.) Kiel represented South Africa in the

Empire Games in Sydney in 1938, but by now his interest in athletics was on the wane. A natural athlete, Kiel was an accomplished competitor in a number of sports, and he successfully returned to cricket, representing Western Province as an opening batsman.[49] Kiel finished his debut season 1939-40 with 524 runs from six matches. In the 1941-2 season, in a match against Transvaal, Kiel came close to carrying his bat, but with his score on 128 his captain, Andrew Ralph, declared at 236/8. Kiel's cricketing career was then interrupted by World War Two. He served from 1942-1946 as a doctor in the South African Medical Corps in the Middle East and India. He managed two matches in the 1945-46 season, scoring 77 against Natal. He played in five out of the six Currie Cup games played in the 1946-47 season, during which he scored three half centuries. According to Maurice Silbert, Kiel was a surprise omission from the Springbok team captained by Jack Cheetham.[50]

Few South Africans are aware that there is an Afrikaans word that derives from the name of a Jewish hurdler who fled Nazi Germany. **Ernst Franz Jokl** was born in Breslau, Germany on 3 August 1907. He qualified as a medical doctor and a physical education teacher in Germany. Jokl was selected for the 1928 German Olympic team in the 400m hurdles. In 1930 he was dismissed as the director of the Institute of Sports Medicine in Breslau on account of being Jewish. At the same time his partner, Erica Lestman, a gold medallist in gymnastics at the 1928 Olympics, lost her job as a high school teacher because she refused to give the Nazi salute at a track meeting in Berlin. That day Jokl and Lestman decided to marry, and two weeks later immigrated to South Africa.

Jokl was appointed at Stellenbosch University and tasked with setting up the first university physical education department. He later established the Department of Physical Education at the Witwatersrand Technical College and pioneered a uniform syllabus and system for physical education in South Africa. Jokl insisted that the physical education curriculum he put in place be implemented for white and black children of both sexes. Jokl stimulated research in physical education, sports medicine and sports physiology.[51]

During World War Two he was a consultant to the South African Defence Force and worked closely with Danie Craven, the legendary Springbok rugby scrum-half and coach, at the Physical Training Battalion.

The Jokls left for the USA after the South African National Party came to power in 1948, because they objected to the implementation of harsh racial policies similar to those of Nazi Germany.

Jokl's successes piled up. He became a faculty member

of the University of Kentucky and from 1952 to 1964 was professor of Neurology and Sports Medicine and director of the university's Medical Rehabilitation Centre. He was also a consultant and team physician for the USA Olympic Committee.

After retirement, Jokl was belatedly recognised in his country of birth. He was bestowed with honorary professorships from the universities of Berlin and Frankfurt, and a street in Cologne was named 'Jokl Strasse'. Jokl died in 1997 but his name lives on in the Afrikaans language—'jokkel' means 'to exercise'.[52]

Henry Laskau and **Shaul Ladany** were both race walkers and two of five Jewish athletes who managed to survive incarceration during World War Two and then compete at the Olympics. The other three survivors were weightlifter, **Ben Helfgott**, swimmer, **Alfred Nakache**, and wrestler, **Yakiv Punkin**. Incredibly, Laskau, Ladany and Nakache set world records following the Holocaust while Punkin won gold in the 1952 Games.

Henry Laskau (1916-2000) was born in Berlin, where he became a top 1500m runner. He was barred from representing Germany and imprisoned in a Nazi forced labour camp in 1938. After about three months he managed to escape and made it to the USA after stays in France and Cuba. Laskau's parents and brother Benno were killed by the Nazis.[53]

Laskau joined the USA army working in counter intelligence in Europe. His knowledge of German made him invaluable as an interpreter in the interrogation of SS officers.

At the conclusion of hostilities, Laskau returned to athletics, but was persuaded by a former national champion race-walker, **Nat Jaeger**, to give up running and take up race walking.[54] Laskau entered his first walking race aged 30 and found immediate success. He went unbeaten in his new discipline in the USA for nine years—from June 1947 until August 1956. He set five national records, won 42 USA national titles and represented the USA at the Olympics in 1948, 1952 and 1956, though failing to win a medal. He broke the outdoor mile world record in 1950 with a time of 6min 19.2s. The record went unbroken for 12 years.

In 1957 Laskau's wife, Hilde, whose family had also fled Germany, pulled the plug on Laskau's racing career by removing one of his shoes from his travel bag. Enough was enough—Hilde wanted Laskau to go out on top.

In 1977 Laskau became the second race walker inducted into the USA National Track and Field Hall of Fame. In 1983 he was named in the USA All-Time track and field team.

Simon Turnbull interviewed **Shaul Ladany** (1936-) and writing in *The Independent*, gave a wonderful description of Ladany's life. Ladany was born in Belgrade. His home was bombed by the Luftwaffe in 1941 and the family spent the next three years on the run. At one time they were in Hungary, where Ladany's parents left him in a Buddhist monastery in Budapest for safe-keeping, warning the terrified child not to let on that he was Jewish. Ladany was eight years old when he, along with his two sisters and parents, was taken prisoner by the Nazis in 1944. After six months in a concentration camp the Ladany family were allowed to flee to Switzerland as part of an exchange deal between the Nazis and the Zionist movement. Ladany was one of the few of Yugoslavia's 70,000 Jews to survive the Holocaust. The Ladany family did not, however, escape unscathed; Ladany's maternal grandparents were killed in Auschwitz.

Ladany was only a child while imprisoned in a concentration camp but his time there was indelibly engraved in his memory. As he reports, 'I was in Bergen-Belsen for six months and I remember every day of it. I mainly remember standing for hours for the roll calls, when the German soldiers made arithmetic errors in adding up the numbers of those alive and those dead. They counted us again and again—for hours and hours, in rain and cold. I remember the barbed-wire fences and the watchtowers and the hunger. Obviously, it all made a tremendous impact on me. Whether it forged my character in one way or another... it's possible'.

After the war the Ladany family returned to Belgrade, but then immigrated to the new nation state of Israel in 1948. Ladany fought in both the 1967 Six Day War and the 1973 Yom Kippur War.

Ladany first competed in the Olympics (50km walk) in 1968. He did not win a medal. Aged 36, Ladany returned to Germany as a race walker, representing Israel in the 1972 Munich Olympics. It was hoped that Jewish athletes would be able to enjoy sporting competition in a now reformed Germany. Gone were the swastikas, uniformed German guards and military personnel. The atmosphere was purposefully relaxed—too relaxed as it turned out. Ladany was about to endure another horror on German soil.

On 5 September 1972, the most infamous day in Olympic history, the Munich Massacre unfolded.

On 3 September 1972 Ladany finished 19th in the 50km walk. The next night the Israeli team watched a theatre production of Fiddler on the Roof. The party returned to the Olympic Village and went to sleep. In the early hours of the morning eight terrorists of the Black September Group entered the apartment block at 31 Connollystrasse in which the Israeli contingent was housed.

The sound of gunfire woke Ladany who was in Unit 2. Simon Reeve, in his book *One Day in September*, describes how Ladany ran from his apartment to the building housing the USA team and alerted the team track coach, Bill Bowerman, to the situation. Bowerman pulled Ladany into his room and called the German police.

The terrorists first attacked Unit 1 which housed sporting officials. **Yossef Gutfreund**, a wrestling referee, noticed the door of the apartment being opened at 4.30am and glimpsed masked gunmen outside. He instinctively threw his 230 pound body against the door while screaming out a warning to his teammates. Gutfreund delayed the entry of the eight terrorists by a precious few seconds, allowing the weightlifting coach **Tuvia Sokolsky** to break a window and escape. **Moshe Weinberg**, the wrestling coach, resisted the terrorists and was shot through the cheek. **Yossef Romano**, a weightlifter and veteran of the 1967 war attacked and wounded an intruder before being shot and killed. The terrorists mutilated Romano's body cutting off his genitals in front of his teammates.[55] The wounded Weinberg was forced to lead the terrorists to where other Israelis were housed. He took them to Unit 3 which housed the wrestlers and weightlifters.

The sleeping athletes were taken by surprise, rounded up and marched back to Unit 1. The injured Weinberg again attacked the terrorists, knocking out several teeth and fracturing the jaw of one of them. In the melee, wrestler **Gad Tsabari** shoved one of the terrorists aside, ran down the stairs and escaped, zig-zagging through the car park while under fire. While reaching for the attacker's gun, which was now on the floor, Weinberg was shot dead by the terrorist who had failed to kill Tsabari.

Following negotiations, the German authorities agreed to transport the terrorists with their hostages to Fürstenfeldbruck airfield, a NATO base, from which the terrorists and hostages would be flown to Cairo. In the fateful hours that followed, all nine Israeli hostages died in a botched German police rescue attempt at the airfield.

Those who died were wrestlers **Mark Slavin** and **Eliezer Halfin**, weightlifters **David Berger** and **Ze'ev Friedman**, wrestling coach **Yossef Gutfreund**, weightlifting coach and judge **Yakov Springer**, shooting coach **Kehat Shorr**, track and field coach **Amitzur Shapira**, and fencing coach **Andre Spitzer**. In total, 11 Israelis lost their lives.

Ilana Romano and Ankie Spitzer, the widows of Yossef Romano and fencing coach Andre Spitzer, fought for decades for the IOC to recognise the 11 Israelis killed by the Palestinian terrorists. Ilana Romano motivated for a minute's silence to be held at the 2012 Games in memory of the fallen Israelis. Her request was denied by the IOC. By 2016, however, the IOC had a change of heart. At the Rio Games the President of the IOC, Thomas Bach, presided over a memorial ceremony and a minute's silence for the slain Israelis. Bach inaugurated a Place of Mourning memorial consisting of two stones from ancient Olympia in a glass case. The memorial is to be a feature at future Games. A memorial describing the Munich Massacre was also put in place in the Olympic stadium in Munich in time for the 2016 Olympics.[56]

Shaul Ladany remains forever an optimist. He said to Simon Turnbull: 'Despite what happened in Munich, I had experience there and in Mexico of barriers being broken down between people of different countries. I am a great believer—a great believer—that the Olympics is a platform for friendship, for mixing. It is almost a utopian situation'.

Ladany won the 100km world title in 1973. He has held the world record (7h 23min 50s) for the 50 mile (80km) walk since 1972. He never won an Olympic medal but is one of only 19 recipients of the Pierre de Coubertin Medal. The medal is named after the founder of the modern Olympics, and is awarded to those who demonstrate outstanding sportsmanship or who have made a notable contribution to the Olympic Games. In awarding Ladany the de Coubertin medal in 2007 the IOC cited his 'unusual outstanding sports achievements during a span covering over four decades'.[57]

Ladany was a Professor of Industrial Engineering at Ben Gurion University of the Negev. He speaks nine languages, holds eight patents, and has written several books and more than a 100 academic articles.

Gerald Ashworth (1942-) is best remembered for running the second leg of the American 4×100m relay that set a world record of 39.0s while taking gold at the 1964 Tokyo Olympics. Paul Drayton, Richard Stebbins and Bob Hayes ran the other legs. Ashworth equalled the world record of 6.1s for the 60y dash in 1961, and with a time of 9.4s broke the 100y world record in 1962. He equalled this record again in 1964.[58]

The Israeli sprinter **Esther Roth** (1952-) just missed out on qualifying for the 100m finals in the Munich Games. Roth was in the semi-finals of the 100m hurdles but never got the chance to contest for a place in the finals because the Israeli team was recalled following the terrorist attack. On being recalled Roth said: 'I didn't even care about what I had to do. I lost my coach, and after all, nothing is more valuable than human life. Everything else was secondary'.[59]

In the 1976 Olympics Roth came sixth in the finals of the 100m hurdles. She was unable to compete in the 1980 Games due to an Israeli boycott of the event. Israel was one of 65 countries that boycotted the Games in solidarity with the USA because of Russia's invasion of Afghanistan.[60]

Ukrainian, **Zhanna Pintusevich-Block** (1972-), ran in the 100m and 200m sprints at the 1996 and 2000 Olympics, reaching the finals in all events except for the 1996 200m. She did not, however, win an Olympic medal.

Block nevertheless shot to fame, becoming the world champion in the 200m when she pipped the USA star Marion Jones in a time of 22.32s at the World Track and Field Championships in 1997.

Block beat Jones again in the 2001 World Championships, but this time over 100m, in a race remembered as one of the greatest upsets in the history of track and field. Block's victory made her the world champion in the 100m dash. She broke the tape in 10.82s, marking Jones's first defeat in four years over this distance. Block was ranked number two in the world in the 100m, behind Jones, between 2001 and 2003.[61]

Then came the Bay Area Laboratory Co-Operative (BALCO) scandal. The founder of BALCO, Victor Conte, along with the vice-President, James Valente, and other company representatives had been providing a performance-enhancing steroid—'The Clear'—as well as growth hormones to athletes. At that time there was no test capable of detecting The Clear. The company was investigated following information given to the United States Anti-doping Agency (USADA) in

June 2003.[62] More than 20 elite athletes were implicated in the scandal that followed, including Block and Jones. In 2011 Block was suspended from competing for two years and her results subsequent to 30 November 2002 were disqualified. Her husband, Mark Block, who supplied the drugs to Block, was banned from sport for ten years.[63] In 2007 Jones was stripped of several medals including the three gold and two bronze medals she won at the Sydney 2000 Olympics.

Jones crossed the line first in the 100m at the Sydney Olympics. After her disqualification it was to be expected that the athlete who took silver would be promoted to gold. That athlete was the Greek sprinter Ekaterina Thanou. Thanou and her partner had, however, been convicted in a Greek court for perjury following an incident during the 2004 Athens Games, when they staged a motorcycle accident in order to avoid a drug test. They were subsequently acquitted on appeal. The IOC, however, deemed that Thanou was not deserving of an Olympic gold. Consequently, there is no name listed in first place in the record books for the Women's 100m final at the 2000 Games. Thanou remains in second place and the other finalists all shifted up a place so that second place is now shared by Thanou and the originally third-placed Tayna Lawrence. Merlene Ottey moved from fourth to third and Block shifted to fourth. The race was described in the *London Eye* as 'the race no one won'.[64]

Performance enhancing drugs create a stark dilemma for athletes. At the start of an event no-one knows who, if any, of the other competitors are fuelled by an illegal accelerant making them stronger and faster. Winning or losing often means the difference between being famous or forgotten. The athlete has to weigh up whether they should cheat or compete clean. Should they take performance enhancing drugs and be caught, their years of training will have come to naught and their reputation ruined. On the other hand, should they compete clean, then their chances of winning are markedly diminished.

Tellingly, four of the first five finishers in the 100m women's final at the Sydney 2000 Games were found to have breached anti-doping laws during or after their competitive days.[65]

In the body-sapping triathlon (swim, cycle and run) **Joanna Zeiger** (1970-) came fourth in Sydney in 2000—the first time the event was held at the Olympics. It was, however, in the even more gruelling non-Olympic event 'The Ironman' that Ziegler had her greatest triumph. She won the 2008 Ironman 70.3 World Championships in Clearwater, Florida in a world record time of 4h 02min 49s.[66] The number '70.3' reflects the total distance of the race—70.3miles (113km). The three legs are the 1.2miles (1.9km) swim, the 56miles (90km) cycle and the 13.1miles (21.1kms) run. In 2000 Zeiger was named the USOC (United States Olympic Committee) triathlete of the year.

Australia's hopes for a medal at the 2021 Olympics in the 400m sprint depend on **Steven Solomon** (1993-). Solomon was a finalist at the 2012 Games. He may be on the podium in 2021.

Before we leave 'Citius,' let us reflect on the irony that in Poland, a country notorious for its anti-Semitism, it is a Jewish woman—Irena Szewińska—who is the most successful Olympian. The analogous situation is found in Hungary, where the Jewish gymnast Ágnes Keleti is that country's mostsuccessful Olympian.

ALTIUS

There are more deceptions and twists to the Nazis' interference in the women's high jump at Hitler's Games than can be found in a spy thriller. The Jewish German high jump champion, **Gretel Bergmann** (1914-2017), was expelled from her club Ulmer FV once the Nazis came to power. In 1933 Bergmann fled Nazi Germany for England, where she became the British high jump champion with a leap of 1.55m in 1934. Hitler countered the threat of a boycott of his Games by the USA and other countries by claiming that Jewish Germans would be able to compete in the Games. Bergmann was enticed back to Germany to try out for the German team so as to demonstrate that Jewish athletes were to be included in the German Olympic contingent. The 'enticement' was more of a warning—family members living in Germany were threatened with reprisals should Bergmann not return. Bergmann went home and won the Olympic trials with a jump of 1.64m. Enraged by the pervasive anti-Semitism, Bergman recalled: 'the madder I got, the better I did'. A fortnight later she received a letter saying that based on her poor performance she had been dropped from the German team. Her records were deleted and her place in the team was given to 'Dora' Ratjen.[67] Ratjen placed fourth in the Olympic finals. Ratjen revealed in 1957 that 'she' was really a man, Herman Ratjen, and had been ordered to pose as a woman for the Games by officials of the Nazi Youth Movement.

Ratjen's name remains in the Olympic record books.[68] Ultimately the Nazi scheme to deny a Jewish athlete a place on the podium failed. The Jewish Hungarian, **Ibolya Csák** (1915-2006), took gold with a jump of 1.60m—4cm less than Bergmann jumped two weeks earlier.

In 1937 Bergmann left for the USA and settled in New York. She vowed never to return to Germany. That same year she won the USA high jump and shot put titles. In 1938 she was again the USA high jump champion. She married a physician, Bruno Lambert.[69]

Germany named a sports complex after Bergmann in Berlin in 1995. Bergmann did not attend the opening ceremony. In 1999 she was awarded the prestigious Georg von Opel-Preis Award for achievement in sport and society. That year the stadium in Laupheim from which she had been barred from competing in the 1930s was named after her. On this occasion Bergmann did attend the ceremony, saying: 'I was not going to participate, but when I was told that they were naming the facilities for me so that when young people ask 'Who was Gretel Bergmann?' they will be told my story, and the story of those times. I felt it [the story] was important to remember, and so I agreed to return to the place I swore I'd never go again. But I had stopped speaking German and didn't even try when I was there. They provided a translator'.[70]

On hearing that Berlin wanted to host the Olympics in 2000, Bergmann wrote to the German Olympic Committee, the USOC and the IOC saying that she had never received an apology for what had been done to her and that Berlin was not ready for the Olympics until the past was redressed. Bergmann was finally acknowledged. She received an apology from Walther Tröger, a former German IOC member and National Olympic Committee (NOC) president.[71]

On 23 November 2009 Bergmann's German high jump record, established in 1936, was officially written back into the German record books. In 2014 a street in the Olympic Park in Berlin was named after her.

Bergmann was immortalised in a documentary *'Hitler's Pawn'* in 2004, and in the film *'Berlin 36'*, directed by Kaspar Heidelbach. Bergmann wrote her own life story in a book, *'By Leaps and Bounds,'* published in 2005.[72] Bergmann died aged 103 in 2017.

Dwight Stones (1953-) is a 6ft 5in American high jumper who broke the world high jump record on three occasions but was never at his best at the Olympics.

Stones won bronze at the 1972 and 1976 Games. He did not compete in the 1980 Moscow Games due to the American boycott. In 1984 he placed fourth at the Los Angeles Games. At the same Olympics he also served as a sports commentator, becoming the first athlete to both compete and commentate at the same Games.

Stones set his first world record on 11 July 1973, clearing 2.30m (7ft 6½in) and becoming the first to break the world record using the technique invented by Dick Fosbury—the Fosbury Flop. In June 1976 Stones lifted the world record to 2.31m (7ft 6¾in) and in August 1976 he added another 1cm to the world record. Stones held the world record for a month short of four years. He also set seven indoor world records for the high jump.[73] Stones commentates on track and field athletics for all three major USA TV networks.

Myer Prinstein (1878-1925) won five Olympic medals—four gold. In the long jump he took silver in 1900, and gold in the 1904 and 1906 Olympics. He took gold in the triple jump in the 1900 and 1904 Games.

Prinstein set two world records for the long jump. On 11 June 1898 he set a world record jumping 7.235m (23ft 87/8in) in New York. The record was broken seven days later by William Newburn. Prinstein regained the world record on 28 April 1900 with a jump of 7.5m (24ft 7¼in).[74]

In the 1900 Games, in a show of solidarity with his non-Jewish teammate, Alvin Kraenzlein, Prinstein agreed not to compete in the finals of the long jump because it was to be held on a Sunday. Syracuse University, for whom Prinstein competed, was a Methodist school and instructed its athletes, as did most other American institutions, not to take part in competition on a Sunday. Unknown to Prinstein, Kraenzlein did however compete, taking gold.[75] Prinstein responded by punching Kraenzlein in the face. Prinstein's jump in the Saturday qualifying event was one cm short of Kraenzlein's uncontested winning jump on the Sunday, allowing Prinstein to take the silver medal. The next day Prinstein won the triple jump (hop, step and jump), setting a new Olympic record.[76] Prinstein subsequently practised law. He died of heart disease aged 46.

Other Jewish athletes to win Olympic medals in jumping events were Irena Szewińska (Poland; long jump), Daniel Frank (USA; long jump), Hugo Friend (USA; long jump), and Charles Jacobs (USA; pole vault).

FORTIUS

The image of a powerfully built woman rotating within the confines of a small circle before releasing a heavy missile with a primal scream would generally be considered an unlikely portrayal of a Jewish woman. It is, however, in the throwing events that Jewish women have compiled an astonishing Olympic record, dominating both the shot and discus over five decades between 1928 and 1980.

Women were first permitted to compete at the Olympics in 1928, but prior to that Jewish women had already made their mark in throwing events in Germany, Canada and the USA.

Lilli Henoch (1899-1942) was considered to be Germany's finest female athlete of the 1920s. She set world records in the shot, discus and 4x100m relay. Her athletic prowess did not save her from deportation from Germany in the Nazi era. Henoch was a proud member of the Berliner Sport-Club. She captained the women's handball team. On 18 January 1933 she was made chairwoman of the women's athletic section. Two weeks later, the 'Aryanisation' policies of the Nazi government forced Henoch out of the club. On 5 September 1942 she and her mother were shot and buried in a mass grave in the woods near Riga, Latvia. Her name lives on in Germany. Several sporting venues in Berlin have been named after her, as well as a street.[77]

German javelin champion **Martel Jacob** was banned from competing in athletics by the Nazi regime. She fled Germany, later to become the English, and then South African, javelin champion.[78]

Lillian Copeland (1904-1964) of the USA won silver in the discus at the 1928 Games. At the 1932 Los Angeles Games she won gold on her final throw, hurling the discus 40.58m—a new world record. At the same event **Jadwiga Wajsówna** (1912-1990), a Jewish athlete from Poland, took the bronze. Between 1925 and 1932 Copeland habitually broke the world record for the discus, shot and javelin. Her career was blighted by Hitler's rise to power. Copeland, boycotted Hitler's 1936 Games. The disappointment of not competing would have been keenly felt by Copeland, as she was unable to defend her own title.[79] The event was won by the German athlete Gisela

Mauermayer, who was a member of the Nazi party and considered in Germany to be the perfect example of Aryan womanhood.

There was, nevertheless, a Jewish athlete sharing the podium with Mauermayer—Jadwiga Wajsówna (whose real name was Pana Weiss). Wajsówna set five world records for the discus between 1932 and 1934, establishing herself as the world's leading discus thrower during this period. Wajsówna, in company with most of the Jewish athletes from Eastern European countries, did not boycott the 1936 Games. She improved from third place in the 1932 Olympics to take silver in 1936.[80] One can only wonder what went through her mind as she was being presented with the silver medal while, next to her stood Mauermayer, arm raised in the Nazi salute. There would have been no thought for the absent Jewish athlete and erstwhile title holder, Lillian Copeland. Equally scant consideration would have been given to another Jewish discus thrower, **Ingeborg Mello** (1919-2009). Mello had been prohibited from competing by the Nazis on account of her religion. She fled Germany for Argentina—one of many elite Jewish German athletes to flee Nazi Germany.[81] She became one of Argentina's most prominent female athletes, winning both shot and discus at the 1951 Pan American Games. Mello represented her new country in the first post war Olympic Games in 1948 and again in 1952. In the 1952 Games, well past her prime, she placed seventh in the finals of the discus—her throw of 41.61m would have placed her third in Hitler's 1936 Games, behind Wajsówna.

Wajsówna next competed after World War Two in the London 1948 Olympics. (The Games were not held in 1940 and 1944.) If she could have duplicated her 1936 throw of 46.22m she would have won gold in 1948 by a margin of 4.3m. Wajsówna was, however, past her prime and placed fourth in the 1948 Olympics.

Micheline Ostermeyer (1922-2001) was born in Pas-de-Calais to a musical mother and a sporting father. She spent her early childhood in Tunisia. The family then returned to France. Her mother coached her at the piano while her father taught her the skills of running and jumping. She continued her education in music under Lazare Levy at the National Conservatorium of Music in Paris.

During World War Two the Ostermeyers went back to Tunisia to escape the Nazi Holocaust. Micheline Ostermeyer gave weekly piano performances on radio Tunis during 1941, and competed in the Tunisian athletic championships, winning five titles.

Ostermeyer returned to France following liberation. She became the French champion at shot put, high jump, the 60m sprint and the heptathlon.[82] Despite the devastating effect of the Holocaust on the numbers and morale of the Jewish population, there were nevertheless three Jewish contestants amongst the eight athletes in the women's discus finals of the 1948 Games—Micheline Ostermeyer, Jadwiga Wajsówna and Ingeborg Mello. In that order they placed first, fourth and eighth. Besides winning gold in the discus, Ostermeyer also won gold in the shot, celebrating her success with an impromptu Beethoven recital at the French team headquarters.

In the high jump Ostermeyer took bronze, using her distinctive rolling style.[83] Her achievements at these Games were second only to the great Fanny-Blankers-Koen, who won four gold medals. Ostermeyer claimed that sport taught her to relax while the piano gave her strong biceps and a sense of motion and rhythm.[84] She continued as a concert pianist long after she packed away her shot and discus. She died aged 79 on 17 October 2001 at Rouen. Ostermeyer is remembered as the most versatile of French Olympic athletes and arguably France's greatest Olympic athlete. She remains the only French athlete to win three medals at a single Olympic Games. It is doubtful that there will ever again be an athlete who can marry the ability to win gold in the shot and discus with a career as a concert pianist.

The Press sisters, Tamara and Irina, represented the

Soviet Union in the Olympics of 1960 and 1964. **Tamara Press** (1937-) was born in Kharkov, Ukraine, and was an engineer by profession. She dominated both the discus and shot events for six years. Over this period she set six world records for each event. Tamara already held the world record for the shot at the time of the 1960 Olympics in Rome. There, she won gold in the shot and silver in the discus, establishing a new Olympic record for the shot. Seven days later, still in Rome, she set a new world record for the discus, so compensating for her failure to win gold at the Games. She won gold in both the shot and the discus in 1964 in Tokyo, setting new Olympic records for both events.[85]

Irina Press (1939-2004) was as successful as Tamara but her events were the 80m hurdles and the pentathlon. Irina won gold in the hurdles event in the 1960 Games in Rome. By 1964 she held the world record in the pentathlon. She won gold in this event in the 1964 Olympics, substantially improving her own world record. She threw the shot (one of the five disciplines of the pentathlon) 17.16m, beating the next best contender, the great Mary Rand, by more than 6m, and managed a credible sixth place in the main shot event.[86] The sisters set a combined total of 26 world records between them,[87] becoming the most successful sisters of all time at the Olympic Games.

Tamara Press's stewardship of the discus and shot put

during the 1960s was taken over by another great Jewish female athlete from the Soviet Union during the 1970s. Born in Bakota, Ukraine, **Faina Melnik** (1945-2016) dominated the discus event from 1971 to 1977. At the 1972 Munich Olympics she won gold in the discus, establishing a new world record of 66.62m. During the event she broke the Olympic record three times. Melnik was the first female to hurl the discus beyond 70m.[88] To break one world record is a remarkable achievement. How does one describe setting eleven new world records in a single sport? This, however, is what Melnik did between 1971 and 1976.

Paul Mayer describes an amusing anecdote with regard to Melnik. A Jewish journalist who was trying to determine whether Melnik was Jewish found that she avoided the direct question. The journalist thought this might have been on account of the surrounding 'minders'. (Many Jews from behind the Iron Curtain were reluctant to discuss their background, given the prevailing anti-Semitism and anti-religious ideology in the Soviet Union.) He therefore changed tack by asking the names of her parents. With a smile she replied, 'Shmuel and Sarah'. He thanked her, to which she replied, 'my pleasure'.[89] Following her athletics career Melnik became a teacher in Moscow and had considerable success coaching the shot.

Svetlana Krachevskaja (1944-) was the most recent Jewish woman to win an Olympic medal in a throwing event. She won silver in the shot in 1980 while representing the Soviet Union.

The most distinguished Jewish male thrower was **James 'Jim' Emanuel Fuchs** (1927-2010). Fuchs competed in the shot, the discus and the decathlon. Although he weighed 215 pounds, he could cover 100y in less than 10s. Fuchs invented a new technique to put the shot in order to compensate for a leg injury. Using his 'sideways glide' he dominated the shot in the early 1950s. His technique was soon adopted by other shot putters. Fuchs set four world records in the shot but peaked between Olympics. He nevertheless won bronze in the shot at the 1948 and 1952 Games.[90]

In later life, Fuchs, with George Steinbrenner, founded the Silver Shield Foundation. The charity was dedicated to assisting children of peace officers killed in the line of duty. Fuchs died aged 82.[91]

Stanley Lampert (1928-2015) did not compete at the Olympics but set a world record for the shot put in 1954, only to lose it some days later. Lampert heaved the shot 59ft 5¾in on 1 May 1954, so becoming the first to pass the 59ft barrier. The legendary Parry O'Brien, using a new technique—the O'Brien glide—broke the record on 8 May 1954 with a winning throw of 60ft 5¼in, becoming the first to break the 60ft mark.[92] O'Brien held the world record from 1953 to 1959.[93] One of few shot putters to beat O'Brien was an American, **Gary Jay Gubner** (1942-). The 6ft 2½in Gubner weighed 120kg and excelled at the shot, the discus and weightlifting. In 1962 he set three world indoor shot put records—on one occasion erasing O'Brien's world record.[94] His best throw of 19.8m (64ft 11½in) gave him the second ranking in the world in 1962. He failed to qualify for the 1964 Tokyo Olympics in the shot, but placed fourth in the super heavyweight lifting event. It is probable that Gubner made a tactical error in hoping to compete in the 1964 Games in both the shot put and weightlifting events. Had he concentrated on one or the other, it is likely he would have won a medal.

Boris 'Dov' Djerassi (1952-) was born in Haifa but emigrated to the USA. He was ranked in the top 10 USA hammer throwers between 1973 and 1981, and in three of these years he was ranked number one. Djerassi was at his peak in 1980 and was chosen as one of three hammer throwers to compete in the 1980 Games, but did not do so because the USA boycotted the Moscow Games. He did receive a Congressional Gold Medal created for athletes prevented from attending the 1980 Olympics. It was also the year that he competed in the *CBS Sports* World's Strongest Man show.[95]

Another American shot putter who was not at his best during the Olympics was **Andy Bloom** (1973-). At the end of 2000 Bloom was ranked number two in the world, finishing the season with a best throw of 21.82m (71ft 7¼in.) In the 2000 Sydney Games, Bloom finished in the agonizing fourth spot with a throw of 20.87m (68ft 5¾in). Arsi Harju of Finland won with a throw of 21.29m (69ft 10¼in.)[96]

Phil Fox (1914-2001), also known as Phil Levy, won the USA discus titles in 1937, 1939 and 1940.[97] His best throw of 172ft 4½in in 1939 was the second best throw in history. In 1939 Fox competed for the USA in Berlin against Nazi Germany. The press gave much publicity to Fox competing against the Nazis. Fox disappointed on the day. Some surmise that the attention unsettled him.[98] His Olympic career was by now over, as the 1940 and 1944 Olympics were cancelled because of World War Two.

In the 1948 Olympics, nerves got the better of American discus thrower, **Victor Frank**. Following a poor throw, two 'no throws' were called, and he was eliminated from the competition. In the following year Frank was ranked three in the world in the discus.[99] During World War Two he served in the USA navy.[100]

It was Baron Pierre de Coubertin—the founder of the modern Olympic Games—who suggested the words 'Citius, Altius, Fortius' (Faster, Higher, Stronger) for the Olympic motto. But for de Coubertin, sportsmanship was more important than winning. He could not have anticipated that the motto 'Citius,

Altius, Fortius' needed a fourth word—'Honoris' (Honour).

SUMMARY

Harold Abrahams won gold in the 100m sprint in the 1920 Olympics equalling the world record. No Australian has won an Olympic 100m race. Abrahams is the best known of Jewish athletes due to his life being immortalised in the film *Chariots of Fire*. Yet there were several Jewish athletes whose successes exceeded that of Abrahams.

Irena Szewińska remains the only athlete, male or female, to have held the world record for the 100m, 200m and 400m sprints—something that even the legendary Usain Bolt has not equalled. No Australian matches the achievements of Irena Szewińska on the track.

Dwight Stones set three world records in the high jump and Myer Prinstein set two world records in the long jump. No Australian athlete has set a world record in the long or high jump.

The greatest discrepancy between Australian and Jewish athletic achievements is, however, in the throwing events. Jewish athletes have won sixteen Olympic medals in these events—six gold. Australians have won three—none of them gold. The Australian medal-winning athletes are Gael Martin (bronze, shot put), Daniela Costian (bronze, discus), and Louise Currey (silver, javelin). Jewish athletes have set 34 world records in the shot put and discus. No Australian has set a world record in throwing events.

MEDAL COMPARISON BETWEEN JEWISH AND AUSTRALIAN OLYMPIC ATHLETES

Jewish track and field athletes have won 54 Olympic medals. Australian athletes have won 85 individual Olympic medals in track and field athletics.

Jewish athletes have won 24 gold medals, as have Australian athletes. Australian athletes have won more Olympic medals than Jewish athletes but Jewish athletes surpass their Australian counterparts in excellence.

JEWISH OLYMPIC MEDALLISTS—TRACK AND FIELD

1896 Athens
Gyula Kellner, Hun. Bronze; marathon

1900 Paris
Myer Prinstein, USA, Gold; triple jump
Myer Prinstein, USA, Silver; long jump

1904 St Louis
Myer Prinstein, USA, Gold; triple jump
Myer Prinstein, USA, Gold; long jump

Daniel Frank, USA, Silver; long jump

1906 Athens
Myer Prinstein, USA, Gold; long jump
Hugo Friend USA, Bronze; long jump
Ödön Bodor, Hun. Bronze; 4x100m

1908 London
Ödön Bodor, Hun. Bronze; 4x100m
Charles Jacobs, USA, Bronze; pole vault

1912 Stockholm
David Jacobs, Great Britain, Gold; 4x100m
Abel Kiviat, USA, Gold; 3000m team
Abel Kiviat, USA, Silver; 1500m
Alvah Meyer, USA, Silver;100m

1916 Cancelled due to World War One

1924 Paris
Harold Abrahams, Great Britain, Gold; 100m
Louis Clarke, USA, Gold; 4x100m
Elias Katz, Finland, Gold; cross-country 3,000m team
Harold Abrahams, Great Britain, Silver; 4x100m
Elias Katz, Finland, Silver; steeplechase 3,000m team

1928 Amsterdam
Fanny Rosenfeld, Canada, Gold; 4x100m
Fanny Rosenfeld, Canada, Silver; 100m
Lillian Copeland, USA, Silver; discus
Ellis Smouha, Great Britain, Bronze, 4x100m

1932 Los Angeles
Lillian Copeland, USA, Gold; discus
Jadwiga Wajsówna, Poland, Bronze; discus

1936 Berlin
Ibolya Czák, Hun. Gold; high jump
Jadwiga Wajsówna, Poland, Silver; discus

1940 and 1944 Cancelled due to World War Two

1948 London
Micheline Ostermeyer, France, Gold; discus
Micheline Ostermeyer, France, Gold; shot put
Steve Seymour, USA, Silver; javelin
James Fuchs, USA, Bronze; shot put
Micheline Ostermeyer, France, Bronze; high jump

1952 Helsinki
James Fuchs, USA, Bronze; shot put

1960 Rome
Irina Press, Russia, Gold; 80m hurdles
Tamara Press, Russia, Gold; shot put
Tamara Press, Russia, Silver; discus
David Segal, Great Britain, Bronze; 4x100m

1964 Tokyo
Gerald Ashworth, USA, Gold; 4x100m
Irena Szewińska, Poland, Gold; 4x100m
Irina Press, Russia, Gold; pentathlon
Tamara Press, Russia, Gold; shot put

Tamara Press, Russia, Gold; discus
Irena Szewińska, Poland, Silver; long jump
Irena Szewińska, Poland, Silver; 200m

1968 Mexico City
Irena Szewińska, Poland, Gold; 200m
Irena Szewińska , Poland, Bronze; 100m

1972 Munich
Faina Melnik, Russia, Gold; discus
Irena Szewińska, Poland, Bronze; 200m
Dwight Stones, USA, Bronze; high jump

1976 Montreal
Irena Szewińska, Poland, Gold; 400m
Dwight Stones, USA, Bronze; high jump

1980 Moscow
Svetlana Krachevskaya, Russia, Silver; shot put

2004
Deena Kastor, USA, Bronze; marathon

CHAPTER 2

SWIMMING

'Jews want to think they're athletes but there's no Jewish athletes. Jews don't go in for athletic activities. In the US I never in my life saw a Jewish athlete... A Jew can't swim'

Jackie Mason, Israel in 1996.[1]

The evidence tells a different story. Let's begin with one of the greatest athletes of all time—**Mark Spitz** (1950-). Spitz's Olympic career began in 1968 in Mexico City where he won four medals (two relay golds, a silver and a bronze, for the 100m butterfly and 100m freestyle). Most would be taken aback to hear that Spitz was disappointed with winning only four medals. Yet disappointment is perhaps appropriate for someone who prior to the Mexico Games held ten world records and was hoping for six golds. Spitz's father had, after all, brought him up to believe that 'swimming isn't everything, winning is'.[2]

In the year that terror came to the Olympics—Munich 1972—Spitz achieved the unimaginable. He won seven gold medals—the 100m and 200m butterfly and freestyle, the 4x100m and 200m freestyle relays and the 4x100m relay medley, all with new world records. To establish one world record is a Herculean achievement. Yet Spitz set an unbelievable thirty-three new world records between 1965 and 1972 and was World Swimmer of the Year in 1967, 1971, and 1972.[3]

The 1972 Games concluded with Spitz a worldwide celebrity. Assisted by George Clooney-like looks, the photo of Spitz in his swimmers with seven gold medals hanging from his neck became an iconic sporting image. He was inducted into the International Swimming Hall of Fame in 1977.

But Spitz was not the only Jewish swimmer to win medals and set new world records at the 1972 Games. The American **Keena Rothhammer** (1957-) beat the great Australian, Shane Gould, into second place in the 800m freestyle, while setting a world record—her second world record for the same distance on two consecutive days. She also took bronze in the 200m freestyle which Gould won. A year later she broke Gould's world record in the 400m freestyle. Rothhammer retired prematurely at the age of seventeen because of migraine headaches. She subsequently worked with children in Special Olympics programmes. She has said that she would rather be remembered for this work than for her swimming achievements.[4]

In the same Games a Hungarian, **Andrea Gyarmati** (1954-), set a world record in the butterfly in the semi-finals, but in the finals only took bronze. She won silver, however, in the 100m backstroke. Gyarmati was named Hungarian Sportswoman of the Year in 1970-1972.

Gyarmati was from an impressive sporting family. Her mother and coach was swimmer **Éva Székely** (1927-2020) and her father, **Dezső Gyarmati**, was a multiple Olympic champion in water polo. Yet it was only by a stroke of luck that Andrea Gyarmati and Éva Székely's names have been inscribed forever in the records of the Olympic Games.

Éva Székely was 17 in 1944 when Hungarian Arrow Head fascists (who killed around 20,000 Hungarian Jews that winter) rounded her up with some other Jews. They were about to be shot when Székely's father, 'under some heavenly influence' (Székely's words), explained that she was a Hungarian swimming champion. 'Tell him your name', her father said. Székely looked at the fascist, seeing one grey and one brown eye, and said her name. She was spared.

Székely again eluded death after Germany entered Hungary. She escaped recruitment into a slave labour battalion by jumping onto a passing car during a forced march. Székely found her way back to her family who were in hiding in a Swiss-run, two-room 'safe house'. The two rooms housed 42 people. Székely kept fit by running up and down the stairs of the five-story building 100 times a day. She was one of only 10 of the 42 who survived the war. In 1945 she was at last able to swim again. In 1948 the woman who as a child had been expelled from her local sports club as 'an undesirable' swam at the Olympic Games. She came fourth in the 200m breaststroke.

In 1950 Székely won the 100m freestyle in an international competition in Budapest. She was awarded the gold medal by the chairman of the swimming association and received a special prize from an important officer of the communist political police. As she was handed the trophy she looked into the major's eyes, to see the unforgettable mismatched eyes—those of the 1944 Arrow Cross leader.[5]

Székely's determination and dedication finally paid off. At the 1952 Games Székely made her mark as an Olympic athlete. She won gold in the 200m breaststroke, setting an Olympic record. In 1956 she took silver in the same event. Székely described her swimming successes as a safehouse against the depredations she had to face under the Nazis and the communists: 'In those days people were stripped of many things: title, rank, property. Millions were humiliated in their dignity. In that world, Olympic gold was like a fixed, shiny star in the universe'.[6]

Many Hungarians shed their Jewish identity in a bid to avoid persecution. In fear of racism, few Hungarian Jewish athletes disclosed their religious background. Székely, however, remained defiantly Jewish. In one television interview, while discussing the anti-Jewish laws of the 1940s, she said that she was unequivocally a Jew.[7]

In 2004, Hungary honoured the athlete they had scorned. Székely was named one of Hungary's Athletes of the Nation. In 2011 she received the Prima Primissima Award.

Éva Székely, Dezső Gyarmati and **Andrea Gyarmati** have all been inducted into the International Swimming Hall of Fame. They remain the only mother, father and daughter family ever to receive this honour.[8]

Few would believe it possible for anyone to win seven golds, all in world record times, in a single Olympics. Fewer still would bet that Mark Spitz's record would ever be broken. Yet, records are broken. It took until 2008 (35 years) for fellow countryman, Michael Phelps, to improve on Spitz's haul of seven Olympic golds. Phelps won eight golds and equalled Spitz in winning seven of them in world record times. Phelps became the fifth member of an exclusive group of Olympic athletes to win nine Olympic gold medals, the others being Mark Spitz, Larisa Latynina (gymnastics), Paavo Nurmi (track) and Carl Lewis (track and field). Phelps won an incredible 23 golds—the only person to have won more than nine.

It was, however, thanks to the Jewish captain of the USA swimming team, **Jason Lezak** (1975-), that Phelps racked up the second of his world-record-breaking golds in the 2008 Games. The pundits had already decided that the French would win the 4x100m freestyle relay. One of their four specialist sprinters—Alain Bernard—was the world record holder for the individual 100m freestyle. The French swimmers themselves were certain of the outcome. Bernard bragged: 'The Americans? We're going to smash them. That's what we came here for'.[9] Boastful words do not, however, decide sporting contests.

Phelps dived in first for the USA, setting a new USA record in a scorching 47.51s. But at the start of the second leg it was Australia in the lead, thanks to Eamon Sullivan, who set a new world record—47.24s for his leg. By the final leg the French were in charge. The contest was now head to head between two swimmers—Lezak and Bernard. Lezak entered the water nearly a body length behind the French favourite, but hung back, drafting in the swell created by Bernard. With 50m to go Bernard remained ahead and most considered the contest over. With 25m left, the 6ft 4in, Lezak began closing in on Bernard 'stroke by stroke' and 'breath by breath', according to Olivier Poirier-Leroy—a former national swimmer for Canada.[10]

The swimmers were almost even under the flags. In the last remaining water—teammates and crowd screaming—Lezak pipped the Frenchman by a barely measurable 0.08 of a second.

This is how commentator and Olympic gold medallist Rowdy Gaines called the finish: 'That might be the most incredible relay split I've ever seen in my entire life. Forty-six flat, not only was that the fastest in history, it *Blew Away* the fastest in history!'[11] Lezak's time of 46.06s broke the world record that Eamon Sullivan had set less than two minutes earlier by more than a second. To top it all the jubilant USA team had set a new 4x100m freestyle relay record.

Phelps was ecstatic. It was the French who made the 4x100m freestyle relay the biggest obstacle to him winning eight golds. As Poirier-Leroy pointed out: 'No relay gold, no hope to beat Spitz's record haul. Simple as that'.[12]

The magnitude of Lezak's swim was diminished in the

excitement of Phelps's phenomenal achievement. Lezak's swim was, however, not lost on swimming aficionados. The swim was voted by *Sports Illustrated* as the most memorable single performance by an American at the Beijing Games. Olivier Poirier-Leroy acclaimed Lezak's anchor leg as the 'greatest relay leg of all time'. Lezak's swim was described in *SwimPro* as 'the greatest swim of all time'. That was no exaggeration. Lezak's record still stands more than a decade later.

Lezak's name entered the swimmers' lexicon: to be 'Lezaked' means that someone who has spent most of a race drafting in your wake beats you with metres to go.[13]

Over a long career Lezak won eight Olympic medals (four gold, two silver and two bronze) between 2000 and 2012. His freestyle relay world record was not his first world record. He was a member of the USA team that set new world records in the 4x100m medley in 2002, 2003, 2004 and 2008. Lezak's swim in the 2008 Olympic 4x100m freestyle relay must, however, rank as his greatest achievement. He is the first athlete in Olympic history to win four medals in the same event in four consecutive Games. Lezak was rightly regarded as a specialist relay swimmer but he also won a bronze in the 100m freestyle in Beijing in 2008. He was inducted into the International Swimming Hall of Fame in 2019.

Phelps got the glory, but Lezak was remembered by swimming connoisseurs as having swum the greatest relay split of all time. There were, however, another two Jewish swimmers in the 4x100m USA world record breaking relay team at the 2008 Games.

Garrett Weber-Gale (1985-) swam the second leg of the race in 47.02s. He won a second gold in the 4x100m medley. He touched the wall in under 48s at the Olympic trials in 2008, becoming the first American to do so.[14]

Ben Wildman-Tobriner (1984-) swam in the preliminaries for the 2008 4x100m relay. In this race, without Phelps or Lezak, the USA set a world record with Wildman-Tobriner swimming the third leg, so making sure the USA qualified for the finals. The record lasted until the next day when the USA again set a new world record in this event. Wildman-Tobriner received gold as one of the team.

Wildman-Tobriner is best remembered for winning the 50m freestyle in the International Swimming Federation (FINA) 2007 World Championships, touching the wall in 21.88s in Melbourne. The Australians nick-named him 'wild man'.[15]

Most people equate Jews and swimming with Mark Spitz. Yet the records show that Jews have excelled in swimming since the first modern Olympic Games. It was a Jewish Hungarian who was the first swimmer to win an Olympic gold. **Alfréd (Hajós) Guttmann** (1878-1955) also known as Alfréd Hajós, was the 1896 swimming equivalent of Mark Spitz.

Guttmann was one of two Jewish swimmers who won the three swimming events at the first Games. Guttmann won the 100m and 1200m races. The Austrian, **Paul Neumann**, won the third Olympic swimming event—the 500m freestyle. The competition was held in bitterly cold weather (13 degree C) in the sea, with waves four metres high. Guttmann won the 100m in 1min 22.2s. Taking the conditions into account Guttmann's time was admirable. The current world record in the controlled environment of an Olympic pool set 104 years later by Eamon Sullivan is 47.05s.

Boats were used to take the competitors into the open water for the 1200m freestyle event. The weather was so bad that the rowing and sailing events were cancelled. In the 1200m race, boats were again used— this time to rescue swimmers in distress. Guttmann described his feelings: 'My will to live completely overcame my desire to win'. Yet he won the race, coming in three minutes ahead of the next competitor.

The Athenian journal *Acropolis* dubbed Guttmann 'the Hungarian dolphin'. Australians would have called him a larrikin on account of a mischievous streak. At a dinner in honour of the Olympic winners the Crown Prince of Greece asked Guttmann where he had learned to swim. 'In the water', he replied.

Guttmann also played soccer for the Hungarian national side and in 1906 coached the national team. He was also the Hungarian 100m sprint champion and held the Hungarian 400m hurdles and discus titles.

Guttmann was, however, much more than a champion athlete. He became a renowned architect, specialising in the design of sport facilities. After he returned to his studies following the 1896 Games, the dean of the university failed to congratulate him on his successes, saying: 'Your medals are of no interest to me, but I am eager to hear your replies in your next examination'. The dean's concerns were misplaced. Guttmann subsequently won another Olympic medal—this time in architecture.

Between 1912 and 1948 the Olympic Games included five categories for creative arts. The entrants were required to link their artistic submission with sport. Together with Dezső Lauber, Guttmann won silver for the design of a sports stadium in the 1924 Olympics—gold was not awarded.

Guttmann was one of two athletes to win Olympic medals in both sport and art. The best known of

Guttmann's sports buildings is the National Swimming Stadium, which was built on Margaret Island in the Danube in 1930. It was home to the 1958, 2006 and 2010 European Aquatic Championships and the 2006 FINA Men's Water Polo World Cup.[16] Today, dotted around Budapest, an architectural legacy to Guttmann's creativity is evident—galleries, hotels, sports stadiums, restaurants and schools.

Guttmann's younger brother **Henrik (Hajós) Guttmann** (1886-1963) took gold in Paris in 1906 in the 4x250m relay.[17]

The greatest hero amongst Jewish swimmers must be **Alfred Nakache** (1915-1983). How does someone survive a Nazi concentration camp and the murder of their family, then return to triumph over man's inhumanity to man? Nakache was born in Constantine in French Algeria but moved to France in 1933. By 1935 he was the French champion in the 100m freestyle and was selected to swim for France in the 4x200m relay in Hitler's 1936 Berlin Games.

The French team finished fourth, the place that Olympians dread—good enough to reach the finals but missing out on a medal. For Nakache the fourth place finish must have been tempered by the French beating the Germans into fifth place.

Following the 1936 Games, Nakache fled Paris with his wife and daughter, moving to Toulouse to avoid the conflict with Germany. During the next few years he set several national records in the 100m and 200m freestyle and the 200m breaststroke.

During the Nazi occupation of France Nakache had to contend with Nazi slurs. 'The Jew Nakache', one journalist wrote, 'polluted the waters of French pools'.

Following Nakache's defeat of the German champion, Joachim Balke, a French journalist wrote: 'The Jew, Nakache, should not be allowed to hold any European titles because he is Jewish'. On 6 July 1941 Nakache broke Jack Kasley's world 200m breaststroke record in a time of 2min 38.8s. It took five years before Joe Verdeur (assisted by a short course pool) beat Nakache's time in 1946. If records were measured as they are today, Nakache's world record would have stood until 1948 before being bettered in a long course pool, again by Joe Verdeur, at the USA Olympic trials.

Meanwhile Nakache was working with the Jewish resistance, helping with the physical training of recruits. In 1942 the French Swimming Federation acquiesced to German demands and shamefully banned Nakache from competing in the 1943 National championships.

In November 1943 Nakache was betrayed by a 'friend'

and he, his wife and his daughter were arrested and subsequently deported to Auschwitz. The Nazis killed Nakache's wife and his daughter, who was two years old. Nakache was transferred to Buchenwald towards the end of the war. He was freed by the Allies weighing only 42kg—one of only 47 Buchenwald survivors.[18]

One would think it impossible to recover from such an experience. Yet less than a year after his liberation Nakache reasserted himself as the French champion in the 200m breaststroke and was included in the national 4x200m freestyle relay team. He was also in the French team that in 1946 broke the world record in the 3x100m relay (3 strokes). In 1948, twelve years after first competing in the Olympics and well past his prime, Nakache again represented France at the Olympics. This time he competed in swimming as well as water polo.

Nakache was one of five men who managed to survive the horrors of Nazi camps and subsequently compete in the Olympic Games. The others are race walkers Henry Laskau and Shaul Ladany (both of whom also set world records following the Holocaust), Yakiv Punkin, who won gold for wrestling at the 1952 Games, and the weightlifter Ben Helfgott.

In a bitter twist, Nakache died by drowning after suffering a heart attack while on his daily swim in the port of Cerberus. His life was the subject of a French documentary: *Alfred Nakache, the Swimmer of Auschwitz.* Several swimming pools in France have been named after him—one of them being the main pool in the city of Toulouse. Nakache was inducted into the International Swimming Hall of Fame in 2019.

It was in the 1912 Games in Stockholm that an Austrian woman first won a medal at the Olympics. Austria took bronze in the 4x100m freestyle event. Three of the four team members were Jewish—**Josephine Sticker** (1894-1963), **Klara Milch** (1891-1970) and **Margarete Adler** (1896-1990).[19] Adler competed in the Games twelve years later in the 10m diving event.

The next trio of great female Austrian Jewish swimmers had to contend with challenges much greater than competitive swimming. These toughest, bravest and most talented of Austrian athletes were **Ruth Langer**, **Judith Deutsch**, and **Lucie Goldner**. All three trained at the Hakoah Jewish club—they were barred from other pools by signs reading: 'No entry for dogs and Jews'.

All three were chosen to compete for Austria in Hitler's 1936 Games despite Austrian officials being uneasy about selecting Jews for their Olympic team. They all refused to go to the Games in protest against Nazi policies, stating: 'we do not boycott Olympia, but Berlin', Langer said in an interview with *Reuters*.

Austria responded by banning the swimmers from all national and international competition.[20] In addition, their names were stripped from the Austrian record books. There was much to delete. Langer held eight national titles and was the Austrian record holder in the 100m and 400m freestyle.

Deutsch dominated Austrian swimming between 1934 and 1936. She held twelve Austrian records, including the 100m, 200m and 400m freestyle events. Her preference, though, was for long distance events. In these races she would carefully ration her energy so as to leave enough strength for a final sprint that would leave her competitors far behind. In this way, she reasoned, there could be no saying that the Jewish swimmer came second. She was the Austrian Outstanding Athlete of the Year in 1935. Deutsch loved to compete and loved to win. In a poignant moment she said: 'eventually I became famous for a race in which I never took part'.[21]

Goldner was the Austrian backstroke champion. When the Nazis took Austria in 1938 Goldner was arrested. She was interrogated and beaten by police, and patched up by the local doctor. The doctor helped her escape through the back door but not before warning her that further displays of courage and defiance would be fatal. Goldner escaped Austria by catching a train to Berlin. The now non-existent German border was the only way Jews could leave Austria without risking arrest. She shared her carriage with several Gestapo agents, Hitler's personal air pilot, and the assassins of the Austrian president, Dolfuss. The assassins were on their way to Berlin to receive their rewards. They were drunk and aggressive. Goldner had dyed her hair blonde and hid her yellow star under her coat. The pilot realised she was Jewish and, surprisingly, protected her. He unclipped his swastika badge and pinned it on her lapel, telling her it would get her safely to Berlin. She got to Berlin but was far from safe, and was forced to risk flying to London without an entry permit. Here she was again lucky. Assisted by a multilingual flight attendant, she related her story to an immigration official who fortuitously recalled her refusal to attend the Berlin Games. She was required to have an English person vouch for her, so she named a club official from Vienna who now lived in London. He gave his full support and Goldner was allowed into England.

Goldner married Henry Gordian who was serving in the free Czech army in England. After the war she joined her husband in Prague. They left Czechoslovakia following the Soviet invasion and got a 'lift' to Australia with a couple of adventurous Canadians in an old World War Two DC3 airplane. In Melbourne, Goldner swam at interstate carnivals and then coached the Victorian team. She died in 2000—two weeks before the Sydney Olympics.[22]

In 1938, after the Anschluss, Ruth Langer used a false baptismal certificate to escape to Italy. In 1939 she moved to England. That year she won the British long-distance swim in the Thames. Once World War Two broke out Langer was sent to Bath as an 'enemy alien'. She was subsequently permitted to return to London, where she met John Lawrence. The two married in 1943. Prior to the 1996 Olympics Ruth Lawrence told Reuters: 'Whenever the Games come up again, I get a heartache. It's something that stays with you for the rest of your life. It was a once in a lifetime opportunity. But being Jewish, it was unthinkable to compete in Nazi Germany, where my people were being persecuted'.

In 1995—fifty years after the war ended—the Austrian government finally apologised and reinstated these women's records and titles. This is what the President of the Federation of Austrian Swimming Clubs said to Goldner: 'When I learned in recent weeks that athletes who refused to serve as window-dressing for the Hitler regime received a lifetime ban…I blushed with anger and shame. I am deeply ashamed of the decision taken at that time. You, who as an irreproachable and decent athlete, did everything you could to achieve success in order to show solidarity with the persecuted, were punished. Those responsible today for the Federation of Austrian Swimming Clubs are glad that you survived that cruel and merciless time and humbly apologise for what our predecessors did. All of your athletic successes and achievements are hereby confirmed and recorded in the perpetual scoring tables. You, Mrs Lawrence, are an example to young people. We are proud that you are there'.[23]

All three women declined to attend the ceremony. In June 1995, Dr. Herbert Karol, the Austrian ambassador to Israel, read out a letter written by the president of the Austrian Parliament. The letter mentioned 'deep sorrow for the event' and continued: 'Perhaps we are apologising too late, but better now than never'. Judith Deutsch replied: 'I am happy to accept your apologies and the withdrawal of sanctions against me… And in no way do I regret having done what I did sixty years ago'.[24] Deutsch settled in Israel.

An American swimmer, **Paul Friesel** (1911-unknown), withdrew from possible selection for Hitler's Games in protest against Nazi policies. Friesel helped make popular a modified breaststroke in the early 1930s. The stroke evolved into butterfly, at which Friesel was a leading exponent. He is credited with giving the stroke its name.

Friesel made an exceptional contribution during World War Two, teaching swimming to thousands of American merchant seamen. Subsequently he became

Director of Lifeguards for the New York Department of Parks.[25]

Jewish swimmers had been winning medals for Austria since the inaugural 1896 Games in which Austria's only two medals were won by Jewish swimmers. The first of these medals went to **Paul Neumann** (1875-1932), who won the third Olympic swimming event—the 500m freestyle. After the Athens Games, Neumann immigrated to the USA and studied medicine, but continued to compete in swimming. Amongst other successes, he set world records in 1897 in the two, three, four and five mile indoor swims.[26]

The second medal was won by **Otto Herschmann** (1877-1942), who took silver in the 100m freestyle, finishing within half a metre of Alfred Guttmann while the rest of the field trailed far behind. Herschmann is one of few Olympians to have won medals in different sports. Sixteen years after winning silver in swimming, and aged thirty-five, he won silver in the 1912 Stockholm Games in fencing as a member of Austria's sabre team. He was president of the Austrian Olympic Committee from 1912-1914 and became the only president of a national Olympic Committee to win an Olympic medal while in office. Later he was arrested by the Nazis and deported to the Sobibor concentration camp, where he died.[27]

Other Jewish Swimming Olympians killed by the

Nazis were the Hungarians, András Székely and Joszef Munk, and the Pole, Ilja Szrajbman.

András Székely (1909-1943) won bronze in the 4x200m freestyle for Hungary in the 1932 Olympics.[28] He was killed at a forced labour camp in Ukraine.[29]

József Munk (1890-unknown) and **Imre Zachár** (1890-1954) won silver as members of the Hungarian 4x200m freestyle relay team in the 1908 Games in London.[30] In 1942 Munk was taken prisoner by the Soviets and was never heard of again.

Ilja Szrajbman (1907-1943) was Poland's 200m freestyle champion and represented Poland at the 1936 Games in the same event. He died in the Majdanek concentration camp.[31]

The Belgian, **Gérard Blitz** (1901-1979), won Olympic medals in swimming and water polo. Blitz competed at the 1920, 1924, 1928 and 1936 Games. He won a bronze medal in the 100m backstroke in 1920. In 1920 and 1924 he won silver medals in water polo, and in Hitler's 1936 Games he took bronze in the water polo event. Blitz also set a world record for the 400m backstroke in 1921. His time of 5min 59.2s was only bettered in 1927. Blitz was inducted into the International Swimming Hall of Fame in 1990.[32]

One of the oddest Olympic swimming events was held

only once. In the 200m obstacle course at the 1900 Paris Olympics, swimmers had to climb over a pole, then over a row of boats, and then swim beneath another row of boats. The race was closely contested, with Fred Lane of Australia narrowly beating Austrian **Otto Wahle** (1879-1963) into second place. Wahle won silver in the 1000m freestyle in the same Games.

Wahle left for the USA in 1901. In 1904 he took bronze in the 400y freestyle at the St. Louis Olympics. He subsequently coached the USA Olympic team for the 1912 Games. One of the athletes Wahle coached for the pentathlon swimming event was to become the legendary USA army general—George S. Patton. Wahle coached the USA water polo team for the 1920 and 1924 Games and was pivotal in the development of competitive swimming in the USA. He was inducted into the International Swimming Hall of Fame in 1996.[33]

The Holocaust devastated European Jewry and brought to an end the run of European Jewish Olympic medallists. In swimming it was now mainly Jewish Americans who came to the fore. We have discussed swimmers such as Mark Spitz, Jason Lezak, Keena Rothhamer, Andrea Gyarmati, and Éva Székely. Let us now consider some of the other great Jewish Olympic swimmers who competed after World War Two.

One could be forgiven for thinking no Jewish swimmer has won more Olympic medals than Spitz's eleven. Yet the Cuban-American, **Dara Torres** (1967-), has done just that. Torres won twelve Olympic medals—four of each colour. She is the first swimmer to represent the USA in five Olympics—1984, 1988, 1992, 2000 and 2008. Torres was 17 when she swam in the 1984 Games and was 41 when she competed in her last Olympics in 2008, making her the oldest swimmer ever to compete in the Olympics. She won at least one medal in each of the Olympics in which she participated. In the 2008 Games she won three silver medals, missing gold in the 50m freestyle by a devastating 0.01s.[34] Torres held the world record for the 50m freestyle in 1983. She had something in common with Jason Lezak. Her split in the 4×100m medley relay (52.27s) in the 2008 Games was the fastest 100m freestyle split in relay history.[35] The Americans, Dara Torres, Jenny Thompson and Natalie Coughlin, have won more Olympic medals than any other women—they are all tied on twelve.

Sports Illustrated named Torres one of the Top Female Athletes of the Decade. Her memoir became one of the best-selling books of 2009. She was inducted into The International Swimming Hall of Fame in 2016.

The American **Marilyn Ramenofsky** (1946-) set the world record for the 400m freestyle on three occasions in 1964. In the same year she took silver in the Tokyo

Olympics in the 400m freestyle. Ramenofsky modified her stroke on realising that by raising her hand high out of the water she could decrease turbulence.[36] Buck Dawson, the director of The International Swimming Hall of Fame, said of her: 'She was the first female to swim a perfect freestyle stroke'.[37] Ramenofsky not only pushed the envelope in swimming but did so as a pioneering scientist working on the physiology and behavior of migratory birds.[38]

It's hard enough to be the fastest man in the water at an Olympic Games but who would bet on anyone winning the 50m sprint on two occasions—16 years apart? **Anthony Ervin** (1981-) won the 50m gold medal (shared with Gary Hall Jr.) at the Sydney 2000 Games. At the same Olympics, Ervin won silver as part of the USA 4x100m freestyle team which included Jason Lezak. Ervin swapped the rigours of competitive swimming for a bohemian existence in 2003 at the pinnacle of his career. He auctioned his gold medal on eBay to help survivors of the 2004 Boxing Day Tsunami. He had his body tattooed, formed a heavy metal band called *Weapons of Mass Destruction*, and sought comfort in religion. He indulged in drugs and alcohol, was involved in a high-speed bike accident while pursued by police, and spent some time in prison.

While studying for a Master's degree in sport, culture and education, Ervin turned his life around. He again focused on swimming and achieved what most would consider impossible. Twelve years after his successes in Sydney, he made it into the USA team for the 2012 Games in London. He came fifth in the 50m freestyle. Four years later, aged thirty-five, this iron-willed champion won his second Olympic gold in the 50m freestyle. He became the oldest individual to win an Olympic gold in swimming.[39] Ervin's story has been released as a memoir: *Chasing Water: Elegy of an Olympian.* It's an inspiring tale about the many facets and challenges of life.

Lenny Krayzelburg (1975-) was born Leonid Krayzelburg in Odessa (now Ukraine). Krayzelburg's parents made the decision to emigrate because they knew that, being Jewish, their son's opportunities would be limited in Russia, especially in sport.[40] The Krayzelburg family left Odessa for the USA in 1989.

In addition to learning a new language the family had to endure financial hardships, requiring Krayzelburg to commute by bus and on foot forty-five minutes each way for swimming training. Krayzelburg became renowned for his powerful strokes and was regarded as one of the most physically strong swimmers. He came to dominate backstroke, setting five world records. In 1999 he broke the world records for the 50m, 100m and 200m events. In addition, Krayzelburg set the short course world records for the 100m and 200m distances and was a member of the world record-breaking medley team at the 2000 Sydney Olympics. In the 2000 Games he also took gold in the 100m and 200m backstroke, making him the first swimmer to take gold in both events since Rick Carey in 1984. In Athens in 2004, as one of the USA 4x100m medley team, he again won gold, giving him a tally of four Olympic golds.

Krayzelburg was named Sportsman of the Year by the USA Olympic Committee in 1998, and was the USA Swimmer of the Year in 1999 and 2000. He was acclaimed as one of the best back-strokers in the history of swimming. He was inducted into the International Swimming Hall of Fame in 2011. Today he runs his own swimming academy teaching children to swim. He also helps underprivileged children learn to swim through his Lenny Krayzelburg Foundation.[41]

Another swimmer who won Olympic medals in medley events is **Scott Goldblatt** (1975-). Goldblatt won silver in the 4x200m freestyle in Sydney in 2000 and gold in the same event four years later in Athens.

Tiffany Cohen (1966-) won gold in the 400m and 800m freestyle in the 1984 Los Angeles Olympics. She set new Olympic records for both distances. She is perhaps best remembered for the 800m victory. Her time was only 0.33s less than the world record held by Australian Tracy Wickham. Cohen was inducted into the International Swimming Hall of Fame in 1996.[42]

Wallace 'Wally' Wolf (1930-1997) was one of the American team that set a world record while winning gold in the 1948 Games in the 4x200m relay. Wolf swam the second leg. He was again in the side that took gold in the 4x200m relay in the 1952 Olympics. Wolf also competed for the USA in water polo at the 1956 and 1960 Games. He was selected for the 1964 team but declined to compete.[43]

Twins **Sarah and Karen Josephson** (1964-) gave the impression of a telepathic display when competing in the duets in synchronised swimming. Search for 'Josephson twins synchronised swimming' on YouTube to see their 1988 Olympic performance. You are bound to come away with increased respect for this unforgiving sport.

The identical twins won silver in the 1988 Seoul Olympics and gold in the 1992 Barcelona Olympics. They are one of only two synchronised swimming duets to have been inducted into the International Swimming Hall of Fame. Between the Seoul and Barcelona Games, the twins never lost a competition. This is their list of victories: The Pan Pacific, the Goodwill Games, the USA Nationals, the Olympic Festivals, the German, Mallorca and Rome Opens, the USA Olympic trials, and the Perth World Championships, where their score set a new world record in duet competition.[44]

South Africa has had several Jewish swimming Springboks. Many of them were unable to compete at the Olympics due to the sporting boycott of South Africa from 1964 to 1992. Two of the many Jewish South African swimming Springboks who missed out on Olympic competition spring to mind.

Carmel Goodman (1956-) captained the South African swimming team. Goodman attended King David School in Johannesburg and first donned a Springbok blazer aged thirteen. Her coach, Bernard Green, described her as having the attributes of a swimming champion—love of the water, ability, dedication to training, and a killer instinct. She was chosen to represent South Africa against West Germany in 1970. Elation was, however, followed by disappointment—the tour was cancelled due to political pressure.

In February to March of 1971, in four scintillating swims, Goodman—a 15 year old schoolgirl—rewrote the South African record books four times in six weeks. She first broke Shirley van der Poel's four year old record for the 100m breaststroke, becoming the first South African to go under 80s. Less than a week later she shaved 1.9s off the 200m breaststroke record, which had also belonged to Van der Poel. This is how Dennis Hands described her swims:[45] 'The achievement is unique in the annals of South African swimming. Never before has an almost unknown swimmer bettered two national records in the same week, swimming against average competition.' He added that what made the twin achievements even more stunning was that both swims were at high altitude. What would Hands have written had he known that Goodman was to break her own 200m breaststroke record on two more occasions in the next five weeks?

There were only six South African swimmers who would have qualified for the 1972 Olympics. Goodman and another Jewish champion, **Roy Abramowitz**, were amongst the six. South Africa had, however, been banned from the Olympics since 1964. We can but imagine the despair of elite South African athletes knowing that they could not compete at the Olympic Games.

In 1972 two South African athletes (one swimmer and one track athlete) received scholarships to train in Australia. Goodman was selected as the swimmer. She was given the opportunity to train under Forbes Carlisle, the Australian Olympic coach, and was permitted to swim in the Australian Olympic trials a month before the 1972 Munich Olympics. In one race Goodman beat the Australian Beverly Whitfield. Her scholarship over, Goodman went back to South Africa. Whitfield went to the 1972 Munich Olympics where she won gold in the 200m breaststroke and bronze in the 100m breaststroke.

Although Goodman could not compete in the Munich Games, she nevertheless received some consolation in the South African Games in 1973. She won the 200m breaststroke, touching 0.5s ahead of Petra Nouws. Nouws, described as one of West Germany's best swimmers, came fifth in the same event at the 1972 Olympics.

By the time South Africa was readmitted to Olympic competition in 1992, Goodman's competitive swimming days were long over. However, she had several strings to her bow. She qualified in Johannesburg as a doctor and married Jon Cartoon, whom she met at Medical School. The family subsequently moved to Australia where Goodman replicated her successes—this time as a specialist in sports medicine. She has been the medical director of the West Australian Institute of Sport (WAIS) since 1990. She is also currently the team doctor to the Australian Olympic and Commonwealth Games teams, a post she has held since 2000. She was awarded the medal for Outstanding Contribution to a Team in the Field of Sports Medicine. She is the author of seventy-four research articles. Citations are in the thousands.[46]

Her coach could have added that the attributes he ascribed to her swimming successes applied to every facet of Goodman's life.

Basil Hotz won more South African swimming titles

and broke more records than even he can remember. Between 1962 and 1965 he won all the South African provincial and national championships in which he competed. He then went to the USA where he placed fourth in the nationals. In 1964 and 1965 Hotz toured Europe as a member of the Springbok team, winning numerous titles, including three British Championships. He was selected for the 1964 and 1968 Olympics but could not attend because of the sporting sanctions against South Africa.

How Hotz came to swimming is itself a story. Hotz was set on a career in soccer and as a young teenager was scouted by the Charlton Athletic soccer club, and was due to attend a 'try-out' camp in London when fate played its hand. Playing for Balfour Park against Marist Brothers, Hotz had the ball and was going at full speed when an opponent called him a f...... Jew. Without thinking Hotz turned and punched his tormentor in the face, breaking his nose. A second opposition player then attacked Hotz. In the melee Hotz fell face-down, with his opponent on his back – both of his wrists and elbows were broken. All three players were suspended for a year. Hotz's upper limbs—wrists to shoulders—were immobilised in plaster casts. Hotz's coach asked the swimming coach at Balfour Park, Jan Kooiman, if they could put Hotz's arms in plastic bags and allow him to swim laps in order to maintain his fitness and lower limb strength.

Several weeks later Hotz was swimming faster than the able-bodied swimmers. Unsurprisingly, Kooiman asked Hotz if he would compete as a swimmer under his coaching that summer. Hotz never returned to soccer—a South African swimming star was born.[47]

The most spectacular achievement of Jewish South African swimmers during the period South Africa was banned from the Olympics belongs to **Jeremy Reingold** (1968-). In September 1980 at 12 years of age Reingold set the world record of 2min 3.01s for the 200m long course individual medley. This event was not held at the 1980 Olympics but it was held at the 1984 Games when Alex Baumann of Canada took gold in a world record time of 2min 1.42s. Silver went to P. Pablo Morales of the USA in 2min 3.05s. Reingold's 1980 world record time would have won him silver at the 1984 Games.

Reingold was, however, more than a swimmer. He played for South Africa's 1985 under-18 rugby union team. It would be a rare achievement to break a swimming world record and play rugby union at such an elite level.

It took sixty-eight years, following the devastation of Germany's Jews, for a South African to make history by returning to her roots to become the first Jewish athlete to again win an Olympic medal for Germany.

Sarah Poewe (1983-) won bronze in the 4x100m medley in the 2004 Athens Games. In the finals of the 100m breaststroke she finished fifth.

Poewe has a South African mother and German father. She grew up in Cape Town and represented South Africa in the 2000 Olympics. She finished fourth in the 100m breaststroke, missing a medal by 0.3s, and sixth in the 200m breaststroke. In 2001 Poewe won the South African 100m breaststroke championships and went on to win the 50m breaststroke title at the World Meet in Barcelona the same year.[48]

Following the 2002 Commonwealth Games, Poewe competed for Germany. From 2002 until 2012 she won 17 German championships, and broke nine German records and three European records.

Following her competitive career in swimming, Poewe was chosen as the German Swimming Patron for the European Maccabi Games. Her interest in these Games was sparked by the likes of Mark Spitz, Lenny Krayzelburg and Jason Lezak. She now runs her own swimming school in Germany.[49]

Two more swimmers I need to mention are the Americans Rebecca Soni and Katie Ledecki. Soni and Ledecki are amongst the best female swimmers ever—both won several Olympic medals and set multiple world records. Neither considers themselves Jewish and Jews do not consider them Jewish. Racists, however, make up their own definitions about what defines a person with to race and religion. Had Soni and Ledecki lived in Nazi Germany or in Nazi aligned countries such as Hungary or Austria they would have been Jewish enough to be persecuted and barred from sport. You only needed one Jewish grandparent to qualify for internment in a concentration camp. Soni had Jewish paternal grandparents—in fact they were Auschwitz survivors.[50] Ledecki is Catholic but has a Jewish grandmother.[51]

SUMMARY

In 1972—the year terror came to the Olympics—Mark Spitz won seven Olympic golds all in world record times. It took 35 years before fellow American, Michael Phelps, broke Spitz's haul of golds.

In a relay leg recognised as possibly the best swim ever Phelps received vital assistance from Jason Lezak in surpassing Spitz's record haul.

Few realise that an American woman, Dara Torres has won more Olympic medals than Spitz.

The successes of the many modern day Jewish swimmers are, however, bland compared to the three female Austrian Olympians who escaped the Nazis.

Alfred Nakache was one of five Jewish athletes who survived internment in a Nazi camp to subsequently compete at the Olympics. Nakache and two other concentration camp survivors subsequently set world records.

South African, Sarah Poewe, returned to her German roots to win an Olympic medal for Germany in 2004—the first Jewish athlete to do so since the Holocaust.

MEDAL COMPARISON BETWEEN JEWISH AND AUSTRALIAN OLYMPIC SWIMMERS

Australia has won more medals in swimming than any other sport. As a country Australia has won 68 Olympic swimming medals. As individuals (each member of a relay team is counted) Australians have won 374 medals (117 gold) in swimming. Jewish swimmers have won 86 medals (44 gold).

In swimming, as in athletics, Australians have won more medals than Jewish athletes, but as in athletics, the Jewish swimmers surpass Australian swimmers in excellence. This difference is made clear by comparing the individual medal tallies of the top five Jewish Olympic swimmers with the top five Australian Olympic swimmers.

Are Jews Really No Good at Sport?

	Gold	Silver	Bronze
Mark Spitz	9	1	1
Dara Torres	4	4	4
Jason Lezak	4	2	2
Lenny Krayzelburg	4	0	0
Anthony Ervin	3	1	0
TOTALS	24	8	7
GRAND TOTAL	39		

	Gold	Silver	Bronze
Ian Thorpe	5	3	1
Dawn Fraser	4	4	0
Libby Trickett	4	1	2
Murray Rose	4	1	1
Liesel Jones	3	5	1
TOTALS	20	14	5
GRAND TOTAL	39		

While the total medal count for the top five Jewish swimmers is equal to that of the top five Australian swimmers, the Jewish swimmers have won 24 gold medals whereas the Australian swimmers have won 20.

JEWISH OLYMPIC MEDALLISTS—SWIMMING

1896 Athens
Alfred (Hajós) Guttmann, Hun. Gold; 100m freestyle
Alfred (Hajós) Guttmann, Hun. Gold; 1,200m freestyle
Paul Neumann, Austria, Gold; 500m freestyle
Otto Herschmann, Austria, Silver; 100m freestyle

1900 Paris
Otto Wahle, Austria, Silver; 1,000m freestyle
Otto Wahle, Austria, Silver; 200m obstacle course

1904 St. Louis
Otto Wahle, Austria, Bronze; 400y freestyle

1906 Athens
Henrik (Hajós) Guttmann, Hun. Gold; 4x250m freestyle
Otto Scheff, Austria, Gold; 400y freestyle
Otto Scheff, Austria, Bronze; 1,500m freestyle

1908 London
József Munk, Hun. Silver; 4x200m freestyle
Imre Zachár, Hun. Silver; 4x200m freestyle
Otto Scheff, Austria, Bronze; 400y freestyle

1912 Stockholm
Josephine Sticker, Austria, Bronze; 4x100m freestyle

Margarete Adler, Austria, Bronze; 4x100m freestyle
Klara Milch, Austria, Bronze; 4x100m freestyle

1916 Cancelled due to World War One

1920 Antwerp
Gérard Blitz, Bel. Bronze; 100m backstroke

1932 Los Angeles
László Szabados, Hun. Bronze; 4x200m freestyle
Albert Schwartz, USA, Bronze; 100m freestyle
András Székely, Hun. Bronze; 4x200m freestyle

1940 and 1944 Cancelled due to World War Two

1948 London
Fritze Wulff-Carstensen, Denmark, Silver;
4x100m freestyle
Wally Wolf, USA, Gold; 4x200m freestyle

1952 Helsinki
Éva Székely, Hun. Gold; 200m breaststroke
Judit Temes, Hun. Gold; 4x100m freestyle
Judit Temes, Hun. Bronze; 100m freestyle
Wally Wolf, USA, Gold; 4x200m freestyle

1956 Melbourne
Éva Székely, Hun. Silver; 200m breaststroke

1964 Tokyo
Marilyn Ramenofsky, USA, Silver; 400m freestyle

Michael Meyerson

1968 Mexico City
Mark Spitz, USA, Gold; 4x100m medley
Mark Spitz, USA, Gold; 4x200m freestyle
Mark Spitz, USA, Silver; 100m butterfly
Semyon Belits-Geiman, Russia, Silver; 4x100m freestyle
Mark Spitz, USA, Bronze; 100m freestyle

1972 Munich
Mark Spitz, USA, Gold; 100m freestyle
Mark Spitz, USA, Gold; 200m freestyle
Mark Spitz, USA, Gold; 100m butterfly
Mark Spitz, USA, Gold; 200m butterfly
Mark Spitz, USA, Gold; 4x100m medley
Mark Spitz, USA, Gold; 4x100m freestyle
Mark Spitz, USA, Gold; 4x200m freestyle
Keena Rothhammer, USA, Gold; 800m freestyle
Keena Rothhammer, USA, Bronze; 200m freestyle
Andrea Gyarmati, Hun. Silver; 100m backstroke
Andrea Gyarmati, Hun. Bronze; 100m butterfly

1976 Montreal
Wendy Weinberg, USA, Bronze; 800m freestyle

1984 Los Angeles
Tiffany Cohen, USA, Gold; 400m freestyle
Tiffany Cohen, USA, Gold; 800m freestyle
Dara Torres, USA, Gold; 4x100m freestyle

1988 Seoul
Karen Josephson, USA, Silver; synchronised pairs

Sarah Josephson, USA, Silver; synchronised pairs
Dara Torres, USA, Silver; 4x100m medley
Dara Torres, USA, Bronze; 4x100m freestyle

1992 Barcelona
Karen Josephson, USA, Gold; synchronised pairs
Sarah Josephson, USA, Gold; synchronised pairs
Dara Torres, USA, Gold; 4x100m freestyle

1996 Atlanta
Lenny Krayzelburg, USA, Gold; 4x100m freestyle

2000 Sydney
Anthony Ervin, USA, Gold; 50m freestyle
Lenny Krayzelburg, USA, Gold; 4x100m medley
Lenny Krayzelburg, USA, Gold; 200m backstroke
Lenny Krayzelburg, USA, Gold; 100m backstroke
Dara Torres, USA, Gold; 4x100m freestyle
Dara Torres, USA, Gold; 4x100m medley
Anthony Ervin, USA, Silver; 4x100m freestyle
Dara Torres, USA, Bronze; 100m freestyle
Dara Torres, USA, Bronze; 100m butterfly
Dara Torres, USA, Bronze; 50m freestyle
Scott Goldblatt, USA, Gold; 4x200m freestyle
Jason Lezak, USA, Gold; 4x100m medley
Jason Lezak, USA, Silver; 4x100m freestyle

2004 Athens
Lenny Krayzelburg, USA, Gold; 4x 100m medley
Jason Lezak, USA, Gold; 4x100m medley

Jason Lezak, USA, Bronze; 4x100m freestyle
Scott Goldblatt, USA, Gold; 4x200m freestyle
Sarah Poewe, Germany, Bronze; 4x100m medley

2008 Beijing
Dara Torres, USA, Silver; 50m freestyle
Dara Torres, USA, Silver; 4x100m medley
Dara Torres, USA, Silver; 4x100m freestyle
Jason Lezak, USA, Gold; 4x100m medley
Jason Lezak, USA, Gold; 4x100m freestyle
Jason Lezak, USA, Bronze; 100m freestyle
Garrett Weber-Gale, USA, Gold; 4x100m freestyle
Garrett Weber-Gale, USA, Gold; 4x100m medley
Ben Wildman-Tobriner, USA, Gold; 4x100m freestyle

2012 London
Jason Lezak, USA, Silver; 4x100m freestyle

2016 Rio
Anthony Ervin, USA, Gold; 50m freestyle
Anthony Ervin, USA, Gold; 4x100m freestyle

TOTAL: 86
Gold 44; Silver 20; Bronze 22

CHAPTER 3

GYMNASTICS—TRAGEDY AND TRIUMPH

'[I] can't think of too many Jewish sporting heroes, if you leave out David's gold-medal skills with the sling-shot'

Philip Adams—Australian journalist.[1]

Besides strength, grace, precision, talent, and endless hours of practice an elite gymnast requires at least two more attributes—a bottomless pit of courage and more than a dash of self-deception. This is what Olympians Nadia Comaneci and Simone Biles said about their sport. Comaneci: 'After a while, if you work on a certain move consistently then it doesn't seem so risky. The idea is that the move stays dangerous and it looks dangerous to my opponents— but it isn't to me'.[2] Biles, more pragmatically, said that you need repeatedly to convince yourself that you are not going to die.[3] Yet for many Jewish Olympic gymnasts, other dangers dwarfed the perils of gymnastic routines. The Nazi regime killed 13 Jewish Olympic gymnasts.

Amongst them were the **Flatow** cousins who participated in the first modern Games in 1896. If you were in the vicinity of the Olympic Stadium in Berlin subsequent to 1997 you might have chanced upon the lane Flatowwallee (Flatow-Avenue). Were you to affix a stamp to a letter in that year, you might have noticed that the stamp portrayed two dashing, bare-chested, mustachioed, young men—Gustav and Alfred Flatow. Along one side of the stamp you would have read the dates *1896-1996*. Had you enquired about the story behind the stamp you would have found that the stamp commemorating the Flatows was one of four issued by German Post to mark 100 years since the first Olympic Games. [4,5] The Flatow cousins won six of the 20 individual medals won by Germany in the first Olympics. Each took gold in the team horizontal and parallel bar events. Alfred won two further medals—gold in the parallel bars and silver in the horizontal bars.

In 1903 **Alfred Flatow** (1869-1942) founded the pioneering Jewish sports organisation in Europe—the Jüdische Turnerschaft. He taught gymnastics and wrote books on the sport. In 1933, this Olympic medallist was made to renounce his membership of his gymnastics club because he was Jewish.

Gustav Flatow (1875-1945) retired from gymnastics to manage a textile company which he founded in 1899.

Following the rise to power of the Nazis, the Flatows fled Germany for Holland. After Germany invaded Holland they were arrested and later sent to the Theresienstadt concentration camp where they were among the 35,000 Jews who died of starvation.[6] After extinguishing their lives it took five decades for Germany to honour their Olympic heroes.

Five of the twelve women who made up the Dutch gymnastics team that competed in the 1912 Stockholm Games were Jewish—all won gold medals. Four of these Olympic medallists—**Estelle Agsteribbe, Annie Polak, Judikje Simons, Helene Nordheim** and their beloved coach **Gerrit Kleerekoper**—lost their lives in Nazi concentration camps. Only **Elke de Levie** survived the Nazi onslaught.[7]

Seven male Jewish Dutch gymnasts who represented Holland in either the 1908 or 1928 Olympics also perished in German concentration camps. They were: **Abraham Mok, Isidore Goudeket, Abraham de Oliveira, Jonas Slier, Mozes Jacobs, Elias Melkman, and Israel Wijnschenk**.[8]

Pearl Perkins was a brilliant American gymnast from South Philadelphia. She would have been better known if she had not boycotted Hitler's 1936 Games. She was chosen for the 1936 USA Olympic team, but on the advice of her Russian Jewish immigrant parents chose to boycott the Games. She subsequently won the USA national championships in the horse and vault in 1941 and 1943 and took the national all-round Amateur Athletic Union (AAU) titles in 1937, 1941 and 1943.[9] It is likely that Perkins would have won a medal at the 1936 Games.

The Hungarian gymnast **Ágnes Keleti** (1921-) was born Ágnes Klein in Budapest, Hungary. Keleti won the Hungarian National Gymnastics championships at the age of 16. She was banned from her gymnastics club in 1941 on account of being Jewish.

Using the identity documents of a Christian girl, Keleti went undercover during the Nazi invasion of Hungary, working as a maid in a small village. Her mother and sister were among the many Jews saved by the heroic Swedish diplomat Raoul Wallenberg. Keleti's father, along with other relatives, was gassed at Auschwitz.[10]

Keleti qualified for the 1948 Games but could not compete due to an ankle injury. At the 1952 Helsinki Games, aged 31, she won four medals: gold in the floor exercise, silver in the team competition, and bronze in the team portable apparatus and the uneven bars. Four years later Keleti was the most successful athlete at the 1956 Melbourne Games. She won six medals—four golds and two silvers. She won golds for floor exercises, uneven bars, balance and team portable apparatus and silvers for all-around performance and the team competition.[11]

Keleti was not the only Jewish Hungarian gymnast to win Olympic medals in the 1956 Games. **Aliz Kertész** (1935-) won gold in the team exercise in portable apparatus events and silver in the team combined exercises event.[12]

During the 1956 Games the Soviet Union invaded Hungary. Keleti, along with several other Hungarian athletes, sought and was granted political asylum in Australia. In 1957 Keleti moved to Israel where she was joined by her mother and sister. In Israel, she worked as a physical education instructor at the Wingate Institute for Sports in Netanya. She also coached Israel's gymnastics team into the 1990s.

In 1991 Hungary honoured the athlete it had treated so shamefully by inducting her into the Hungarian Sports Hall of Fame. Keleti was inducted into the International Gymnastics Hall of Fame in 2002.[13]

We can best appreciate Keleti's achievements by contrasting her Olympic successes with those of her countrymen and women. Of the top twenty Hungarian Olympic athletes, Keleti ties in first place with Aladar Gerevich[14] in terms of the total number of medals won—ten. She is fourth in terms of gold medals—five. No Hungarian woman has won as many medals, or more golds than Keleti, making her the most distinguished female Hungarian Olympian of all time.

There are, however, four other Jewish athletes who feature amongst the twenty most successful Hungarian Olympians. They are: **Jenő Fuchs** (9th) (fencing), **Dezső Gyarmati** (13th) (water polo), **Endre Kabos** (18th) (fencing) and **György Kárpáti** (19th) (water polo). Jewish athletes comprise five (25%) of the twenty most successful Hungarian Olympians. Consider that prior to the Nazi era Jews comprised only 6% of the Hungarian population. Subsequent to World War Two Jews comprised about 1.45% of Hungarians and today about 0.11%.

We now need to consider the contribution of the decimated Hungarian Jewish population to the 1956 Games in Melbourne. Hungary won 26 medals, placing fourth behind the Soviet Union, the USA and Australia. Of Hungary's 26 medals, 17 were won by individuals. Of the 17 individual medals, the now minute Hungarian Jewish population won five. Ágnes Keleti won three of Hungary's five golds and one of Hungary's eight silvers. **Éva Székely** won another of Hungary's silvers for swimming.

Hungarian Jewish athletes were also over-represented in team events. Hungary won nine team medals. There were three Jewish water polo players in the victorious water polo team—**György Kárpáti, Mahaly Mayer** and **Dezső Gyarmati**. **László Fábián** took gold in the 10,000m pairs canoeing, and **Ágnes Keleti** and **Aliz Kertész** took silver in the combined team exercises.

Hungary is not the only Eastern Bloc country from which great Jewish gymnasts have emerged. From Russia there have been several Jewish gymnasts who have succeeded in the Olympics. One of the most successful was **Maria Gorokhovskaya** (1921-2001), who won more medals at the 1952 Games in Helsinki—two gold and five silver—than any other athlete, male or female. No woman has won more medals in a single Olympic Games than Gorokhovskaya. She remains (along with Mark Spitz) on the list of the 10 athletes who have won the most medals in a single Olympics. No Australian features in this list.

Gorokhovskaya was ranked the world's best gymnast in 1952 and 1953.[15] She was awarded the Honorary Master of Sport as well as the Order of the Red Banner—the Soviet Union's most prestigious sports award. She retired in 1954 after competing as part of the victorious Soviet team in the World Championships. In 1957 Gorokhovskaya was depicted on a Soviet stamp.

During World War Two Gorokhovskaya enrolled in the Russian army and served as a nurse in Leningrad during the three year siege of the city by the Germans. She was awarded the Order of the Great Patriotic War. In 1990 she immigrated to Israel. Only then did it become known that she was Jewish.[16] Here, she coached gymnastics until her death in 2001.

As Gorokhovskaya's star was rising in 1952, the star of another great Jewish Russian gymnast was setting. **Galina Urbanovich** (1917-2011) would undoubtedly have won several Olympic medals had the Soviet Union taken part in the Olympics prior to 1952. She was considered probably the world's best female gymnast of the 1940s. She won the following Soviet titles: all-around—seven times; rings—seven times; uneven bars—five times; pommel horse—three times; horse vault, balance beam and floor exercises—twice; and horizontal bars—once. Aged 34, she finally got her chance to compete at the Olympics, winning gold in the team all-around and silver in the team Portable Apparatus at the 1952 Helsinki Games. Following these Games Urbanovich retired from competitive gymnastics to become a coach.[17]

Yelena Shushunova (1969-2018) is one of five women who have won all-around titles at all major competitions—the Olympics, the World Championships and the European/Continental Championships. Shushunova was considered a certainty to mount the podium at the 1984 Olympics but could not compete because Russia boycotted the

Games. In the 1988 Seoul Olympics, Shushunova won two golds, a silver and a bronze. She scored three perfect '10's to take gold in the individual and team all-around events. She took silver on the balance beam and bronze on the uneven bars. In 2004 she was inducted into the International Gymnastics Sports Hall of Fame[18]. Shushunova died at only 49, of pneumonia.

Other Jewish Soviet gymnasts who have won Olympic medals are **Mikhail Perelman, Vladimir Portnoi, Natalia Laschenova, Valeri Belenky, Tatiana Lysenko, Yana Batyrshina,** and **Yulia Raskina.**

Mitchell Gaylord (1961-) led the USA gymnastics team to gold in 1984. At these Games Gaylord became the first American gymnast to score a perfect '10' and then went on to win silver in the vault and two bronzes for rings and parallel bars. As well as his individual triumphs, Gaylord led the men's team to gold for the first and only time in Olympic history. Gaylord's crowning glory was his invention of two skills that are named after him. The Gaylord Flip and the Gaylord Two are regarded as the most difficult and spectacular feats in gymnastics.

Following the 1984 Games, President Reagan appointed Gaylord to the President's Council for Physical Fitness where he served two terms. In 1986 Gaylord made his debut as an actor in the movie

American Anthem, playing a gymnast training for the Olympics. He also worked as a stunt double in the 1995 movie *Batman Forever* and appeared in several commercial advertisements. Gaylord created *Gold Medal Fitness* and the *Melt it OFF! With Mitch workout program*.[19] In 2006 he was inducted into the USA Olympic Hall of Fame.

American women have won 48 Olympic medals in gymnastics. Three Jewish gymnasts Aly Raisman, Kerri Strug and Phoebe Mills have won nine of these medals (19%), while Jews make up only 0.02% of the American population. Of American female gymnasts, Raisman's tally of six Olympic medals is second only to Shannon Miller, who has won seven. Raisman has, however, won three golds compared to Miller's two.

In the London 2012 and Rio 2016 Olympic Games, **Aly Raisman** (1994-) captained the USA women's team, nicknamed the 'fierce five' and 'final five', to win gold in the team competitions. At the 2012 Games, Raisman also won gold in the floor event and bronze on the balance beam, making her the most successful USA gymnast at these Games.[20]

In the 2012 Olympics Raisman became the first American woman to win gold for the floor exercise event.[21] She dedicated her routine—performed to the tune of 'Hava Nagila'—to the 11 Israelis who were killed by terrorists at the 1972 Munich Games.[22]

In 2016 in Rio de Janeiro, Raisman took gold in the team event and silver for the all-around and floor exercise competition. Her gymnastics coach Márta Károlyi said of Raisman: 'I really love to have this kind of gymnast. She gives her heart'.[23]

We all know the pain and hobbling limp that comes with a twisted ankle. Imagine, then, having to ignore such an injury and vault again for your team to stay in the running for a medal. This is what happened to **Kerri Strug** (1977-) during her first vault in the team Olympic finals in Atlanta in 1996. Strug's coach Béla Károlyi urged her on, saying, 'Kerri, we need you to go one more time. We need you one more time for the gold. You can do it, you better do it'.[24]

Strug now limped to the runway to start her second vault. America held its breath as Strug ran, vaulted and landed on both feet, almost instantaneously hopping onto her good foot. Strug saluted the judges and collapsed. She scored 9.712, guaranteeing gold for her team and the USA. In an image burnt into the minds of the world, Károlyi carried the tiny gymnast with the huge heart to join her team on the podium. Her injury compelled her to withdraw from the subsequent events. Strug, however, had a gold medal to add to the bronze she won four years before in Barcelona, aged 14, and the youngest member of the USA team.

Strug's vault made her a national hero. She visited

President Clinton, appeared on television shows and featured on the cover of *Sports Illustrated*. Kenny Thapoung, in March 2015, listed Strug's vault as third in 'The Eight Greatest Moments for Women in Sports'. Nadia Comaneci was listed first for achieving the first perfect '10' in gymnastics and Billie Jean King was second for thumping Bobby Riggs at tennis.

Phoebe Mills (1972-) was another Jewish gymnastics star coached by the husband-and-wife team of Márta and Béla Károlyi. Mills was the only American gymnast (male or female) to win a medal at the 1988 Seoul Olympics.[25] She took bronze on the balance beam behind Daniela Silivas and **Elena Shushunova**. In 1988 she was the USA Olympic Committee's Gymnast of the Year. Mills was also a competitive diver (10m-board), snowboarder and speed skater. She was one of a talented sporting family. Her sister Jessica was the 1989 World Junior Figure Skating champion. Her brother Nathaniel competed in speed skating at the 1992, 1994 and 1998 winter Olympics.[26]

SUMMARY

After athletics and swimming, gymnastics is the third most popular of Olympic sports. Gymnastics at the Olympic Games is a story of tragedy and triumph for Jewish Olympians. Thirteen Jewish Olympian gymnasts were killed by the Nazis.

Of those killed, the Flatow cousins won six of Germany's individual medals in the first modern Olympics in 1896. Germany subsequently honoured them.

Hungary, a country with a very dark past, has as its greatest Olympic athlete the Jewish gymnast, Ágnes Keleti.

Sixty-seven years after winning seven Olympic medals in 1952, Maria Gorokhovskaya still features (with Mark Spitz) in the list of the ten Olympic athletes to win the most medals in a single Games.

In more recent times Jewish gymnasts from the USA and Russia have made their mark. Mitch Gaylord's crowning glory was his invention of two skills that are named after him. The Gaylord Flip and the Gaylord Two are regarded as the most difficult and spectacular feats in gymnastics.

Aly Raisman is recognised as America's second most successful Olympic gymnast. Kerri Strug's pain-defying vault in Atlanta in 1996 will never be forgotten.

The Russian, Yelena Shushunova, is one of only five gymnasts to win the all-around event at every major gymnastics competition.

MEDAL COMPARISON BETWEEN JEWISH AND AUSTRALIAN OLYMPIC GYMNASTS

Jewish gymnasts have won a total of 65 Olympic medals—32 gold, 22 silver and 11 bronze.

By comparison Australian athletes have won a single medal in gymnastics. Ji Wallace took silver in 2000 for the individual competition.

JEWISH OLYMPIC MEDALLISTS—GYMNASTICS

1896 Athens
Alfred Flatow, Ger. Gold; parallel bars
Alfred Flatow, Ger. Gold; parallel bars team
Alfred Flatow, Ger. Gold; horizontal bar team
Gustav-Felix Flatow, Ger. Gold; parallel bars team
Gustav-Felix Flatow, Ger. Gold; horizontal bar team
Alfred Flatow, Ger. Silver; horizontal bar

1904 St. Louis
Herman Glass, USA, Gold; rings

1912 Stockholm
Samuel Fóti, Hun. Silver; combined exercises team
Imre Gellért, Hun. Silver; combined exercises team

1916 Cancelled due to World War One

1928 Amsterdam
Estelle Agsteribbe, Hol. Gold; team

Elke de Levie, Hol. Gold; team
Helena Nordheim, Hol. Gold; team
Judikje Simons, Hol. Gold; team
Annie Polak, Hol. Gold; team

1932 Los Angeles
George Gulack, USA, Gold; rings
Philip Erenberg, USA, Silver; club-swinging

1940 and 1944 Cancelled due to World War Two

1948 London
Ágnes Keleti, Hun. Silver; team

1952 Helinski
Maria Gorokhovskaya, Russia, Gold; combined exercises team
Maria Gorokhovskaya, Russia, Gold; portable apparatus (PA) team
Ágnes Keleti, Hun. Gold; floor exercises
Mikhail Perelman, Russia, Gold; combined exercises team
Maria Gorokhovskaya, Russia, Silver; asymmetrical bars
Maria Gorokhovskaya, Russia, Silver; floor exercises
Maria Gorokhovskaya, Russia, Silver; horse vault
Maria Gorokhovskaya, Russia, Silver; balance beam
Maria Gorokhovskaya, Russia, Silver; PA team
Ágnes Keleti, Hun. Silver; combined exercises team
Ágnes Keleti, Hun. Bronze; asymmetrical bars
Ágnes Keleti, Hun. Bronze; PA team

Galina Urbanovich, Russia, Gold; all-around team
Galina Urbanovich, Russia, Silver; PA team

1956 Melbourne
Ágnes Keleti, Hun. Gold; floor exercises
Ágnes Keleti, Hun. Gold; balance beam
Ágnes Keleti, Hun. Gold; PA team
Aliz Kertész, Hun. Gold; PA team
Ágnes Keleti, Hun. Silver; combined exercises
Ágnes Keleti, Hun. Silver; combined exercises team
Aliz Kertész, Hun. Silver; combined exercises team

1960 Rome
Vladimir Portnoi, Russia, Silver; combined exercises team
Vladimir Portnoi, Russia, Bronze; horse vault

1984 Los Angeles
Mitch Gaylord, USA, Gold; combined exercises team
Mitch Gaylord, USA, Silver; horse vault
Mitch Gaylord, USA, Bronze; rings
Mitch Gaylord, USA, Bronze; parallel bars

1988 Seoul
Natalia Laschenova, Russia, Gold; team
Yelena Shushunova, Russia, Gold; team
Yelena Shushunova, Russia, Gold; all-around
Yelena Shushunova, Russia, Silver; balance beam
Yelena Shushunova, Russia, Bronze; uneven bars
Phoebe Mills, USA, Bronze; balance beam

1992 Barcelona
Tatiana Lysenko, Unified, Gold; team
Tatiana Lysenko, Unified, Gold; balance beam
Valeri Belenki, Unified, Gold; team
Valeri Belenki, Unified, Bronze; all-around
Kerri Strug, USA, Bronze; combined exercises team
Tatiana Lysenko, Unified, Bronze; vault
(In 1992 the Unified team consisted of the sports teams of the former Soviet Union except for the Baltic States).

1996 Atlanta
Kerri Strug, USA, Gold; combined exercises team
Yana Batyrshina, Russia, Silver; all-around

2000 Sydney
Yulia Raskina, Russia, Silver; all-around

2012 London
Alexandra Raisman, USA, Gold; team
Alexandra Raisman, USA, Gold; floor exercises
Alexandra Raisman, USA, Bronze; balance beam

2016 Rio
Alexandra Raisman, USA, Gold; team
Alexandra Raisman, USA, Silver; all-around
Alexandra Raisman, USA, Silver; floor exercises

TOTAL: 65

CHAPTER 4

MARTIAL ARTS

'There never was a prominent Jewish athlete in history'

> American representative to the International Olympic Committee in 1936, General Charles H. Sherrill.[1]

FENCING

In the prologue to his fascinating book, *By the Sword,* Richard Cohen discusses the many ways in which fencing influences our lives. Cohen notes that since 3000 B.C. our language has conjured images of thrusting, slashing and cutting. We shake hands to show we are not reaching for a sword. A gentleman offers a lady his right arm because at one time his sword was at his left hip. A man's coat has the buttons on the right, so that a duellist may unbutton it with his left, unarmed hand. The two main parties in the House of Commons are separated by the precise length of two sword blades. Each MP's locker still contains a loop of silk on which to hang their sword. Kamikaze pilots took their samurai swords with them into their cockpits.

From the earliest times the sword has served as a symbol of justice, power and righteous authority. With the touch of a sword a man is knighted; with the breaking of his sword he is disgraced. Whole armies are surrendered by the giving up of a single sword. There can be no other sport that so permeates our daily lives.[2]

There are three weapons in fencing. The foil is a thrusting weapon and has a flexible rectangular blade. Hits are scored with the point and are only counted if they contact a metallic conductive jacket which covers the trunk.

The épée has a rigid triangular blade. Hits are scored with the point of the sword on any part of the body. The épée is the traditional duelling sword.

The sabre has a flexible triangular blade. Hits are scored both with the point and cutting edge. Hits are scored on the mask or on a metallic jacket covering the body above the waist. All weapons are linked to an electrical scoring system.

For 2000 years, Jews have had to defend themselves against anti-Semitic attacks. During the late nineteenth and early twentieth centuries, Eastern European countries, in particular, were ridden with anti-Semitism. Proficiency at martial arts provided Jews not only the opportunity to try gain acceptance in society but gave Jews a means of defence. It should therefore be unsurprising that Jews excelled in martial arts—particularly fencing. Not only did fencing skills help in climbing the social ladder; they also provided the perfect means of defending one's honour.[3] Challenging an antagonist who had insulted one to a duel was an effective means of restoring one's dignity. An adversary who refused such a challenge suffered the humiliation of being regarded as a coward. It was clearly in the interests of Jews to acquire fencing skills.

The most intriguing of the Jewish Olympic fencers is **Helene Mayer** (1910-1953). Almost six foot tall and blonde, Mayer epitomised the 'Aryan' woman in looks and physique—yet she was Jewish. Mayer was the world's number one foil fencer when Hitler came to power and she was idolised in Germany. Fencing experts who saw Mayer in action, or footage of her fencing, describe her technique as so perfect that many still consider her to be the best ever female foil fencer. A New York filmmaker, Semyon Pinkhasov, himself a fencer, said of Mayer: 'When I see footage of her fencing I can't believe what I see. She is a huge talent. She is phenomenal. If she was alive today and between 20 and 30 [years old], she would win the Olympics. There is nobody better than her'. She was, according to Pinkhasov, as big in Germany in the late 1920s as Michael Jordan is in the USA today.[4]

Mayer won gold in the individual foil in the 1928 Olympic Games at 18 years of age. She was the German foil champion from 1924 to 1930 and World Champion in 1931.

This Jewish German sporting hero created a dilemma for Hitler. Hitler's barring of Jews from sporting clubs meant that even Mayer was forced out of her club. Consequently, Mayer left Germany for the USA. Hitler's announcement that Jews would be banned from competing for Germany in the Berlin Games resulted in some countries, the USA in particular, threatening to boycott the 1936 Games. Hitler's response was to tone down the racist rhetoric, remove the signs barring Jews and dogs from public spaces, and invite Mayer to compete as part of the German contingent. No other Jews were chosen to compete for Germany in the summer Olympics despite there being many Jewish athletes who merited selection. The inclusion of Mayer in the German team and the now subdued Nazi racist propaganda were enough for the Games to proceed without a boycott.

That Jewish athletes can compete and win at the top level was emphatically demonstrated at Hitler's Games by the most dramatic fencing contest of all time—the women's foil event.

The contest ended with Mayer taking the silver medal. Ironically, she shared the winners' podium with two other Jewish fencers. Hungary's **Ilona Elek** won the gold medal and Austria's **Ellen Preis** won bronze. What happened next has been indelibly preserved in a photograph. On receiving her medal Mayer raised her right arm in the Nazi salute in the manner expected of German medal winners.

The Nazi, Reinhold Heydrich, loudly and publicly abused Mayer for not winning the event, calling her a 'Jewish c...t'. Mayer apologised to Heydrich for her failure. Shortly after the Games Mayer returned to the USA.[5]

Mayer must have been deeply troubled by the predicament in which she found herself. Should she, in keeping with many Jewish athletes, have boycotted the Games, knowing that she would possibly then not get another chance to participate in an Olympics? Or should she have followed the example set by other Jewish athletes—of competing in order to disprove Hitler's lie that Jews lack athletic ability? And what made her give the Nazi salute?

Following the 1936 Games, Mayer attended and graduated from Mills College in Oakland with a Masters degree in French. She then taught German and coached fencing at Mills College. We will never know what went on in her mind because she lived a reclusive life, refusing to discuss the 1936 Berlin Games and her Nazi salute. Mayer died in 1953 of breast cancer.[6] She will forever remain an enigma.

In the late 1930s it became impossible for Jews in Central and Eastern Europe to take part in competitive sports. **Ilona Elek** (1907-1988) was banned from competitive fencing for a period of six years.[7] Before and after being sidelined Elek won ten gold, five silver and two bronze medals at the World Championships.[8] The Olympic Games were cancelled in 1940 and 1944 but Elek returned in the 1948 Olympics to win gold in the individual foil, and in the 1952 Games she won silver in the same event. Elek's 1948 gold medal win made it five times in a row that a Jewish woman won an Olympic gold in individual foil. Elek received the Olympic Order in 1982—an award given for a particularly distinguished contribution to the Olympic movement. Her sister **Margit** also had her fencing career interrupted by the Nazi ban. She too subsequently took part in the 1948 and 1952 Olympics.

Ellen Preis (1912-2007) won a gold medal in the individual foil in the 1932 Olympics and bronze medals in the same event in the 1936 and 1948 Olympics. She won the World Championships in 1947, 1949 and 1950.[9] She won 17 Austrian titles and in 1949 was declared Austrian female athlete of the year. Mayer, Elek and Preis remain amongst the greatest female fencers ever.

They were, however, not the only Jewish fencers to mount the podium at Hitler's Games. Hungarian, **Endre Kabos** (1906-1944), retired from fencing due to the virulent anti-Semitism in Hungarian fencing society. He had already won gold and bronze (team and individual sabre) in the 1932 Olympics. He subsequently had a change of heart and returned to competition, winning two golds (individual and team sabre) at Hitler's 1936 Games. During World War Two he was deported to a labour camp, where a Captain Konrad, an officer at the camp, on realising Kabos was a former national hero, arranged for him to return to Budapest. Kabos was driving a supply truck over the Margaret Bridge when he was killed by an explosion that destroyed the bridge.[10]

Hungarians regard themselves as descendants of sabre-wielding warrior ancestors. Consequently, it was at sabre fencing that Hungarians most prided themselves. The height of distinction for a Jewish Hungarian fencer was therefore success with the sabre.

Jenő Fuchs (1882-1955) was the first of the brilliant Jewish Hungarian fencers—a reclusive and eccentric fencing celebrity. His success can be accounted for by a combination of meticulous defence and rapid counter attack. Fuchs won four Olympic medals—golds in the individual and team sabre events at both the 1908 and 1912 Games.

Three other Jewish Hungarian fencers won gold in the team sabre at the 1908 and 1912 Games. **Oszkár Gerde, Dezsö Földes** and **Lajos Werkner** fenced with Fuchs in the gold medal winning teams of the 1908 and 1912 Olympics.

Following the 1912 Games, **Oszkár Gerde** (1883-1944) judged international fencing competitions and worked as a medical doctor. He was deported to the concentration camp, Mauthausen, in Austria, where he perished in 1944.[11]

Dezsö Földes (1880-1950) left for the USA after the 1912 Olympics. He founded a medical clinic for the under-privileged in Cleveland, where he died in 1950.[12] **Lajos Werkner** (1883-1943) survived the Holocaust and died in Budapest, aged 60.

The good looking and flamboyant **Attila Petschauer** (1904-1943) won gold in the sabre team event with fellow Jewish Hungarians **Sándor Gombos** (1895-1968) and **János Garay** (1889-1945) He won silver in the individual sabre event in the 1928 Games and another gold in the sabre team event in 1932 with Endre Kabos.

Petshauer was deported to a Hungarian labour camp towards the end of the war. Here a previous Olympian, the horseman Kalman Czeh, now a colonel, recognised Petschauer and ordered his subordinates to make life difficult for 'the Jew'. On a bitterly cold day Petschauer was ordered to climb naked up a tree. Fellow inmates were forced to watch as he was commanded to crow like a rooster while the guards hosed him with cold water. He fell, frozen stiff, to the ground and died shortly afterwards of hypothermia. Petschauer's death was immortalised in the film *Sunshine*.[13]

János Garay (1889-1945) won silver in the sabre team event and bronze in individual sabre in the 1924 Games. In the 1928 Games he won gold in the sabre team event with **Petshauer** and **Gombos** (1895-1968). Garay perished in the Mauthausen concentration camp.[14] Gombos was the Hungarian sabre champion in 1930. He survived the Holocaust.

George Worth (1915-2006) was born György Woittitz in Budapest. Anti-Semitism drove Woittitz to leave Hungary in 1937. His move was prescient. He was unable to immigrate directly to the USA because he was Jewish and so spent two years in Cuba. While in Cuba he won the Cuban national sabre championship. When he finally got to the USA at 22 years of age, he changed his name to George Worth. Worth enrolled in the USA forces in World War Two and won Bronze Stars fighting in the Battle of the Bulge 1944-45. Subsequently he was made a captain in the South Orangetown Ambulance Corps in New York and Chief Commissioner of the Orangeburg New York Fire Department. Worth competed in four

Olympics for the USA between 1948 and 1960, winning a bronze in 1948 in the sabre team event.[15] He was inducted into the USA Fencing Hall of Fame in 1974.

In 1922 and 1930 the German National champion in épée was **Hans Halberstadt** (1885-1966), a decorated hero from World War One. He was also the German team sabre champion in 1924 and 1925. He was unable to compete in the 1924 Games due to Germany's exclusion from the Games. In 1928 he represented Germany at the Olympics in individual épée, team épée, and team sabre events, coming fourth in the sabre team event. Following Kristallnacht,[16] the Halberstadt's family business was confiscated by the Nazis and Halberstadt was taken to the Bergen-Belsen concentration camp. He was released because of his status as a fencer and allowed to leave Germany, aged 56, with whatever he could carry. He went via London to the USA where he continued fencing as an instructor. One of his students was **Helene Mayer**. The two were from the same town and fencing club in Germany—Offenbach Am Main (Frankfurt).[17]

Ironically, the Gestapo General Reinhard Heydrich, whom even Hitler described as having a 'heart of iron',[18] came to the assistance of two Jewish fencers. Heydrich helped the former German Jewish fencing champion **Paul Sommer** escape to the USA.[19] He also helped **Roman Kantor** (1912-1943), a Polish

Olympian. Kantor competed in Hitler's 1936 Games in the épée event. In the preliminary rounds he beat both the eventual silver and gold medallists but did not reach the finals. Heydrich provided Kantor with travel papers and money after Kantor had fled the Soviet occupation zone in 1939.[20] There is an explanation for Heydrich's moments of compassion: he was passionate about fencing, although not particularly adept at the sport. He assisted the two Jewish fencers out of admiration and respect for their fencing skills. Heydrich's 'compassion' did not, however, save Kantor, who was later arraigned and killed in the Majdanek concentration camp in 1943.

Otto Herschmann (1877-1942) was a rarity—one of few Olympic athletes to win medals in two unrelated sports. In 1896 he won silver for Austria in the 100m freestyle swim. In the 1912 Olympics he again won silver, but this time it was in the sabre team event.[21] He served as President of the Austrian Olympic Committee from 1912-1914 and is the only president of a National Olympic Committee to win a medal while in office.[22] He was also for a time President of the Austrian Swimming Federation (1914-1932). He was arrested by the Nazis in 1942 and killed in the Sobibor concentration camp.

The Dutch Olympic épée and foil fencer, **Simon Okker** (1881-1944), was sent to Auschwitz where he was killed.[23]

Yves Dreyfus (1931-) eluded the Nazis as a child in occupied France by taking the name Yves Doucet. He won Olympic bronze medals in 1956 and 1964 in the épée team event and was the French épée champion in 1964. Dreyfus was decorated by Charles de Gaulle in 1966, and in 1967 received the National Order of Merit. Later he became a Master of Arms.

Albert Wolff (1906-1989) qualified for the French Olympic team for Hitler's 1936 Games. His disgust with Hitler was so great that he turned down the opportunity to compete in Berlin, saying: 'I cannot participate in anything sponsored by Adolf Hitler, even for France'.[24] Instead he joined the French army in the fight against the Germans. He fought with distinction but was captured by the Germans and interned in a war camp from which he escaped. He was awarded the Croix de Guerre for bravery while defending the Maginot Line. He arrived in the USA in 1941 and again enlisted to fight the Nazis. He served for two years in Africa, receiving a battlefield commission. At the end of hostilities he returned to fencing, becoming the American national épée champion in 1946. In 1948, aged 42, and the oldest member of the USA team, Wolff finally realised his dream of competing in the Olympics. He carried the USA flag in the opening ceremony in London in 1948 and competed in the individual and team épée events. In 1952 he fenced at the Helsinki Games. He failed to add an Olympic medal to an otherwise heroic life.[25]

Ivan Osiier (1888-1965) was a Danish Olympic medallist and World Champion fencer. Osiier was equally at home with the foil, épée and sabre and won 25 National Championships and several Scandinavian Championships. He represented Denmark in seven Olympic Games between 1908 and 1948 and would have competed in eight had he not refused to attend Hitler's 1936 Games. Osiier is one of only four athletes to have competed in the Olympics over a span of 40 years. In 1912 he won a silver medal at the Stockholm Olympics in individual épée. He was one of the few athletes to be awarded the Olympic Diploma of Merit.[26] When the Nazis occupied Denmark, Osiier fled to Sweden. Here he continued working as a surgeon at Saint Goran hospital.

Other fencers who refused to compete in Hitler's Games were the Romanian **Endre Altmann**[27] and the Canadian **Julius Polack**, who was due to captain the Canadian team.[28]

Between 1908 and 1936 Jewish Hungarian fencers won 26 Olympic medals—19 gold, of which 16 were in sabre fencing. In 1941 the population of Hungary was about 10 million, of which about 400,000 (4%) were Jewish. In 1949, following the Nazi devastation of Hungary's Jews, the population of Hungary remained at about 10 million, of which now only about 130,000 were Jewish (1.3%). The number of Jews in Hungary at the time of the 2011 census was only 10,965. The decimation of the Hungarian Jewish population brought to an end the domination of Hungarian Jews in sports such as fencing, wrestling, gymnastics, swimming, water polo, and soccer.

It is more than 70 years since the Holocaust almost destroyed Hungary's Jews. Yet the list of the 20 Hungarian athletes who have won the most Olympic medals contains the names of five Jews, two of whom were fencers. **Ágnes Keleti** (gymnastics) is in the top spot (shared with Aladar Gerevich), **Jenő Fuchs** is 9th (fencing), **Dezsö Gyarmati** is 13th (waterpolo), **Endre Kabos** is 18th (fencing) and **Györgi Kárpáti** is 19th (water polo).

Following the Holocaust, the few surviving Hungarian Jews continued to win Olympic medals in fencing (and other sports). Between 1948 and 1972 six Hungarian Jewish fencers won 12 Olympic medals.

Íldiko Ujláky-Réjtö (1937-) was a stand-out, competing in every Olympics between 1960 and 1976 and winning seven medals. Ujláky-Réjtö had to contend with the handicap of being born profoundly deaf. She learned her fencing technique from written instructions from her coach.[29] She was Hungarian Sportswoman of the Year in 1963 and 1964.[30]

Edgar Seligman (1867-1927) of Great Britain first fenced at the Olympics at the age of 39 in 1906. He nevertheless competed at five Olympic Games, winning silver in team épée at the 1906 Olympic Games (also known as the Intercalated Games) as well as at the 1908 and 1912 Olympiads. He remains the only man to twice win the British fencing championships in all three weapons (foil, épée and sabre). Seligman was also a distinguished artist. He submitted his work in the Olympic Art competitions in the 1928 and 1932 Games.[31] Seligman fought in the Boer War with the Imperial Yeomanry. His brother **Herbert Seligman** was a brigadier general in the Royal Artillery and fought in both the Boer War and World War One.[32]

In recent times it has been Jewish Russian fencers who have made their mark. From 1952-2004 10 Jewish Russian fencers won 24 Olympic medals—12 gold. They are **Grigory Kriss, Mark Rakita, Mark Midler, Yakov Rylsky, Maria Mazina, David Tyshler, Eduard Vinokurov, Yosif Vitebsky, Vadim Gutzeit** and **Sergey Sharikov**.

Born in Kherson, Ukraine, **David Tyshler** (1927-2014) was an athlete, a coach and an academic. During World War Two his family fled to Moscow. Tyshler was one of the first of the wave of internationally successful Soviet fencers. He won bronze in the 1956 Games in the sabre team event and was the Soviet individual sabre champion in 1960. He won several World Championship medals between 1955 and 1959.

He also won acclaim as a coach. From 1961-1973 Tyshler was head coach of the Russian national sabre team. Some of the champions he coached were **Sergey Sharikov, Mark Midler, Mark Rakita,** Victor Sidjak, Victor Krovopulskov and Victor Bazhenov. He received the award of 'Honoured Master of Sport'.

In 1984 Tyshler became Professor of Fencing and Modern Pentathlon at Russian State University of Physical Education, Sport, Youth and Tourism.

Tyshler has published more than 170 academic papers and has written over 40 books on fencing. Several of his works have been translated into other languages.[33] Tyshler started fencing schools in Russia and South Africa. He orchestrated the fencing scenes in many Moscow theatres and Soviet movies.

Grigory Kriss (1940-) was born in Kiev and is the most successful of the Russian Jewish fencers. Kriss won gold in the individual épée in the 1964 Olympics. In 1968 he collected silver in both the individual and team épée events. He won his last Olympic medal in 1972, taking bronze in the team épée event.[34] Kriss served as an officer in the Soviet Red Army.

Other Jewish Russian fencers to achieve Olympic

success via the military were **Eduard Vinokurov** (1942-2010) and **Mark Rakita** (1938-). Both men trained at the Armed Forces Sports Society in Leningrad. Vinokurov won gold medals in the sabre team event at the 1968 and 1976 Olympics. In the 1972 Games he had to settle for silver in the same event.[35] Mark Rakita competed in three Olympic Games. In 1964 and 1968 he won gold in the sabre team event. In 1968 he won silver in individual sabre event and in 1972 he won silver in the sabre team event. He won the World Championships in the individual sabre event in 1967.

Rakita earned the titles Honoured Master of Sport and USSR Honoured Coach. Four of his students won Olympic medals. He also coached **Sergey Sharikov** and **Maria Mazina** to gold medals at the 2001 Maccabiah Games. He was the honorary President of Maccabi Russia in 2004.[36]

Rakita mentioned in an interview with Lev Krichevsky that when he competed, he was made to feel inferior because he was Jewish. He felt that in order to feel accepted as being on par with the others he had to be clearly better than they were.[37]

Vadym Gutzeit (1971-), was born in Kiev, and was another Russian fencer to compete at the Maccabi Games. Gutzeit took part in three Olympics, winning gold in the sabre team event in the 1992 Games.

Gutzeit coached the Ukrainian sabre team and was President of the Ukrainian Fencing Federation. [38] He officiated as an international referee from 2002 in many major fencing tournaments.

Mark Midler (1931-2012) captained the Soviet foil team at the 1960 and 1964 Olympics. He won gold in the foil team event on both occasions. Midler also took to coaching the Russian Olympic side. He was appointed head coach of the 1980 Soviet Olympic foil team.[39] Later he was awarded the Order of the Badge of Honour.

Sergey Sharikov (1974-2015) was one of the world's best sabre fencers. He was in Russia's national fencing team from 1994-2005. Sharikov competed in three Olympic Games between 1996 and 2004 and won four Olympic medals in sabre fencing. In 1996 and 2000 he won gold in the sabre team event. In 1996 he also won silver in the individual sabre event. In 2004 he won bronze in the sabre team event. He died at 40 from injuries sustained in a car crash.[40]

Most recently, Muscovite **Maria Mazina** (1964-) won bronze and gold in the épée team events in the 1996 and 2000 Olympics. She won the World Women's Épée Championship on five occasions. She has taught fencing at Maccabi Moscow since the club first opened in 1995. In 2001 she won gold in the Maccabiah Games. Mazina has also been coach to the Russian

Federation's épée team.

While Jewish Russian fencers swept to success after success at the Olympics following World War Two, Jewish American fencers were mostly confined to the wings. This was not for lack of numbers. The list of Jewish American Olympian fencers **includes Soren Thompson, Allan Kwartler, Harold Goldsmith, Nathaniel Lubell, Eugene Glazer, Paul Makler** and his sons **Paul Makler junior** and **Brooke Makler, Dan Kellner, Robert Blum, Joel Gluckman, Stephen Kaplan, Martin Lang, Eli Dershwitz, Tamir Bloom, Robert Blum, Byron Krieger, Nick Bravin**, father and son **Daniel and Jeff Bukantz**, brothers **John** and **Paul Friedberg**, brothers **Abe** and **Herb Cohen**, sisters **Sada** and **Emily Jacobson, Albert Axelrod, Norman Armitage** and **Tim Morehouse**.

Of these fencers, Bukantz, Lubell, Axelrod, Goldsmith, Krieger, Armitage, Kwartler and Blum all finished in the agonising place of fourth in team foil or sabre events—some on more than one occasion. Goldsmith competed in the 1952, 1956 and 1960 Games. His family fled Nazi Germany in 1938 when he was eight years old. He served as an officer in the USA army.[41]

Only four of the 29 American Jewish Olympic fencers have won medals at the Olympic Games. The five-times Olympian **Albert Axelrod** (1921-2004), son of immigrants who fled the Russian pogroms, won bronze in the individual foil event at the 1960 Olympics. He was the only American to reach the finals at the World Championships in foil until Gerek Meinhardt took bronze in 2010. During World War Two, Axelrod saw action in the USA navy in the Pacific theatre. He was ranked the number one fencer in the USA in 1955, 1958, 1960 and 1970. From 1986 to 1990 Axelrod edited the magazine *American Fencing*. In a 1988 interview he said that one of the nicest compliments he ever received was from the Russian team after the 1958 World Championships. As a group they approached him and said that he fenced like a tractor. Although this may not sound very complimentary, according to Russian ideology the tractor is considered to be the backbone and heart of farms and industry.[42]

Norman Armitage (1907-1972) was one of America's greatest sabre fencers. He competed in six Olympics over a 28 year period (1928 to 1936 and 1948 to 1956). He won a bronze medal in the sabre team event in the 1948 Games and carried the USA flag at the Opening Ceremony in 1948, 1952 and 1956. He was the first person inducted into the USA Fencing Hall of Fame. He won the USA national sabre title on 17 occasions—more than any other American sabre fencer.[43]

In more recent years **Sada Jacobson** (1985-) won bronze in the individual sabre event at the 2004 Olympics and in 2008 she won silver in the individual sabre event and bronze in the sabre team event. In 2016 Sada and her sister **Emily** were inducted into the USA Fencing Hall of Fame.

Tim Morehouse (1978-) was the number one USA sabre fencer from 2008 until 2011. He was a member of the American fencing teams at the 2004, 2008 and 2012 Olympics. He took silver in the sabre team event at the 2008 games.

Morehouse's maternal grandmother and two of her sisters escaped Nazi Germany in the 1930s. Morehouse's grandmother subsequently became a Quaker, having been impressed by their relief work in Germany following World War Two. Morehouse, however, has an affinity for Judaism based on his grandmother's courage and determination in the face of difficulty.

In 2011 Morehouse founded the not-for-profit 'Fencing in the Schools'—an organisation which introduces fencing to poorly serviced communities.[44]

Australia has never won an Olympic medal in fencing, although it would have done so had **Allan Jay**, MBE (1931-) not returned to Great Britain. Jay competed for Australia at the 1952 Games but did not win a medal. He subsequently returned to his country of birth and competed in four more Olympic Games, winning two silver medals (for the individual and team épée events) for Great Britain at the 1960 Rome Olympics. In 1964 Jay was the flag bearer for Great Britain at the Tokyo Olympics. He was Britain's first world champion in foil and is one of the most successful fencers in Britain's history.[45]

James Wolfensohn, KBE AO (1933-) also fenced for Australia. He competed at the 1956 Olympics but failed to win a medal. Wolfenson is better known as President of the World Bank (1995-2000), making him probably the only Olympian to be head of the World Bank. He served as an officer in the Royal Australian Air Force.[46]

MEDAL COMPARISON BETWEEN JEWISH AND AUSTRALIAN OLYMPIC FENCERS

Jewish fencers have won 109 Olympic medals of which 50 are gold.

Australia is yet to win an Olympic medal in fencing.

JEWISH OLYMPIC MEDALLISTS—FENCING

1900 Paris
Siegfried Flesch, Austria, Bronze; sabre

1906 St Louis
Edgar Seligman, Great Britain, Silver; épée team

1908 London
Dezsö Földes, Hun. Gold; sabre team
Jenő Fuchs, Hun. Gold; sabre
Jenő Fuchs, Hun. Gold; sabre team
Oszkár Gerde, Hun. Gold; sabre team
Alexandre Lippmann, France, Gold; épée team
Eugene Olivier, France, Gold; épée team
Jean Stern, France, Gold; épée team
Lajos Werkner, Hun. Gold; sabre team
Alexandre Lippmann, France, Silver; épée
Edgar Seligman, Great Britain, Silver; épée team
Paul Anspach, Belgium, Bronze; épée team

1912 Stockholm
Henry Anspach, Belgium, Gold; épée team
Paul Anspach, Belgium, Gold; épée
Paul Anspach, Belgium, Gold; épée team
Dezsö Földes, Hun. Gold; sabre team
Jenő Fuchs, Hun. Gold; sabre
Jenő Fuchs, Hun. Gold; sabre team
Oszkár Gerde, Hun. Gold; sabre team
Jacques Ochs, Belgium, Gold; épée team
Gaston Salmon, Belgium, Gold; épée team
Zoltan Schenker, Hun. Gold; sabre team
Lajos Werkner, Hun. Gold; sabre team
Otto Herschmann, Austria, Silver; sabre team
Ivan Osiier, Den. Silver; épée
Edgar Seligman, Great Britain, Silver; épée team
Salomon Nardus, Holland, Silver; épée team

Albert Bogen, Hun. Bronze; sabre team

1916 Cancelled due to World War One

1920 Antwerp
Paul Anspach, Belgium, Silver; épée team
Alexandre Lippmann, France, Silver; épée
Alexandre Lippmann, France, Bronze; épée team

1924 Paris
Alexandre Lippmann, France, Gold; épée team
Ellen Osiier, Den. Gold; foil
Paul Anspach, Belgium, Silver; épée team
János Garay, Hun. Silver; sabre team
Zoltan Schenker, Hun. Silver; sabre team
János Garay, Hun. Bronze; sabre
Zoltan Schenker, Hun. Bronze; foil team

1928 Amsterdam
János Garay, Hun. Gold; sabre team
Sándor Gombos, Hun. Gold; sabre team
Helene Mayer, Ger. Gold; foil
Attila Petschauer, Hun. Gold; sabre team
Attila Petschauer, Hun. Silver; sabre

1932 Los Angeles
Endre Kabos, Hun. Gold; sabre team
Attila Petschauer, Hun. Gold; sabre team
Endre Kabos, Hun. Silver; sabre

1936 Berlin
Endre Kabos, Hun. Gold; sabre
Endre Kabos, Hun. Gold; sabre team
Ilona Elek, Hun. Gold; foil
Helene Mayer, Germany, Silver; foil
Ellen Preis, Austria, Bronze; foil

1940 and 1944 Cancelled due to World War Two

1948 London
Ilona Elek, Hun. Gold; foil
Karen Lachmann, Denmark, Silver; foil
Ivan Osiier, Denmark, Silver; épée
Norman Armitage, USA, Bronze; sabre team
George Worth, USA, Bronze; sabre team
Ellen Preis, Austria, Bronze; foil

1952 Helsinki
Claude Netter, France Gold; foil team
Ilona Elek, Hun. Silver; foil
Karen Lachmann, Denmark, Bronze; foil

1956 Melbourne
Claude Netter, France, Silver; foil team
Yves Dreyfus, France, Bronze; épée team
Armand Moyal, France, Bronze; épée team
Yakov Rylsky, Russia, Bronze; sabre team
David Tyschler, Russia, Bronze; sabre team

1960 Rome
Mark Midler, Russia, Gold; foil team
Allan Jay, Great Britain, Silver; épée
Allan Jay, Great Britain, Silver; épée team
Ujláky-Réjtö, Hun. Silver; foil team
Albert Axelrod, USA, Bronze; foil

1964 Tokyo
Tamás Gábor, Hun. Gold; épée team
Mark Midler, Russia, Gold; foil team
Grigory Kriss, Russia, Gold; épée
Mark Rakita, Russia, Gold; sabre
Íldiko Ujláky-Réjtö, Hun. Gold; foil
Íldiko Ujláky-Réjtö, Hun. Gold; foil team
Yakov Rylsky, Russia, Gold; sabre team
Yves Dreyfus, France, Bronze; épée team
Yakov Rylsky, Russia, Bronze; sabre

1968 Mexico City
Eduard Vinokurov, Russia, Gold; sabre team
Grigory Kriss, Russia, Silver; épée
Grigory Kriss, Russia, Silver; épée team
Mark Rakita, Russia, Silver; sabre
Íldiko Ujláky-Réjtö, Hun. Silver; foil team
Yosif Vitebsky Russia, Silver; épée team
Íldiko Ujláky-Réjtö, Hun. Bronze; foil
Peter Bakonyi, Hun. Bronze; sabre team

1972 Munich
Sándor Erdos, Hun. Gold; épée team
Mark Rakita, Russia, Silver; sabre team

Íldiko Ujláky-Réjtö, Hun. Silver; foil team
Eduard Vinokurov, Russia, Gold; sabre team
Grigory Kriss, Russia, Bronze; épée team
Peter Bakonyi, Hun. Bronze; sabre team

1976 Montreal
Eduard Vinokurov, Russia, Gold; sabre team
Íldiko Ujláky-Réjtö, Hun. Bronze; foil team

1980 Moscow
Johan Hamenberg, Sweden, Gold; épée
Eduard Vinokurov, Russia, Gold; sabre team

1992 Barcelona
Vadim Gutzeit, Unified, Gold; sabre team

1996 Atlanta
Sergey Sharikov, Russia, Gold; sabre team
Sergey Sharikov, Russia, Silver; sabre
Maria Mazina, Russia, Bronze; épée team

2000 Sydney
Maria Mazina, Russia, Gold; épée team
Sergey Sharikov, Russia, Gold; sabre team

2004 Athens
Sergey Sharikov, Russia, Bronze; sabre team
Sada Jacobson, USA, Bronze; sabre

2008 Beijing
Sada Jacobson, USA, Silver; sabre

Tim Morehouse, USA, Silver; sabre team
Sada Jacobson, USA, Bronze; sabre team

BOXING

Jews have been involved in boxing since its earliest days. **Daniel Mendoza** (1764-1836) had 27 straight victories in bare-knuckle boxing. Weighing 73kg he became the first middleweight to win the World Heavyweight crown. Mendoza was inducted into the Bare Knuckle Boxing Hall of Fame in 2017 and into the International Boxing Hall of Fame in 1990. Mendoza's great-great-grandson is the actor **Peter Sellers**. Sellers is proud of his heritage—in the *Pink Panther* films portraits of Mendoza are displayed on the walls of Inspector Clouseau's apartment.[47]

It may come as a surprise to realise the number of Jews who have won a professional world boxing title. Daniel Bodner writes that between 1910 and 1940 there were 26 Jewish world champions.[48] I have counted the number of Jewish world champions up to the present time and have found 35 of them.[49] You would be correct in assuming that since there have been 35 Jewish World Boxing champions there must have been a very large pool of Jewish professional boxers. Bodner says that by 1928 Jews formed the dominant 'nationality' in professional prizefighting. Jewish fighters dominated boxing for several decades in the mid 20th century.

Many of these boxers are remembered as legends—none more so than **Max Baer** (1909-1959). On 8 June 1933, in perhaps the most intriguing boxing match ever, Baer fought Hitler's favourite, Max Schmeling, a former world heavyweight champion, in New York. Hitler himself approved of the bout, assuming Schmeling would win. Hitler expected Schmeling to deny the persecution of Jews in Germany yet just prior to the fight Hitler banned Jews from boxing and instituted a boycott of Jewish businesses.[50]

The fight drew a huge crowd of 60,000. Baer fought with the Star of David on his trunks and gave Schmeling such a beating that the referee stopped the bout after he knocked Schmeling down in the 10th round.[51] The Nazi tabloid *Der Sturmer* attacked Schmeling for fighting a non-Aryan, calling it a 'racial and cultural disgrace'.[52] Had Schmeling won, you can be sure that *Der Sturmer* would have called the bout a triumph of Aryans over the inferior races. Baer held the World Heavyweight crown from 14 June 1934 to 13 June 1935.

A surprising twist to this story became known many years later. Terrified by the Nazi brutality during the Kristallnacht pogrom in November 1938, David Lewin, a friend of Schmeling, asked him to hide his two sons. Schmeling hid the boys in his apartment in the Berlin Excelsior Hotel. Once the Kristallnacht rage abated, he helped the boys reach safety in the USA.

The episode only became public in 1989 when Henry Lewin invited Schmeling to Las Vegas to thank him for saving his life.[53]

The German Jewish boxer **Erich Seelig** (1909-1948) was Germany's amateur middleweight boxing champion in 1931. He then turned professional and won the German lightweight and middleweight titles. In March 1933 the Nazis stripped him of his titles because he was Jewish. In May 1933 the Nazis gave Seelig an hour to leave Germany, failing which they said they would kill him and his family. Seelig and his parents fled penniless to France. Here, Seelig lost in a close contest to World Champion Marcel Thiel. In 1935 he reached the USA where he fought nearly every top middleweight of the era. Amongst his successes were victories over Ken Overlin and Mickey Walker—both World Champions. He was ranked as high as fifth middleweight in the world by *The Ring*. He was inducted into the New Jersey Boxing Hall of Fame on 11 November 1999.[54]

In the USA Seelig met a German Jewish hurdler, Greta Meinstein. Meinstein fled to the USA after the Nazis prevented her from competing in the 1936 Games. The two athletes married in 1940. Meinstein fought for years for Germany to restore Seelig's titles—this never happened. Instead, Germany suppressed the story of the persecution of one of their best boxers long after the fall of the Nazi regime. *The World Sports*

Encyclopedia, published in Essen in 1956, wrote that Seelig relinquished his title in March 1933 due to weight gain.[55]

The Canadian boxers **Sammy Luftspring** (1916-2000) and **Benjamin Yakubowitz** (1925-1987) were certainties for the 1936 Games. Luftspring was considered to have a good chance of winning the gold medal.[56] The two wrote a letter to the *Toronto Globe* explaining why they would not be attending the trials for the Canadian team. They wrote: 'We know that we, as Canadian boys, would be personally safe and perhaps well received in Germany. But can we forget the way the German government is treating the Jewish boys in Germany? No athlete or sportsman would think of engaging in a sporting contest with a bully who would ill-treat even a dumb animal. The German government is treating our brothers and sisters worse than dogs.' Showing remarkable prescience, the two boxers also wrote that Germany would exterminate Jews if they had the opportunity.[57]

Luftspring was well acquainted with the mentality of racists. He partook in the infamous Christie Pits riot in which young Jewish men came to blows with Canadian Nazi sympathisers from the Swastika Club.

Luftspring turned professional in 1936. In 1938 he knocked out Frank Genovese to win the Canadian welterweight title. He was ranked three in the world in the welterweight division but never got a shot at the world title because he had to retire following a boxing injury that resulted in loss of sight in one eye.[58]

Luftspring wrote an autobiography—*Call me Sammy*—published in 1975. He was inducted into Canada's Sports Hall of Fame in 1985.

Yakubowitz was a ferocious bantamweight who fought under the name 'Baby Yack'. He won the Canadian bantamweight title in 1937. Yack had an enviable boxing record, winning 90 out of 100 amateur fights. In 1937 he turned professional becoming the fourth ranked bantamweight in the world. After hanging up his gloves he served in World War Two.

Like many ex-fighters Yack struggled with alcohol. He worked as a taxi driver, then spent some time in prison, and lived out the rest of his life in cheap lodgings. He died in 1987.[59]

The Dutch boxing champion **Ben Bril** (of whom more later), the Australian boxer **Harry Cohen** (1918-unknown), and American featherweight **Louis Gevinson**[60] also boycotted the 1936 Games. Cohen turned professional a few days after announcing he would not take part in the Berlin Games. Two weeks later he defeated Young Nelson to win his first professional bout. As a professional boxer Cohen held both the Australian bantamweight and featherweight titles.⁶¹ He was the only Australian athlete to boycott Hitler's Games.

The Hungarian boxer **Imre Mándi** (1916-1943) competed in Hitler's Games. He reached the quarterfinals of the welterweight division, losing to the eventual gold medalist Sten Stuvio.⁶² Mándi perished in a Nazi labour camp.⁶³

Heinz Levy (1904-1944) was a Dutch boxer and veteran of the 1924 Olympics. He died in Auschwitz.⁶⁴

The Tunisian **Victor Perez** (1912-1945) left Tunisia for France in 1927 where he won the French lightweight crown in 1930. Perez became the world's youngest ever world boxing champion when he won the world flyweight crown in October 1931. In 1943 he was arrested by the Gestapo in France and was transported to Auschwitz where he was forced into hard labour and made to take part in boxing matches to entertain the Nazis. He had to fight men sometimes a foot taller and 50 pounds heavier. In these matches the victor would receive extra soup and bread while the loser would be killed. Perez would share his extra rations with other inmates although this was punishable by death. He was forced to go on the death march from Auschwitz on 18 January 1945. While on the march he was shot dead by the Nazis. His life was portrayed in the film *Victor Young Perez* screened in 2013.⁶⁵

Perez was not alone when it came to prisoners fighting for their lives for the entertainment of their Nazi guards. **Ben Bril** (1912-2003) was one of Holland's best boxers. He competed in the 1928 Olympic Games, coming fifth in the flyweight division, and won the Dutch title eight times. He was blocked from competing in the 1932 Games by a Dutch Nazi in charge of the Dutch Olympic Committee. Bril based his decision to boycott the 1936 Games on what he had seen in Germany on a boxing tour in 1934. After Germany occupied Holland, Bril, his wife, and their son Albert went into hiding above what was their sandwich shop. They were, however, betrayed by a 'good friend', who was also the temporary owner of the business, and deported to the Vught transit camp. Father and son were later transported to the Bergen-Belsen concentration camp. Bril realised that, as a famous boxer, he needed to make use of his boxing skills if he were to have any chance of survival. His dilemma is described in the book *Dancing to Survive* by Steven Rosenfeld. Should one give up or hang in? Should one resist or cooperate? Should one beat up the Germans in the ring or let them win? How does one choose what to do in a predicament where no choice is correct? Bril's will to live and save the lives of his family meant more to him than his pride. He fought the Nazis with bare hands, allowing them to win. By humouring these men Bril managed to survive Bergen-Belsen. He could not, however, save the lives of his family. His sister and four brothers were murdered in the camp.⁶⁶

After the war Bril did return to the Olympics—this time as a referee. He officiated as a referee in Olympic matches between boxing legends such as Joe Frazier, George Foreman and Teofilo Stevenson. He also refereed several professional fights. The most intriguing of these must have been the ones involving the German heavyweight champion Karl Mildenberger.⁶⁷ Did Mildenberger know that his referee was a former boxing champion who fought Nazis to survive Belsen-Belsen?

A biography titled *Ben Bril—Decorated with the Star of David* was published in 2006. The first copy was presented to his son, Albert, by the Dutch Olympic swimmer Erica Terpstra. Bril died aged 91 in Amsterdam. He has been memorialised by a boxing tournament held each October in Amsterdam—the Ben Bril Memorial Boxing Gala.⁶⁸

At 17 **Salamo Arouch** (1923-2009), from Thessalonika, was the middleweight champion of Greece and the All Balkans Middleweight champion. Strong and stocky, Arouch was nevertheless nicknamed 'the ballet dancer' because of his nimble footwork. Arouch registered 24 wins (all by knock out) before joining the Greek army and becoming a member of the army boxing team. Following the German occupation of Greece the Nazis exterminated almost the entire Jewish population of Thessalonika. Only 2,000 of 47,000 Jews from Thessalonika survived. In 1943 Arouch and his family were arrested and sent to Auschwitz. On arrival Arouch's mother and three sisters were immediately dispatched to the gas chambers. Arouch's father and brother were also killed. His brother was shot for refusing to extract gold teeth from the dead. On realising that Arouch was a boxer, the Germans forced him to fight other inmates up to three times per week in conditions reminiscent of Roman era gladiatorial combat. The loser was shot or sent to the gas chamber. In such a contest the choice was stark. Arouch said simply: 'If I didn't win, I didn't survive'. Arouch won more than 200 of these bouts. Fights would end when one boxer went down or the Nazis became bored. The rare fight ended in a draw. On one occasion Arouch fought a German-Jewish inmate—Klaus Silber. Silber was an undefeated amateur boxer. Arouch knocked him out and never saw Silber again.

He was finally liberated by the allies in 1945. After the war, while searching liberated concentration camps for surviving relatives, Arouch met Marta Yechiel, also from Thessalonika. They married and migrated to Mandatory Palestine in 1945, where Arouch fought again—this time in the 1948 War of Independence.

The 1989 film *Triumph of the Spirit* was shot in Poland. The film was based on Arouch's time in

Auschwitz. He returned to Poland to advise the director, Robert M. Young. Here, in a tearful reunion, Arouch met with a Polish Olympian and rare survivor of one of his bouts.

The two had fought 50 years before in a blood-stained, bare-knuckled bout in the middle of the night.[69] After the film was released, Arouch met with boxing greats such as Mohammed Ali and Mike Tyson. He died in 2009, happy that the story of his life would not be forgotten.

Jacko Razon, Leone Efrati and **Harry Haft** were also amongst those who fought for the entertainment of depraved Nazis. As with Arouch, Razon (1921-1997) held the middleweight title in Greece. He also kept goal for the Salonika soccer side Olympiakos in the Greek National Football League. Razon was transported to Auschwitz in 1943 and was required to box weekly, often against heavyweights. Thanks to his kitchen connections (the boxers had access to more rations) Razon helped other prisoners. It is estimated that hundreds owe their lives to him. He was liberated in May 1945.

Razon returned to Greece and helped organise Holocaust survivors planning to migrate to Palestine. A group numbering 356 survivors set sail on the Henrietta Szold on 30 July 1946. They were met by British warships in Haifa. The refugees, led by Razon, attempted a revolt against the British navy in May 1945. The revolt was put down and the Holocaust survivors were deported to Cyprus where they were again interned. Razon eventually made it to Palestine where he fought in Israel's War of Independence. He was a founder of the Organisation of Greek Concentration Camp Survivors in Israel.[70]

Italian **Leone Efrati** (1916-1944) boxed professionally in Rome in the 1930s. It is likely that Efrati would have won a European title while in Italy, but as a writer with the *Milwaukee Sentinel* pointed out, Jews were not allowed to box in fascist Italy. By 1938 Efrati was boxing in the USA. In December of 1938 he fought for the world featherweight title against Leo Rodak.

The fight went the full distance and in a contentious decision, Rodak was declared the winner. The fight was a turning point for Efrati. He failed to win another bout, losing his last match in the USA in November 1939 to Jackie Callura.

At the commencement of World War Two, all Italians living in the USA who were not citizens were expelled or given the chance to leave the USA. Efrati was in this group. It is not known if he was deported or returned voluntarily to Italy. It is known that he was arrested in Rome in 1943 and sent to Auschwitz. Here he too was forced to fight much heavier men for the entertainment of the Nazis, before his death in April 1944.

When Efrati fought Rodak in 1938 he was in reality fighting for more than a world title—he was fighting for his life. Had he won the bout and become the world champion it is unlikely that he would have had to leave the USA.[71]

Harry Haft (1925-2007) stepped into the ring on 18 July 1949 to fight the boxing heavyweight legend Rocky Marciano. Most of us would recoil in horror at the thought of climbing into the ring with Rocky Marciano—a man who would go on to demolish Joe Louis to become the world heavyweight champion. For Haft, however—as we will see—this bout was nowhere near as terrifying as most of his previous fights.

Born in Belchatow, Poland, Haft was arrested by the Nazis while searching for his brother during the German occupation of Poland in 1939. (Unbeknown to him, his brother had already been rounded up.) As a teenager just shy of 16, Haft found himself in the Nazi death camps. He was chosen to become a boxer because of his physique and brute strength. He had to fight fellow Jewish prisoners in contests which ended when one fighter could no longer stand. The loser was typically executed. Every Sunday Haft squared off against three or four Jewish prisoners. He won all his fights. The Nazis called him 'the Jew animal'. Haft's son, Allan, estimates that at least 76 men were killed after losing to Haft.

Haft managed to escape from a death march in 1945. While on the run he killed a German soldier and by donning the German uniform managed to survive the remaining weeks of the war.[72] In 1948 he immigrated to the USA where he earned a living competing as a heavyweight prizefighter. It must have come as a relief to Haft that his fight with Marciano was his last. On being inducted into the National Jewish Sports Hall of Fame and Museum he was asked if he had any regrets. His son recalled that he looked at his giant fists with broken knuckles and replied that his regrets were the lives that passed through his hands.

Haft died in 2007 but his story has been preserved in the book *Harry Haft: Survivor of Auschwitz, Challenger of Rocky Marciano* written by his son.[73]

Nathan Shapow (1922-2018), working with writer Bob Harris, told his story about boxing in the Nazi concentration camps in the book *The Boxer's Story: Fighting for My Life in the Nazi Camps*. Shapow was born in Riga, Latvia and was a boxing champion. There were about 40,000 Jews in Riga when the Nazis captured the city in 1941. Thousands were murdered.

Those who survived were sent into the Riga Ghetto as forced labourers. Shapow was one of 4,400 Riga Jews assigned to forced labour. His strong physique drew the attention of SS Officer, Obersturmführer Hoffman, who took pleasure in beating defenceless

Jews. On one occasion Shapow was alone with Hoffman and assumed that Hoffman was readying to kill him. Shapow decided that he could die like a coward or die as a warrior. When he saw Hoffman reach for his gun Shapow let his training take over. With all his strength he threw a fast, round-arm left hook. He followed with a classic right to Hoffman's chin. Hoffman went down in shock and pain, his mouth hanging open. Shapow finished the job by cracking Hoffman's skull open with a heavy stool. The murder was the first of several physical encounters, including multiple boxing matches Shapow endured in order to stay alive.

In 1943 Shapow was transferred to a Nazi concentration camp from which he was finally liberated by American forces in April 1945. He lost his mother and two brothers in the Holocaust.[74]

After the war Shapow went to Palestine and joined the Irgun in the fight against the British Mandate. He then fought in the War of Independence. Subsequently he migrated to California where he died, aged 96, in 2018.

For eccentricity alone it would be hard to beat the Olympic bouts of the American **Jackie Fields** (1908-1987) and the South African **Harry Isaacs** (1908-1961). Jackie Fields, whose real name was Jacob Finkelstein, was 16 years of age at the 1924 Olympics, and the youngest competitor in boxing. In the finals

Fields had to fight his best friend, Joe Salas, with whom he had grown up in Los Angeles.

The two shared a dressing room and when they were called to fight they hugged each other and started crying. Minutes later they were beating each other up.[75] Fields was so upset about defeating his mate that he continued crying in the dressing room after the match. Fields is the youngest ever Olympic boxing champion.

As a professional Fields won the World Welterweight Crown, defeating Joe Dundee in July 1929. He lost his title to Young Jack Thompson but regained it against Lou Brouillard in January 1932. Fields and his good friend Joe Salas died eight days apart in June 1987.[76]

Harry Isaacs is one of 19 South Africans to have won Olympic medals in boxing. Isaacs took bronze in the bantamweight division in the 1928 Games. His semi-final bout was spoilt by mean-spirited behavior amongst the spectators. Isaacs was initially declared the winner against the American John Daley. Once the decision was announced, however, Daley's supporters stormed the judges' table demanding that the decision be reversed. It was then announced that one of the judges had transposed his figures and Daley was declared the winner. The fracas was described in the London *Daily Express* as 'an example of vacillation unprecedented in the history of a meeting of such worldwide scope'. In the finals, the decision was again given to Daley's opponent and again the American mob screamed in protest. One reporter described the situation as more than two hours of clatter, screeching, raving and several skirmishes with police. This time the judges stood by their decision. Isaacs returned to South Africa convinced he had been robbed of at least the silver but possibly the gold medal.[77] You have to feel for him.

MEDAL COMPARISON BETWEEN JEWISH AND AUSTRALIAN OLYMPIC BOXERS

Jewish boxers have won thirteen Olympic medals—seven golds and six bronze.

Australians have won four Olympic medals in boxing—one silver and three bronze.

JEWISH OLYMPIC MEDALLISTS—BOXING

1904 St Louis
Samuel Berger, USA, Gold; heavyweight

1916 Cancelled due to World War One

1920 Antwerp
Albert Schneider, Can. Gold; featherweight
Samuel Mosberg, USA, Gold; lightweight
Montgomery Herscovitch, Can. Bronze; middleweight

1924 Paris
John Jackie Fields, Gold; featherweight

1928 Amsterdam
Harold Devine, USA, Bronze; featherweight
Harry Isaacs, South Africa, Bronze; bantamweight
Michael Jacob-Michaelsen, Denmark, Bronze; heavyweight

1932 Los Angeles
Nathan Bor, USA, Bronze; lightweight

1940 and 1944 Cancelled due to World War Two

1960 Rome
Gyula Török, Hun. Gold; flyweight

1976 Montreal
Victor Zilberman, Romania, Bronze; welterweight

1972 Munich
György Gedó, Hun. Gold; light-flyweight

1980 Moscow
Shamil Sabirov, Russia, Gold; light-flyweight

WRESTLING

The wrestling match between the Austrian heavyweight **Fred Oberlander** (1911-1996) and the

German champion Kurt Siebert was reminiscent of the heavyweight boxing encounter between Max Baer and Max Schmeling. The match took place in the first round of the 1935 World Wrestling Championships. Oberlander recalled the German coach objecting to the Hakoah emblem on his wrestling outfit, saying it was a political insignia. Oberlander pointed out that the emblem was that of his club. After much deliberation the referee ruled that the swastika on Siebert's jersey was also a political insignia and the match could proceed. Oberlander mused that the bout started and ended in his favour. So did the entire competition—Oberlander won the World Wrestling Championships.

Oberlander and **Nikolaus Hirschl** (1906-1991) were childhood friends in Vienna. Both became heavyweight wrestling champions and both competed for the Jewish Hakoah Vienna—a club that won 127 wrestling titles between 1929 and 1934. In 1935 Oberlander was offered a place in the Austrian team for the 1936 Berlin Games but declined on account of the Nazis' treatment of Jews. Oberlander's wrestling successes spanned two continents and four countries. Between 1930 and 1950 he won two Austrian junior titles, five French Heavyweight Championships, the 1944 Allied Championships, and in 1948 he won the Heavyweight Wrestling Championships at the Commonwealth Games while captaining the British side. In that year he represented Great Britain in the London Olympics as captain of the team. Oberlander then emigrated to Canada where he founded the Canadian Maccabi Association.[78] His son Philip wrestled in the 1964 Olympics.[79]

Hirschl also chose to boycott Hitler's Games. Hirschl's parents ran a kosher butchery and his father was president of a synagogue. Hirschl was the Austrian junior champion in shot put, discus and heavyweight weightlifting. It was, however, in wrestling and the pentathlon that he had astounding success.

Hirschl won the Austrian heavyweight wrestling championships at 18 years of age and held that title for 10 years. He also held the European heavyweight wrestling title. He won the Austrian pentathlon title, aged 17, and held it for seven years.

Pentathletes are amongst the most skilled of athletes. They compete in five events chosen to mirror the skills required of a soldier in battle. In the 1928 Games pentathletes competed in shooting, swimming (300m freestyle), fencing, equestrian and a 4000m cross country race.

In the 1932 Los Angeles Games Hirschl won bronze medals in heavyweight Greco-Roman and freestyle wrestling.

In an interview with Milt Sherman, Hirschl described how on his return from the 1932 Olympics he was congratulated by the Austrian president but was 'hated by the Nazis', and following a number of dangerous confrontations with Nazis, began carrying a gun for protection. One night while walking his girlfriend home through a park the couple were accosted by Nazis. A fight ensued and Hirschl shot one of the assailants dead. The couple returned home safely but later that night the police knocked on their door and told Hirschl that they knew about the incident but would not arrest him. They added, however, that they could not protect him and that he was a marked man. Hirschl fled by train to Italy and then by ship to Palestine. He later enrolled with the British army and was trained as a commando because of his superb physical condition and his fluency in German.

He could not have foreseen that his pentathlete and martial arts skills would be put to use in real battle. He has described an attack on a German fuel depot in North Africa. Under cover of darkness the commandos paddled ashore, intent on destroying the depot. Hirschl described how two guards had to be killed—one by him and the second by another commando. Once the guards were taken care of the commandos laid mines with timers on the fuel dumps. They then left for their own lines, walking at night and burying themselves in the desert sand during the day.

During the second night they were attacked by a German truck. The commandos blew up the truck using a hand grenade, but nine of the twelve commandos died during the attack. Hirschl sustained a leg wound but managed to carry an injured comrade towards the British lines where they had to endure friendly fire before being recognised as allies. Most of Hirschl's family died in the Holocaust.

The war over, Hirschl married and settled in Australia, operating a successful meat business. In 1984 he and his old mate Oberlander met at the Olympics in Los Angeles.[80] If only one could have been a fly on the wall!

Abraham Kurland (1912-1999) of Denmark won a silver medal at the 1932 Games and was a favourite for the lightweight Greco-Roman event at the 1936 Games. He too boycotted the 1936 Games.[81] He participated again in the 1948 Olympics at 45 years of age.

Hitler's 1936 Games forced Jewish athletes to make an uncomfortable decision. Some boycotted the Games while others attended the event—many of the latter refuting through their performances the Nazi propaganda that Jews made inferior athletes. **Károly Kellner** (1906-1996) is one of the latter. Kellner won his first Hungarian national junior wrestling title in 1925. That year the sports clubs of his town refused entry to Jews. Kellner was devout in his faith and unlike many Hungarian Jews refused to convert to Catholicism, instead adopting the Hungarian name Kárpáti. Under this name he was permitted to compete. He won several European lightweight wrestling crowns and at the 1932 Olympics took the silver medal. He was now in the Hungarian team for the 1936 Games. The devoutly Jewish Kárpáti went to compete in Berlin—a city draped in swastikas, and crowded with SS men—while knowing that Hitler was in the stands. Kárpáti was, however, on a personal mission. En route to the finals he defeated the Frenchman Charles Delporte, out-wrestled the Australian champion Dick Garrard, pinned down Italy's Paride Moragnoli and beat the Olympic champion Hermanni Pihlajamaki of Finland. The final was against the unbeaten Nazi champion Wolfgang Ehrl. Hitler and some of his generals attended the deciding bout—no doubt expecting a German victory. The huge and partisan crowd roared triumphantly when the German won a move and jeered Kárpáti's counter-moves. Prior to the match Kárpáti had announced to his teammates: 'I either come out of this with the gold medal or I don't come out at all'. He came out with the gold.

Back in Nazi-aligned Hungary, Kárpáti had to endure the ire of a nation maddened with hate. On one occasion Kárpáti escorted a rabbi home and the pair were attacked by Nazi thugs. Kárpáti routed the thugs. He was later forced into a labour camp in Poland.

Here he witnessed the cruel murder of the champion fencer **Attila Petschauer** (see section on fencing). In 1944 Kárpáti escaped from the camp and was reunited with his wife, who was being sheltered by a Hungarian, Viktor Papp. While in hiding Kárpáti's wife became pregnant. Papp arranged forged papers so she could give birth in a hospital. Undeterred by what he had endured, Kárpáti remained in Budapest following the war. He became coach to the Hungarian national team for the next 20 years and wrote five books on wrestling. He is buried in a Jewish cemetery in Budapest. Victor Papp was declared 'Righteous Among the Nations' by the Yad Vashem.[82]

Another indomitable individual was **Yakiv Punkin** (1921-1994). Punkin joined the Soviet Army during World War Two. He was captured by German forces and remained in POW camps until the war ended. During his years of captivity Punkin avoided being shot as a Jew (unlike many of his cellmates) by claiming to be an Ossetian Muslim. He weighed only 36kg on being liberated by Soviet troops in 1945.

Punkin rejoined the Soviet army between 1945 and 1948. He won the army wrestling championships in 1947 and took four Soviet titles between 1949 and 1955. In 1952 he won gold at the Helsinki Games. Punkin was once asked whether he felt fear during a match. He replied that at one time he had, but that his fear had been depleted by his time in concentration camps. A wrestling tournament is held annually in Zaporizhzia in his honour. His son Grigory lives in Israel.[83]

The Dutch wrestler **Jacob van Moppes** (1876-1943) competed in the Greco-Roman lightweight division in the 1908 Games.[84] He was killed by the Nazis in the Sobibor concentration camp in March 1943.[85]

Paul Yogi Mayer, whose athletic career as an Olympic standard athlete was ruined by Hitler, described the **Baruch** brothers, **Julius** and **Hermann**. Mayer knew the brothers as odd job men who worked for his parents. They were two of the 100,000 German Jews who fought in World War One for Germany. (80,000 of these men were at the frontline. 12,000 died.[86] Despite the prevailing anti-Semitism, 35,000 Jewish soldiers were decorated for bravery.18,000 were awarded the Iron Cross.)[87] The brothers were both German champions in wrestling. Hermann was also a European weightlifting champion. Germany was barred from competing in the Olympics from 1920 to 1928 as punishment for its part in World War One. This meant that the Hermann brothers were unable to compete in those Games. They were both badly injured by Nazi thugs during the 1938 pogroms. They were later sent to Buchenwald and Auschwitz before being killed in the Theresienstadt concentration camp. At Mayer's urging a new road in Bad Kreuznach was named the 'Gebruder Baruch Strasse' with a small sign explaining the fate of the brothers.[88]

Not long after the Holocaust another Jewish world wrestling champion emerged, this time on the other side of the world. **Henry Wittenberg** (1918-2010) came to wrestling after his swimming coach said: 'Kid, forget it. You'll never be a swimmer. You've got no intestinal fortitude'. The instructor elaborated: 'You know what that means? You've got no guts'. He could not have been more wrong. Unperturbed by the coach's insult, Wittenberg switched to wrestling. This was an astute move befitting the captain of the high school chess team. Wittenberg dominated his division in national and international freestyle wrestling, winning more than 300 consecutive matches and eight Amateur Athletic Union championships between 1939 and 1951.

He won two Olympic medals while serving as a New York City police officer. In the first Olympics following the war he took gold in the light heavyweight class (195.5 pounds). He reached the final in the 1952 Olympics but, now on the decline, only managed to take silver. Had World War Two not brought about the cancellation of the 1940 and 1944 Games during Wittenberg's prime, his display cabinet would have contained more Olympic hardware.

Wittenberg's record nevertheless established him as one of wrestling's all-time greats. When his competitive days were over Wittenberg coached the USA Greco-Roman team for the 1968 Mexico City Olympics. He also coached the teams of Yeshiva University and the City College of New York (CCNY).

While serving as a police officer Wittenberg received citations for bravery on five occasions. In one instance he disarmed a man brandishing a gun and an axe on a Manhattan rooftop. He retired from the police force in 1954.

Wittenberg visited Israel prior to the 1972 Munich Games and gave coaching tips to the Israeli wrestlers. On 4 September 1972 Wittenberg and his wife Edith spent time one evening with Yosef Gutfreund, an Israeli wrestling referee, in a Munich hotel. The next day Palestinian terrorists attacked the Olympic village, killing Gutfreund and 10 other Israeli athletes and coaches.

Unlike many other amateur wrestlers Wittenberg never dabbled with the lucrative hair-pulling and stamping of professional wrestling. 'I was a wrestler. I wasn't an actor', he declared. Wittenberg's wife also served as a New York City police officer. She fenced for Hunter College in New York and coached fencing at CCNY. She died in 2008.[89] In 1977 Wittenberg was inducted into the National Wrestling Hall of Fame.

I described the 1972 Munich massacre in the chapter on

athletics. **Mark Slavin** was the more accomplished of the two wrestlers who died in the attack. He took up wrestling to defend himself against anti-Semitic hoodlums in his home town of Minsk. Slavin was regarded as one of Russia's most gifted young athletes after winning the Soviet Junior Greco-Roman wrestling championships in 1972. He left for a new life in Israel only four months before the Munich games and was to make his Olympic debut at 18 years of age. He and **Eliezer Halfin** both lost their lives in the botched German rescue attempt at the Furstënfeldbruck airbase.

As with fencing and boxing, there are eccentrics amongst Jewish wrestlers. People in their millions have walked down Broadway Street and along St. James Park and Fleet Street in London. Many would have noticed the sculpture—the two winged masks of 'Past and Future'—decorating the former *Daily Telegraph* building in Fleet Street and the sculpture of the 'West Wind' decorating the former Transport for London Headquarters Building at 55 Broadway, St. James. Few, however, would know about the artist who created these sculptures. **Samuel Rabin** (1903-1991) was born in Manchester to a poor Russian family who had fled Imperial Russia. Rabin won a scholarship which made him, at eleven years of age, the youngest pupil to study at the Manchester Municipal School of Art. Rabin was, however, much more than a sculptor.

He had a fine baritone voice and often sang on music

radio programmes. During World War Two he sang with the Army Classical Music Group. The group travelled throughout England, Scotland and later Germany with Rabin singing operatic arias. In 1949 he became Teacher of Drawing at Goldsmith's College of Art in London. Rabin rarely exhibited his art but he did have an exhibition at the Leicester Galleries in 1960. A retrospective was held at Dulwich Picture Gallery in 1985-86.[90]

So what connection did this highly talented man have with wrestling? As with many artists, Rabin struggled to make ends meet. He had, however, a unique solution. Blessed with an unusually powerful physique, Rabin took to wrestling and boxing to support his creative talents He was as successful in the martial arts as he was in the creative arts. In 1928 he represented Great Britain at the Olympic Games, winning a bronze in wrestling. He turned professional in 1932 and fought as 'Rabin the Cat' and 'Sam Radnor the Hebrew' Jew across Great Britain. To top it all he also acted. He was cast, appropriately as a wrestler, in the 1933 film *The Private Life of Henry VIII* and in 1934 had the part of the Jewish prize fighter Daniel Mendoza in *The Scarlet Pimpernel*.[91]

Wrestling and fencing were the two disciplines in which Hungarians took the most pride. Andrew Handler described the events as a coalescence of athletic, Christian and nationalistic values. No

Hungarian had won a medal in either wrestling or fencing until 1908. At the 1908 London Games, however, Hungary's red, white and green flag was raised to the sound of the national anthem for both of these events. Two proud Hungarian champions stood on the podium to receive their gold medals. One was the fencer **Jenö Fuchs** and the other was wrestler **Richárd Weisz** (1879-1945). Both were Jewish. Weisz won gold in the Greco-Roman heavyweight division. In the final he defeated the immensely powerful Russian, Petrov. After an hour of struggling, the bout was extended by three periods of overtime—ten, twenty and a further ten minutes, before Weisz was announced the winner. Built like a bear—Weisz's neck measured 20 inches and his chest 50 inches—Weisz was also Hungary's first weightlifting champion. He was the Hungarian champion in the heavyweight division from 1903 to 1909.

Despite his successes as a Hungarian Olympian, the growing insanity of Hungarian anti-Semitism before and during the war caught up with Weisz. He too was forced into a ghetto. He did, however, manage to survive the Nazi era.

Samuel Norton Gerson (1895-1972) was born in Russia but came to the USA to live with relatives when aged 11. Gerson captained the University of Pennsylvania chess team but it was at wrestling that he excelled. He won silver in the featherweight class in freestyle wrestling at the 1920 Antwerp Olympics. He left the Games in a state of unease after an official told him that he may have been unfairly judged because he was Jewish. Gerson had believed that the Olympics were about fostering peace. In 1945 he founded Olympians International with the intent of encouraging peace between nations through their athletic associations. The group has grown to include former Olympians from all parts of the globe. His grief at the killing of the Israeli athletes by Palestinian terrorists is said to have brought on the heart attack that caused his death in 1972—a month after the Munich Massacre.[92]

The Holocaust ended the tradition of Jewish wrestlers in Europe. Since 1948 the only Jewish Olympic medallists in wrestling have been Russian or American.

MEDAL COMPARISON BETWEEN JEWISH AND AUSTRALIAN WRESTLERS

Jewish wrestlers have won fifteen Olympic medals—seven gold.

Australia has won three Olympic medals in wrestling—one silver and two bronze.

JEWISH OLYMPIC MEDALLISTS—WRESTLING

1908 London
Richárd Weisz, Hun. Gold; Greco-Roman heavyweight

1916 Cancelled due to World War One

1920 Antwerp
Samuel Gerson, USA, Silver; featherweight
Fredrick Meyer, USA, Bronze; freestyle heavyweight

1928 Amsterdam
Samuel Rabin, Great Britain, Bronze; freestyle middleweight

1932 Los Angeles
Károly Kárpáti, Hun. Silver; Greco-Roman lightweight
Abraham Kurland, Den. Silver; Greco-Roman lightweight
Nikolaus Hirschl, Austria, Bronze; freestyle heavyweight
Nikolaus Hirschl, Austria, Bronze; Greco-Roman heavyweight

1936 Berlin
Károly Kárpáti, Hun. Gold; freestyle lightweight

1940 and 1944 Cancelled due to World War Two

1948 London
Henry Wittenberg, USA, Gold; freestyle, light-heavyweight

1952 Helsinki
Yakiv Punkin, Sov. Union, Gold; Greco-Roman, featherweight
Henry Wittenberg, USA, Silver; light-heavyweight freestyle
Boris Gurevich, Sov. Union, Gold; Greco-Roman flyweight

1960 Rome
Oleg Karavaev, Sov. Union, Gold; Greco-Roman bantamweight

1968 Mexico City
Boris Gurevich, Sov. Union, Gold; freestyle middleweight

JUDO

The American **James Bregman** (1941-) and the Russian **Aron Bogolyubov** (1938-) are Jewish judokas (experts in judo) who won bronze medals in the 1964 Tokyo Games—the first Olympics to host judo. (The sport was omitted in 1968 but has been included in all subsequent Olympics.)

In 1992 Israeli judokas began an Olympic medal-winning streak that has continued in current times. **Yael Arad** (1967-) was the first Israeli to win an Olympic medal, taking silver at the 1992 Barcelona Games in the women's lightweight division. She dedicated her medal to the 11 victims of the 1972 Munich terrorist attack. At the post-match press conference Arad said: 'Today we proved that the abominable murder did not succeed in eradicating Israeli sports: we are continuing'. Arad won silver in the World Championships in 1993.[93]

In the 1992 Olympics **Oren Smadja** (1970-) won bronze in the men's lightweight division.

Heavyweight **Arik Ze'evi** (1977-) competed in the 2000, 2004 and 2008 Games, taking bronze in 2004. Only days after the UN Secretary–General Ban Ki-moon announced the traditional Olympic truce requiring people and nations to 'set aside their differences', an Iranian, Javad Mahjoub, pulled out of the 2012 London Games. Mahjoub was due to compete against Ze'evi. The reason given for his withdrawal was 'weakness, nausea and vomiting'.

This was not the first time Mahjoub had refused to fight an Israeli. In the Judo 2011 World Cup in Tashkent Mahjoub declined to compete against Israel's Or Sasson. The Olympic Charter states: 'Any form of discrimination with regard to a country or a person on grounds of race, religion, politics, gender or otherwise is incompatible with belonging to the Olympic Movement'.[94] Behaviour not in keeping with Olympic ideals was also visited upon Israeli **Ehud Vaks** (1979-) at the 2004 Games. Vaks was drawn to fight the Iranian, Arash Mirasmaeli. Mirasmaeli was, however, disqualified for being over the weight limit. Vaks expressed sympathy for the Iranian, saying that he was forced out of the match because of Iranian national policy.[95] It is widely believed that Mirasmaeli conspired to be disqualified in order to avoid competing against Vaks. Mirasmaeli's own comments support this view. He said: 'Although I have trained for months and was in good shape, I refused to fight my Israeli opponent to sympathise with the suffering of the people of Palestine and I do not feel upset at all'. The Iranian President Mohammad Khatami was quoted as saying that Mirasmaeli's actions would be 'recorded in the history of Iranian glories' and that he was considered by the Iranian nation to be 'the champion of the 2004 Olympic Games'.[96]

The 120kg, 6ft 4in heavyweight, **Or Sasson** (1990-), took gold at the World Cup in Prague in 2012. At the 2016 Rio Olympics he fought Egypt's Islam El Shahaby in the first round.

After losing to Sasson, Islam El Shahaby refused to shake hands with the victor. El Shahaby's unsportsmanlike behavior was rewarded with loud boos and jeers from the near capacity crowd. Sasson said that he wanted to shake his opponent's hand because he had been educated to respect his opponents, no matter who they are. He went on to take the bronze.[97]

Yarden Gerbi (1989-) won gold at the World Judo Championships in 2013 in Rio in the under 63kg class. In the final Gerbi defeated Clarisse Agbegnenou of France. Using her infamous chokehold, she not only rendered Agbegnenou unconscious but dislocated her shoulder. She so impressed her fans that she received three marriage proposals.[98]

At the Rio Olympics in 2016 Gerbi won bronze. On retiring in 2017 Gerbi recalled at a news conference how at three years of age she watched the 1992 Olympics on television and, seeing the Israelis Oren Smadja and Yael Arad take medals, she asked her mother how you buy a ticket to the Games. Her mother answered that you can't buy a ticket but have to work hard to get there. That was the start of Gerbi's dream. Gerbi added that people always ask her whether it's better to be a world champion or an Olympic medallist. Her answer is that she didn't have to choose as she'd done both.[99] For Gerbi her childhood dream became reality.

Alice Schlesinger (1988-) is another Israeli Olympian to win gold at the World Judo Championships without fulfilling her potential at the Olympics. Schlesinger took bronze in the 2009 World

Championships but won gold in 2013 and 2014. In 2008 she competed for Israel at the Beijing Games in the under 63kg division but failed to win a medal. Because Schlesinger's mother is British she was able to subsequently fight for Great Britain. Since 2015 she has won several judo medals for Great Britain but again disappointed at the Olympics, failing to win a medal at the 2016 Games.

Sagi Muki (1992-) won the World Championships in 2019 in Tokyo in the under 81kg class. He competed for Israel in the 2016 Olympics but failed to win a medal.

One could be forgiven for thinking that in judo—a sport only recently included in the Olympics—Jewish athletes may have competed unhindered by bigotry and hate. Sadly, that has not been the case.

MEDAL COMPARISON BETWEEN JEWISH AND AUSTRALIAN OLYMPIC JUDOKAS

Jewish judokas have won 10 Olympic medals—two silver and eight bronze.

Australian judokas have won two Olympic medals—both bronze.

JEWISH OLYMPIC MEDALLISTS—JUDO

1964 Tokyo

James Bregman, USA, Bronze; middleweight
Aron Bogolyubov, Russia, Bronze; lightweight

1984 Los Angeles
Mike Berger, Canada, Bronze; heavyweight
Robert Borland, USA, Silver; middleweight

1992 Barcelona
Yael Arad, Israel, Silver; lightweight
Oren Smadja, Israel, Bronze; lightweight

2004 Athens
Arik Ze'evi, Israel, Bronze; heavyweight

2012 London
Felipe Kitadai, Brazil, Bronze; half-lightweight

2016 Rio
Or Sasson, Israel, Bronze; heavyweight
Yarden Gerbi, Israel, Bronze; lightweight

TAEKWONDO

Taekwondo was first included as a sport in the Sydney Games in 2000. No Jewish athletes have won a medal in this discipline.

Australia has won two medals.

Michael Meyerson

SUMMARY

Jewish involvement in martial arts is rich in stories that go beyond standard contests in the ring or on the mat. Jewish inmates in concentration camps fought each other for survival. An Austrian wrestling champion became a war hero fighting against the Nazis.

Max Baer humiliated Hitler by pulverising German heavyweight hope Max Schmeling to take the world heavyweight title in June 1933. Jewish athletes defeated their German opponents in fencing and wrestling at Hitler's 1936 Games.

A sculptor, short of money, both boxed and wrestled to help make ends meet. In so doing he won an Olympic medal in wrestling. Millions of people walk past Samuel Rabin's sculptures in London. Few know the fascinating details of the sculptor's life.

With the Holocaust still fresh in the minds of Jews the Olympics returned to Germany in 1972. At these Games Israeli Olympians were attacked by terrorists with the wrestlers and weightlifters bearing the brunt of the onslaught.

Jewish Olympians have won more medals than Australians in fencing, boxing, wrestling and judo. Who would believe the huge number of Olympic medals won by Jewish fencers, if there were no records of their successes?

OVERALL MEDAL COMPARISON BETWEEN JEWISH AND AUSTRALIAN ATHLETES IN MARTIAL ARTS

Jewish Olympians have won 147 medals in martial arts—64 gold.

Australian Olympians have won 11 medals in martial arts—none is gold.

CHAPTER 5

WEIGHTLIFTING

'The Germans are not discriminating against Jews. The Jews were eliminated because they are not good enough athletes'

Frederick Rubien, secretary of the USA Olympic Committee.[1]

Weightlifting was established as a sport in the late 19th Century. The first world champion weightlifter was the Jewish Englishman—**Edward Lawrence Levy**. Between 1891-1894 Levy set 14 world records. Levy's intense passion for sport is evident in his words: 'A person who does not engage in sport is not worth educating'.[2] The tradition of lifting impossibly heavy metal discs was continued by several Jewish strongmen.

Olympic success for Jewish weightlifters began with the Austrian **Hans Haas** (1906-1973), who took gold and silver in the 1928 and 1932 Olympics in the lightweight division.[3]

Another Jewish Austrian, **Robert Fein** (1907-1975), defied Nazi propaganda in the most incisive way by competing in Hitler's 1936 Games. He took gold in the lightweight division, setting a new Olympic record for the press (105kg).[4]

I discussed the German wrestling champions and brothers, **Julius** and **Hermann Baruch**, in the chapter on martial arts. Hermann was also a European weightlifting champion. The brothers could not compete in the Olympics from 1920 to 1928 because Germany was barred from the Games as punishment for its part in World War One. The brothers perished in the Theresienstadt concentration camp.[5]

Ben Helfgott (1929-)—later Sir Ben Helfgott, MBE—was born in Poland. He is one of five Jewish athletes who survived internment by the Nazis to later compete in the Olympics. (The other four are the swimmer, **Alfred Nakache**, the wrestler, **Yakiv Punkin**, and the race walkers **Henry Laskau** and **Shaul Ladany**. Incredibly, Nakache, Laskau and Ladany also set world records following the Holocaust.)

Helfgott was liberated by the Allies from the Theresienstadt concentration camp in 1945 and sent to England along with 700 other children—most of them survivors of concentration camps. His parents and youngest sister were shot by the Nazis.[6]

Helfgott was the British lightweight champion from 1954-1960. He captained the British weightlifting team at the 1956 and 1960 Games. He did not win an Olympic medal but took bronze in the 1958 Commonwealth Games.[7] Helfgott was knighted in November 2018 in recognition of his service to Holocaust remembrance and education.

Three Jewish weightlifters, **Ze'Ev Friedman, David Berger**, and **Yossef 'Yossi' Romano**, had their lives stolen by the Palestinian terrorists who attacked the Israeli contingent at the 1972 Olympics.

Ze'ev Friedman (1944-1972) was born in Prokopyevsk, Russia but moved to Israel in 1960. He won bronze at the 1971 Asian Weightlifting Championships and placed 12th in his class in the Munich Olympics.[8]

Yossef 'Yossi' Romano (1940-1972) was born in Benghazi, Libya. His family migrated to Mandatory Palestine when he was six years old. Romano was Israel's light and middleweight weightlifting champion for nine years. He had to withdraw from the competition at the Munich Games because he ruptured a knee tendon during one of his lifts. He was due to fly home the day the terrorists attacked the Israeli athletes. After his death his mother committed suicide. [9]

David Mark Berger (1944-1972) immigrated to Israel

after competing in the 1969 Maccabi Games for the USA.[10] Berger had an enviable academic record, including a combined MBA-law degree from Columbia University. His father, Benjamin, a physician, has been quoted saying that he used to tell Berger: 'You may not be the best weightlifter in the world, but you're certainly the smartest'.[11]

Berger went to the Munich Games to compete for Israel as a light heavyweight weightlifter. His body was flown back to the USA in an Air Force jet on the orders of President Nixon. The ten other murdered Israeli Olympians were repatriated to Israel for burial.

Isaac 'Ike' Berger (1936-)—the son of a rabbi—was born in Jerusalem and immigrated to the USA in his teens. Berger won three Olympic medals in the featherweight class of press, snatch and jerk. In Melbourne in 1956 the total of Berger's three lifts—press (107.5kg), snatch (107.5kg) and jerk (137.5kg)—was 352.5kg (776.5lb), giving Berger not only an Olympic gold, but the world record.

In 1960 Berger won silver at the Rome Games. Weighing 59kg (130 pounds), Berger again took silver at the 1964 Games. His lift of 152.5kg (336lb) in the clean and jerk made him pound-for-pound the strongest man in the world. It took nine years for this record to be bettered.

Berger established other world firsts. He was the first featherweight to lift a total of 362.8kg (800 pounds) in the press, snatch and jerk and was also the first weightlifter to press double his body weight.[12]

He was one of few weightlifters to consistently defeat the Russians. At the 1960 Games it took Yevgeny Minayev 10 hours of dogged competition to reverse his loss to Berger at the 1956 Olympics. The contest finally ended at 4am with Berger failing to jerk 152.5kg (336lb) and having to be content with silver.[13] Berger came back, however, to win the World Championships in 1958 and 1961, relegating Minayev to second place on both occasions.

In 1957, at the Maccabi Games, Berger became the first athlete to set a world record in Israel with a press of 117.1kg (258 pounds).[14] Berger held eight world records—four were official.

It is fitting that Berger was featured in a stamp series with the great Jesse Owens—the American athlete who destroyed the concept of 'Aryan' athletic superiority at Hitler's 1936 Games.[15]

Berger lived his own dream and advised others to do the same. His advice: 'Believe in yourself and your dream. The lady who wants to become a schoolteacher or a television newscaster. The guy who wants to write a book or start his own business. Go ahead. Whatever you dream, make that your gold medal'. He was inducted into the USA Weightlifters Hall of Fame in 1965.[16]

It would be hard to better Berger's tally of world records, yet **Grigory Novak** (1919-1980) of the Soviet Union set more than 50 world records during his career—18 of them officially recognised. In 1946 he was the world light heavyweight champion. Novak was less successful as an Olympian but did win silver in the middle-heavyweight division at the 1952 Helsinki Games.

Novak's muscles were honed as a child by working alongside his father as a builder. Before embarking on his weightlifting career he was employed in a circus as an acrobat and juggler. After he retired from competition in 1952 he returned to the circus—this time as a strongman, weight juggler and choreographer. He lifted platforms upon which several performers would engage in different acts, such as, cycling, weightlifting and acrobatics. He also juggled with 30-40kg weights![17]

Novak served as an officer in the Russian army in World War Two. He was cited for bravery on four occasions.[18]

Two American strong men were **Frank Spellman** and **Gary Gubner**. **Spellman** (1922-2017) was placed in an orphanage at seven years of age after his father died.

He entered the USA army at 20 and fought against the Nazis in France and Germany.[19] In 1948 he competed in the first post war Olympics in London, winning gold in the middleweight category. On his way to the gold he set two Olympic records. In 1954 he set a world record in the squat at the USA National Squat Championships. Spellman had a long and successful career in weightlifting, winning several USA Championships before retiring at the age of 49. He has been inducted into the USA Weightlifting Hall of Fame, the Helms Athletic Foundation Hall of Fame, and the Porterville Quarterback Hall of Fame.[20]

The 6ft 2½in American **Gary Jay Gubner** (1942-) weighed 120kg and excelled at the shot, discus and weightlifting. He placed fourth in the super heavyweight lifting event in the 1964 Games.[21] He failed to qualify for the 1964 Olympics in the shot. It's probable that Gubner made a tactical error in hoping to compete in the 1964 Games in both shot put and weightlifting. Had he concentrated on one of the disciplines it's likely he would have won a medal. He is one of few shot putters to beat the legendary, William 'Parry' O'Brien. In February 1962 he set two indoor shot put world records—on one occasion erasing O'Brien's world record.[22] In the same year his best throw of 19.8m (64ft 11½in) gave him the second ranking in the world.

Other Jewish Olympic medallists in weightlifting

include lightweight **Igor Rybak** and heavyweight **Valery Shary**—both Russians. These lifters each took gold in the 1956 and 1976 Games.

SUMMARY

Jewish weightlifter Robert Fein defied Nazi propaganda taking gold at Hitler's 1936 Games. Sir Ben Helfgott survived the Nazi concentration camps to compete at the Olympics. Three Israeli weightlifters and a weightlifting judge were killed in the terrorist attack at the 1972 Munich Games.

Russian Grigory Novak's success in winning silver at the 1952 Games was dwarfed by his ability to set world weightlifting records. Novak was also a circus acrobat, juggler and strongman.

Isaac Berger had a stellar career and was pound for pound the strongest man in the world.

MEDAL COMPARISON BETWEEN JEWISH AND AUSTRALIAN OLYMPIC WEIGHTLIFTERS

Jewish weightlifters have won ten Olympic medals—six gold and four silver.

Australian weightlifters have won four Olympic medals—one gold, one silver and two bronze.

JEWISH OLYMPIC MEDALLISTS—WEIGHTLIFTING

1928 Amsterdam
Hans Haas, Austria, Gold; lightweight

1932 Los Angeles
Hans Haas, Austria, Silver; lightweight

1936 Berlin
Robert Fein, Austria, Gold; 67.5kg

1952 Helsinki
Grigory Novak, Russia, Silver; middle heavyweight

1956 Melbourne
Isaac Berger, USA, Gold; featherweight
Igor Rybak, Russia, Gold; lightweight

1960 Rome
Isaac Berger, USA, Silver; featherweight

1964 Tokyo
Isaac Berger, USA, Silver; featherweight
Rudolf Plyukfelder, Russia, Gold; light heavyweight

1976 Montreal
Valery Shary, Russia, Gold; light heavyweight

CHAPTER 6

WATERSPORTS—ROWING, SAILING AND PADDLING

'No Jew in crew'

> Phrase associated with rowing at American universities.[1]

ROWING

It is not uncommon to hear of someone discovering their Jewish background late in life, but what if you were told that you are Jewish as you were setting off to compete in Hitler's 1936 Olympic Games?

This happened to **Robert 'Bobby' Moch** (1914-2005). The story of the 1936 USA rowing crew, who bonded as lifelong friends, has been told by Daniel James Brown in the gripping book, *The Boys in the Boat*.

Moch knew that his family had relatives in Switzerland and Alsace-Lorraine. Assuming he would be picked to cox the USA's 1936 eight man rowing crew, he asked his father, Gaston, for the contact details of these relatives. He intended to look them up once in Europe. After some hesitation Gaston replied that he would supply the details should Moch's crew really go to Berlin. Moch's Seattle University crew was duly chosen to row in Berlin. Shortly thereafter he received a sealed envelope containing the family details from his father. Within the envelope there was, however, another envelope which had on it the words, 'read this in a private place'. Now anxious, Moch sat alone under a tree to read the letter. Before he had finished he was in tears. He had learned that he and his family were Jewish. It was, however, not this discovery that brought Moch to tears. It was realising the pain his father must have endured while concealing his true identity in order to succeed in America.

Brown details the rigours of rowing. Rowing requires all the muscles in your body to work against an unrelenting resistance of water and wind while maintaining perfect balance so that the 24in wide vessel remains on an even keel. This requires your body to burn calories and consume oxygen at a rate unequalled in almost any other human endeavour. Moreover, the start and end of each race require flat-out sprints, calling for the anaerobic use of energy.

Every athlete who competes in a sport requiring anaerobic respiration knows the agony of having to keep going full throttle while their muscles scream in protest at the lactic acid build up. The journalist Royal Brougham described rowing like this: 'Nobody ever took time out in a boat race. There's no place to stop and get a satisfying drink of water or a lungful of cool, invigorating air. You just row until they tell you it's all over…It's no game for a softy'.

Furthermore, rowing differs from other team sports in one vital aspect. In sports such as cricket or rugby, a team can still triumph despite one or two players being off form. In rowing each individual has to row in perfect synchrony with the rest of the team. One rower's mistake can destroy the rhythm and pace of the entire boat.

Moch's crew had been trained to keep the stroke count low at the start of a race and to increase the intensity towards the end. They would usually be trailing at the halfway mark but as the stroke rate lifted they would surge past their rivals. It was up to Moch, as cox, to call out the stroke rate to the oarsman, Don Hume. Hume would respond by setting the pace for the other oarsmen behind.

On the way to the 1936 Olympic finals the USA beat the favourites—Great Britain. Both teams were pushed to their limits but the USA won, setting new Olympic and World records. The regatta's final event was also the final event of the Games. 75,000 spectators gathered around Lake Grunau at 6pm on the 14 August 1936 to watch the contest. In the grandstand were Hitler and his henchmen—among them Hermann Goering and Joseph Goebbels. The event was to be broadcast around the world.

Germany shot ahead at the start—then came Italy followed by Great Britain. America was at the back of the field. At the halfway mark (1,000m) the Italians and Germans were in front by more than a boat length. Great Britain had fallen back and was level with the USA in last place—they were five long seconds behind the leaders. The Americans' stroke rate was held at 36. But now the cadence of the Americans began to increase. With 500m to go, the USA moved to third place. With 200m to go the roar along the water's edge drowned out Moch's call of the stroke rate. The crowd was chanting 'Deutsch-Land! Deutsch-Land!' in time with the German oarsmen. His megaphone now useless, Moch resorted to beating out the cadence for his eight on the side of the boat— a cadence much softer, but faster and more effective than the chant of the German crowd.[2]

Moch pushed the stroke rate to a near impossible 44. The Americans overtook the Germans in the final 10 strokes, crossing the line with the Italians. No one knew who had won. The crowd, now still, awaited the decision. It was finally announced that the USA won (6:25.4mins) with Italy second (6:26.0mins) and

Germany third (6:26.4mins). After almost six and a half minutes of agony, only a second separated first and third places.

The contest ended to the tune of the USA national anthem rather than the German 'Horst Wessel'. Moch and his eight-man crew stood quietly while the American flag was raised and the 'Star-Spangled Banner' played. Moch was given credit for the victory. His teammates, who could have been excused for cursing him during the race, now acknowledged that he drove them to achieve the impossible. 'Bob got some things out of the crew that I didn't think were there' recalled Roger Morris, who rowed in the eight-seat. 'We owe him a ton for helping win that race in Berlin,' McMillin said. 'We were in deep trouble and he was able to pull us out of it'.[3] We will never know what went through Moch's mind as he pummelled his exhausted crew to victory. Did the discovery that he was Jewish enhance Moch's will to succeed? Probably. The pity is that Hitler never knew that a Jewish coxswain denied the Nazis victory at the final event of the Berlin Games.

The morning after the race the boys agreed to be filmed by Leni Riefenstahl, the Nazi sympathiser and film director, for her movie *Olympia*. Riefenstahl already had good footage of the race but she now wanted close-ups of the victorious coxswain, Bobby Moch, and the stroke, Don Hume. The results were spectacular—the eight-oared rowing footage contributed some of the most dramatic scenes in *Olympia*. Riefenstahl made use of long shots of the boats with close-ups of Moch shouting commands point blank at the camera. Riefenstahl's movie premiered in Berlin on 20 April 1938. The lavish occasion was attended by Hitler, the Nazi elite, representatives of more than forty countries as well as military leaders, film stars and athletes. How would Riefenstahl, Hitler and their fellow Nazis have reacted had they known that their propaganda movie immortalised Bobby Moch, a Jewish athlete who had coxed an American crew to victory against all odds?

There is yet another oddity to the Bobby Moch story. The phrase 'No Jew in crew' was long associated with American universities in the days that Moch competed. When the American eight was selected for the 1936 Games, none of the crew, including the Jew Bobby Moch, knew there was a Jew in the crew. Had it been known that Moch was Jewish he may not have been selected. Without Moch, as tactician, it's unlikely that the USA would have taken gold at Hitler's Games.

Moch later coached the rowing team at MIT and practised as a lawyer. He died in 2005.

Joshua West (1977-) is a dual British-American citizen and rowed for Great Britain in the eights at the 2004 and 2008 Olympics, winning silver in the 2008 Games. During the period that West rowed he was, at

6ft 9½in (2.07m), the tallest rower ever to have participated in the yearly Oxford vs Cambridge race.[4] He is a four time Cambridge Blue (1999-2002) and was on the winning Cambridge crew in 1999 and 2001.[5] He owns two World Championship silver medals and one bronze.[6] West is an Associate Professor in the Department of Earth Sciences at the University of Southern California.[7]

Zoe De Toledo (1987-) is only 5ft tall and coxed the women's British eight to silver in Rio in 2016. De Toledo has the distinction of also coxing the men's Oxford eight in the Oxford vs. Cambridge race. This is what De Toledo is reported to have said about her job of shouting out the stroke rate to seven hefty men: 'Maybe it's a role that a Jewish woman is better at doing—ordering men around'.[8] Her rowing days over, De Toledo studied medicine at Oxford.

New Zealand has a population of about 4.8 million, of which about 10,000 are Jews. Of this tiny Jewish population, two athletes—rower Nathan Cohen and sailor Jo Aleh—won three Olympic medals.

Nathan Cohen (1986-), with Joseph Sullivan, won the doubles sculls World Championships in 2010 and 2011. In 2012 they teamed up to win gold in the sculls at the 2012 London Games.[9] In the finals they were coming last at the 500m mark but in a desperate sprint managed to cross the line ahead of Italy to take gold.[10]

Their victory gave them New Zealand's Favourite Sporting Moment award.[11]

In 2013 Cohen was made a Member of the New Zealand Order of Merit for services to rowing.[12]

(I have counted Cohen as Jewish because others have done so and he has been listed in the International Jewish Hall of Fame.[13] I can, however, not vouch for his being Jewish. Cohen, himself, denies Jewish heritage. I doubt, however, that he would have escaped the attention of the Nazis with the name 'Nathan Cohen'.)

SAILING

With wars come heroes. **Robert Halperin** (1908-1985) won bronze in sailing at the 1960 Olympics and gold at the 1963 Pan American Games. But he was much more than a brilliant yachtsman. He also played professional football at quarterback for the Brooklyn Dodgers in the National Football League (NFL).

Most impressive, however, are the medals he won in battles much more serious than sporting contests. Halperin was one of 550,000 Jewish Americans who enrolled in the military during World War Two.[14] He joined the navy at the start of the war as a seaman and rose to the rank of commander.

In November 1942 he sailed his scout boat in pitch

darkness from seven miles off the coast to locate and mark, with landing signals, the beaches on which attacking troops were to land in French Morocco. While being strafed by enemy planes Halperin guided the assault troops to their landings. He was the first American in the invasion to capture two of the enemy—both officers. He was rewarded with the Navy Cross—the Navy's second highest honour.[15] Halperin was awarded every Navy theatre campaign ribbon, including Sicily, Italy, Europe and the Pacific.

June 6th 1944 will always be remembered as D Day—the day allied troops poured onto the beaches of Normandy in France. Newspapers described Halperin as one of the first Americans to go ashore—perhaps the first.[16] Part of Assault Force 'U', he guided the boats from the transport area to the beaches, helping them avoid both allied bombing and enemy attack. The war correspondent Willian H. Stoneman described Halperin's work as an intricate job calling for as much brain as courage and barrels of both. He described Halperin as 'certainly making a hero of himself again this morning [D day] doing a job on which not one man in a thousand would have'. Halperin received a bronze star for heroic service in combat. The citation for his award described troops being rescued from swamped boats and dispatched to the beaches under his direction as well as the saving of two men from drowning thanks to his exceptional initiative and quick action.[17]

In 1945 Halperin was sent to China where he led a team of Americans who trained 3,500 Chinese troops in guerrilla warfare against the Japanese. The Nationalist Chinese government recognised his valour by awarding him its highest honour—the Yun Hui 'Cloud Banner'.[18]

In 1960 Halperin sailed under more relaxed conditions to win the bronze medal at the Rome Olympics in the star-class.

Halperin died on 8 May, 1985 aged 77. He was buried at the Arlington National Cemetery.

Following the terrorist attack at the 1972 Munich Games, all Jewish athletes were warned to leave Munich. Two Israelis who were due to compete in sailing therefore had to return home. They handed their blue and white flag inscribed with 'Sports Federation of Israel XXth Olympiad Munich 1972' to the American sailing Olympian **Donald 'Don' Cohan** (1930-2018) and told him that he was now their representative and he needed to win a medal for them. Cohan did just that—aged 42, he took bronze as helmsman in the mixed three-person Dragon Class.

Cohan's celebration was marred by having the Nazi sympathiser Avery Brundage—head of the USA Olympic Committee and IOC President—drape his medal around his neck. In Cohan's case Brundage's deceit and bigotry were of a personal nature. Besides preventing the Jewish sprinters Glickman and Stoller from running at Hitler's Games, Brundage dropped Cohan's beloved uncle, Hy Seldin, from the 1936 USA Olympic fencing team, using Seldin's mild ear infection as an excuse to expel him. Seldin had helped care for Cohan after his father died at a young age. In a bitter-sweet moment Seldin, with tears streaming down his face, was there to applaud Cohan as he received his medal.

Another poignant moment for Cohan occurred as he walked alone along the water after the closing ceremonies. He noticed a shadow approaching from behind and with the terrorist attack in mind quickly moved under a light to face the approaching figure. He saw a worn-looking and stooped, but well dressed, older man. The man explained that he had been Germany's Dragon Class champion during the 1930s and had been set to represent Germany in the 1936 Olympics, but instead he was sent by the Gestapo to work in a forced labour camp. He told Cohan that he kept his sanity by 'reliving every race he ever raced and went to sleep at night dreaming of winning an Olympic medal'. The old man then took out his solid gold Champion of Germany pin and pinned it on Cohan's jacket saying: 'Thank you for living my dream'.[19]

Between 1968 and 1980 a Russian, **Valentyn Mankin** (1936-2014), set a sailing record that is yet to be equalled. Mankin is the only sailor ever to win three different classes at the Olympics. Mankin took gold in Finn (1968), Tempest (1972) and Star (1980). His fourth Olympic medal was a silver in 1976 (Tempest). Mankin subsequently moved to Italy where he trained a generation of top sailors.[20]

New Zealander **Jo Aleh** (1986-) was a national, world and Olympic champion in the two-woman 470 dinghy. '470' refers to the length of the dinghy. which has both a spinnaker and a trapeze. Along with Olivia 'Polly' Powrie, Aleh won gold in 2012 and silver in the 2016 Olympics, sailing in the 470 Class. Aleh and Powrie won the 420 World Championships in 2007 and 2013. Aleh was born in Auckland to an Israeli father and a British-born mother who served in the Israeli Defence Force. In 2008 and 2013 Aleh was ranked No. 1 in the world in Women's Laser and the Women's 470 respectively.[21]

In 2013 Aleh was appointed a Member of the New Zealand Order of Merit for her services to sailing.[22]

Of the watersports it is in windsurfing that Israel has been most successful. **Gal Fridman** (1975-) won bronze in the 1996 Atlanta Olympics and gold in the 2004 Games. Another Israeli to win an Olympic windsurfing medal is **Shahar Tzuberi** (1986-), who won bronze in 2008 in Beijing. Tzuberi is a nephew of Gad Tsabari, the Olympic wrestler who escaped the terrorists at the Munich Games in 1972.

The Israeli, **Lee Korzits** (1984-), could be forgiven for thinking that when it comes to the Olympics she has been jinxed. Korzits won the windsurfing World Championships on four occasions—2003, 2011, 2012 and 2013. Yet she competed in the 2004 and 2012 Olympic Games without winning a medal, her best result being sixth in the London 2012 Olympics.[23]

Australia is yet to win a medal in windsurfing.

PADDLING

In slalom events the racing paddlers navigate through a number of gates while contending with roaring waters, powerful eddies, swirls and stoppers (a stopper is water that flows over a drop, hits the bottom and then recirculates back upwards.)

French born **Jessica Fox** (1994-), known as 'The Flying Fox', competed in both K1 and C1 events for Australia (K refers to the kayak and C refers to the canoe. The number that follows the K or C refers to the number of paddlers and the next number is the race distance.) What makes Fox unique is that she has perfected the different techniques required to race both the kayak and the canoe. She is the greatest individual canoe slalom paddler in history—male or female. This is a summary of her major results up to 2019.

4xC1 World Champion (2013, 2014, 2015, 2018)

3xK1 World Champion (2014, 2017, 2018)

Olympic silver and bronze medals (2012 and 2016)

U 23 World Champion K1 (2014, 2015, 2016, 2017)

U 23 World Champion C1 (2013, 2014, 2016)

Junior World Champion K1 and C1 (2010, 2012)

Fox has also won several World Championship titles in the team events. Two of these have been won with her younger sister **Noemie**.

It is as hard to keep track of Fox's awards as it is to keep track of her medals. Some of her awards include: New South Wales Athlete of the Year 2013, 2017 and 2018; Australian Institute of Sports Athlete of the Year 2018; and World Paddle Awards Sportswoman of the Year 2017 and 2018. This last award recognises the most outstanding female athlete in any paddle sport in the world. Furthermore, by winning the award twice in a row Fox is the most awarded athlete at the World Paddle Awards.[24]

For Jessica Fox a family precedent has been set for winning Olympic and World Championship medals. In the 1996 Olympics Fox's mother **Myriam** won bronze in the K1 event. Her father, Richard, also an Olympian, was a five-times World Champion. The family joke is that someday Richard may be the only family member without an Olympic medal.[25]

SUMMARY

When the USA's eight was selected for Hitler's 1936 Games none of the crew, including the Jew, Bobby Moch, knew there was a Jew in the crew. Had it been known that Moch was Jewish he may not have been selected. The phrase 'No Jew in crew' was long associated with American universities in the days that Bobby Moch competed. Without Moch as the tactician, it's unlikely that the USA would have taken gold. We can only wonder how Hitler and his cronies would have reacted had they known that Leni Riefenstahl's Nazi propaganda movie inadvertently showcased Jewish athlete, Bobby Moch.

Robert Halperin won Olympic and military medals. He was a war hero and possibly the first to land on the Normandy beaches on D day. The Nationalist Chinese government recognised his valour by awarding him their highest honour.

Donald Cohan's bronze medal was steeped in emotional significance. He was bonded to the Israeli yachtsmen ordered to return home after the 1972 Munich Games terror attack. His Olympic medal was draped on his neck by Avery Brundage the president of the USA Olympic committee, Nazi sympathiser, and the man who blocked Cohan's beloved uncle from competing in the 1936 Games.

Russian Valentyn Mankin set a sailing record that is yet to be equalled. Mankin is the only sailor to ever win three different classes at the Olympics.

Today, Australia's Jessica Fox's achievements in paddling make her the most successful paddler in the world—male or female.

MEDAL COMPARISON BETWEEN JEWISH AND AUSTRALIAN ATHLETES IN WATERSPORTS

In watersports Jewish athletes have won a total of 44 Olympic medals. Twelve Jewish paddlers have won a total of twenty Olympic medals—seven gold. Most of these athletes are from East European countries. The most impressive statistic belongs to the Hungarian Jewish canoeists. Four paddlers from the remnant Hungarian Jewish population of about 11,000 (in 1941 about 400,000) have won seven Olympic medals between 1956 and 1992.

Australia has won 24 Olympic medals in paddling but as individuals Australians have won 40 medals (two of them belonging to Jessica Fox).

Rowing and sailing are Australia's fourth and fifth

most successful Olympic sports. Australia has won forty medals in rowing—11 gold, 8 silver and 13 bronze. Jewish rowers have won eleven medals—3 gold, 5 silver and 3 bronze.

In sailing Australia has won 27 medals—11 gold, 8 silver and 8 bronze. Jewish sailors have won 13 medals—4 gold, 5 silver and 4 bronze.

If, however, a count of individual medals were made for Australians in rowing and sailing, then this tally would be much higher, because several medals have been won by Australia with teams of 4 or 8 rowers.

JEWISH OLYMPIC MEDALLISTS—WATER SPORTS ROWING

1908
Károly Levitzky, Hun. Bronze; single sculls

1924
Sidney Jelinek, USA, Bronze; coxed fours

1936
Robert Moch, USA, Gold; eights

1952
Leonid Gissen, Russia, Silver; eights

1960
Guy Nosbaum, France, Silver; coxed fours
Jean-Claude Klein, France, Silver; coxed fours

1964
Boris Dubrovsky, Russia, Gold; double sculls

1988
Seth Bauer, USA, Bronze; eights

2008
Josh West, Great Britain, Bronze; eights

2012
Nathan Cohen, NZ Gold; double sculls

2016
Zoe De Toledo, Great Britain, Silver; eights

SAILING

1932
Peter Jaffe, Great Britain, Silver; yachting star
Robert Halperin, USA, Bronze; yachting star

1968
Valentin Mankin, Russia, Gold; yachting finn

1972
Valentin Mankin, Russia, Gold; tempest pairs
Donald Cohan, USA, Bronze; dragon team

1976
Valentin Mankin, Russia, Silver; tempest

1980
Valentin Mankin, Russia, Gold; star pairs
Nicolai Polyakov, Russia, Silver; soling team

1984
Daniel Adler, Brazil, Silver; soling team
Jay Glazer, USA, Silver; tornado

1996
Gal Fridman, Israel, Bronze; windsurfing

2000
Gal Fridman, Israel, Gold; windsurfing

2008
Shahar Tzuberi, Israel, Bronze; windsurfing

PADDLING (CANOEING AND KAYAKING)

1956
Imre Farkas, Hun. Bronze; C2 10,000m
László Fábián, Hun. Gold; K2 10,000m
Leon Rotman, Rom. Gold; C1 1,000m
Leon Rotman, Rom. Gold; C1 10,000m

1960
Leonid Geishtor, Russia, Gold; C2 1,000m
Klára Fried-Bánfalvi, Hun. Bronze; K2,500m
Imre Fárkas, Hun. Bronze; C2 1,000m
Leon Rotman, Rom. Bronze; C1 1,000m

Michael Meyerson

1968
Naum Prokupets, Russia, Bronze; C2 1,000m
Anna Pfeffer, Hun. Silver; K2 5,000m

1972
Anna Pfeffer, Hun. Bronze; K1 500m

1976
Alexandr Vinogradov, Russia, Gold; C2 500m
Alexandr Vinogradov, Russia, Gold; C2 1,000m
Anna Pfeffer, Hun. Silver; K2 500m

1988
David Berkoff, USA, Silver; K4 four 1,000m

1992
Joe Jacobi, USA, Gold; C2 slalom

1996
Miryam Fox-Jerusalmi, France, Bronze; K1 slalom

2000
Michael Kalganov, Israel, Bronze; K1 500m

2012
Jessica Fox, Australia, Silver; K1

2016
Jessica Fox, Australia, Bronze; K1

Fanny Rosenfeld 1928 Olympics

Faina Melnik breaking the world record for discus in 1975

Irena Szewińska - winner of seven Olympic medals

Gretel Bergmann - German high jump champion banned from Hitler's 1936 Games

Althea Gibson and Angela Buxton, London August 1975

Éva Székely in breaststroke finals - Helsinki Olympics 1952

Mark Spitz swimming to world record in the 200m butterfly at USA Olympic trials

Hakoah Vienna swimmers - from left: Judith Deutsch, Heddy Bienenfeld, Fritzi Loewy and Lucy Goldner with coach Zsigo Wertheimer

Helene Mayer giving Nazi salute 1936

Max Baer vs Joe Louis, heavyweight title fight 1935

Victor Perez - world flyweight champion killed by the Nazis

Ben Bril Dutch boxer and referee

Béla Guttmann legendary Hungarian soccer player and coach

Endre Kabos - Hungarian fencer

CHAPTER 7

WATER POLO

'I'm Jewish. I don't play sport'

Comedian Mel Miller speaking at the 2016 South Coast Lions Show.

The water polo match between Hungary and Russia at the 1956 Melbourne Olympics is known as the most infamous water polo contest of all time. Not so well known is that four out of the fourteen contestants were Jewish.

Russia had just invaded Hungary, savagely putting down an anti-Soviet uprising. Hungarians were killed in their hundreds—thousands were imprisoned. The two countries were now to meet in the semi-finals of the 1956 Melbourne Olympics. Three Jewish Hungarians took to the water. They were **Dezsö Gyarmati** (half Jewish)[1], **György Kárpáti** and **Mihály Mayer.** For Russia **Boris Goikhman** kept goal.

The match was more than a sporting contest. The

Hungarian players were bent on salvaging national pride and showing their defiance at the Soviet invasion of their country. Play soon deteriorated into a violent brawl. **Dezsö Gyarmati** (1927-2013) was instrumental in Hungary's win. He opened the scoring and set up Hungary's other three goals. The match was dubbed 'blood in the water' because a head-butt from Russian, Valentin Prokopov, on Ervin Zador caused blood to swirl in the pool. Zador, blood streaming down his face, was helped out of the pool for medical treatment. The violent play forced the referee to halt the contest. Hungary was ahead 4-0 and therefore declared the winner.[2] The police were required to prevent a riot and protect the Russians from further punishment from the 5,500 spectators.[3] Hungarians were again elated when their team defeated Yugoslavia in the finals to take gold.

Gyarmati is rated by many as the best water polo player of all time. He is the only water polo player to win Olympic medals in five successive Games. Between 1948 and 1964 he won three Olympic golds, a silver and a bronze.[4]

Gyarmati duplicated his playing successes as a coach. He coached Hungary to win silver, gold and bronze at the 1972, 1976, and 1980 Olympics. Gyarmati wrote several books on water polo including a history of Hungarian water polo. Following the dissolution of the Soviet Union and the Eastern Bloc, he became a

Member of Hungary's Parliament.

Gyarmati was inducted into the International Swimming Hall of Fame in 1976 and was given an Athlete of the Nation Award in 2004.

He was one of three Olympic champions in his family. His wife **Éva Székely** won gold in breaststroke in the 1952 Games and their daughter **Andrea Gyarmati** won silver in the 100m backstroke and bronze in the 100m butterfly at the Munich 1972 Games (see chapter on swimming).

In addition to gold at the 1956 Games, **Mihály Mayer** (1933-2000) won three more Olympic medals in water polo. He took bronze in 1960, gold in 1964 and bronze in 1968.

György Kárpáti (1935-) also competed in four Olympics, winning gold in the 1952, 1956 and 1964 Games. In 1960 he won bronze.

1956 was not the only occasion that Hungarian Jews competed in water polo in trying conditions. At Hitler's 1936 Games, two Jewish Hungarians, **György Bródy** (1908-1967) and **Miklós Sárkány** (1908-1998), competed for Hungary. The finals, between Hungary and Germany, drew an intensely partisan crowd of 20,000. The match ended in a draw but Hungary was awarded the gold on account of their superior goal difference. The hero of the Hungarian team was György Bródy, who was the goalkeeper. Both Bródy and Sárkány had previously won gold for Hungary in the 1932 Los Angeles Games, but for these two men there could have been no sweeter victory than their 1936 win against Germany.

In the inter-war years Hungary achieved pre-eminence in water polo under the legendary Jewish coach **Béla Komjádi**. Komjádi was a renowned water polo player himself but an injury sustained in World War One forced him into retirement. At the 1928 Games Komjádi was responsible for coaching the Hungarian team which lost narrowly to Germany in the final. Komjádi died in 1933 and thus never saw his team avenge their 1928 defeat.[5] Half of the 1936 Hungarian team were veterans trained by 'Uncle Komi'. On returning from Berlin the Hungarian water polo heroes held a monumental salute at Komjádi's gravesite.[6]

György Bródy came to be revered as one of the greatest goalies of all time. Bródy and his wife escaped from behind the Iron Curtain and settled in South Africa in 1948. Bródy trained the South African national squad for the 1960 Rome Games.[7]

A third Jewish water polo player who went home from Hitler's Games with a medal was the Belgian, **Gérard Blitz** (1912-1990). This was Blitz's final Olympic appearance. The bronze medal that Blitz won was his third Olympic medal for water polo. Blitz spearheaded the Belgian team to the silver medal in the 1920 Antwerp Games and they again took silver in the 1924 Paris Games. He was one of Belgium's best water polo players in the period up to the World War Two, when the Olympics were halted. Blitz also won bronze for the 100m backstroke in Antwerp and set a world 400m backstroke record in 1921. The record stood for six years.[8]

Gérard's brother, **Maurice Blitz** (1891-1975), took silver medals alongside Gérard in the 1920 and 1924 Games. Maurice's son was also called Gérard and he was also an international water polo player. He founded the hotel chain Club Med.

Kurt Epstein (1904-1975) played for Czechoslovakia in the 1928 Olympics and again competed in Hitler's 1936 Games. Epstein was a military man and served as an officer in the Czech army. During the 1938 mobilisation Epstein was stationed at the Terezin garrison.

Three years later the Germans sent Epstein back to Terezin as a prisoner to rebuild and transform the garrison into the Theresienstadt concentration camp. He was subsequently sent to a Polish labour camp. The once strapping 6ft 1in Olympic athlete survived the German concentration camps to emerge weighing 90lb (41kg). Epstein then returned to Prague and was elected to Czechoslovakia's Olympic Committee. Following the Communist take-over in 1948, Epstein migrated to the USA. He married a survivor from Auschwitz, Franci Rabinek Solar. The New York Athletic Club refused to allow the ex-Czech officer and Olympian to coach their water polo team because it did not accept Jewish members.[9]

Frank Fisher was a Czech water polo player who refused to participate in Hitler's Games.[10]

The Canadian water polo team, which had several Jewish players, also boycotted the Nazi Games.[11]

The most recent Jewish water polo Olympian is the American goalkeeper **Merrill Moses** (1977-). His success as a goalie is partly attributed to his 6ft 8in wingspan.[12] The goal in water polo is 10 feet wide, meaning that with outstretched hands Moses's fingertips were only 20 inches short of the post on either side. The perennial Moses has competed in three Olympics. His first, in 2008, was his most successful, with the USA team taking silver. He was again in the USA team for the 2012 and 2016 Games.

SUMMARY

The water polo semi-final–dubbed 'blood in the water'–between Hungary and Russia at the 1956 Games is the most infamous water polo contest ever. Four of the fourteen players were Jewish. Three were Hungarian.

The belligerence was a result of Russia's invasion of Hungary and brutal suppression of the anti-Soviet uprising that ensued. The Hungarians won the match and took gold in the finals. One of the Hungarian players, Dezsö Gyarmati, is still regarded as the best water polo player of all time.

The Belgian, Gérard Blitz, won three Olympic medals in water polo including one at Hitler's Games. Blitz also won bronze for the 100m backstroke in the 1920 Antwerp Games and set the world record for 400m backstroke in 1921.

In more recent times Merrill Moses's enormous wingspan made him a huge asset as goalkeeper for the USA team.

MEDAL COMPARISON BETWEEN JEWISH AND AUSTRALIAN OLYMPIC WATER POLO PLAYERS

Jewish athletes have accumulated 33 Olympic medals for water polo—16 of them gold. Twenty of the 33 medals belong to Hungarians.

No Australian man has won an Olympic medal in water polo. Australian women won gold at the Sydney Olympics in 2000 and bronze in 2008 and 2012. Australian women as individuals have won 39 Olympic water polo medals.

Michael Meyerson

JEWISH OLYMPIC MEDALLISTS—WATER POLO

1900
Henri Cohen, Belgium, Gold

1912
Jean Hoffman Belgium, Bronze

1920
Gérard Blitz, Belgium, Silver
Maurice Blitz, Belgium, Silver

1924
Gérard Blitz, Belgium, Silver
Maurice Blitz, Belgium, Silver

1928
István Barta, Hun. Silver

1932
István Barta, Hun. Gold
György Bródy, Hun. Gold
Miklós Sárkány, Hun. Gold

1936
György Bródy, Hun. Gold
Miklós Sárkány, Hun. Gold
Gérard Blitz, Belgium, Bronze

1948
Dezsö Gyarmati, Hun. Silver

1952
Róbert Antal, Hun. Gold
György Kárpáti, Hun. Gold
Dezsö Gyarmati, Hun. Gold

1956
Dezsö Gyarmati, Hun. Gold
György Kárpáti, Hun. Gold
Mihály Mayer, Hun. Gold
Boris Goikhman, Russia, Bronze

1960
Boris Goikhman, Russia, Silver
Mihály Mayer, Hun. Bronze
György Kárpáti, Hun. Bronze
Dezsö Gyarmati, Hun. Bronze

1964
Mihály Mayer, Hun. Gold
György Kárpáti, Hun. Gold
Dezsö Gyarmati, Hun. Gold

1968
Mihály Mayer, Hun. Bronze

1972
Nicolai Melnikov, Russia, Gold
Peter Asch, USA, Bronze
Barry Weitzenberg, USA, Bronze

2008
Merrill Moses, USA, Silver

CHAPTER 8

SOCCER

'It is rare for the JC [Jewish Chronicle] to be able to hail the role of a Jewish sportsman in one of the definitive sporting achievements of our time. But Steven Reingold's net bowling to Ben Stokes prior to his innings of 258 was a major contribution. [Here are] some previously hidden examples. The tailor who sewed the elastic band on Pele's trousers; the accountant who checked how many clubs were in Jack Nicklaus's golf bag; the doctor who put a plaster on Lasse Viren's arm after his transfusion. And, of course, the Blooms waiter who served Mohammed Ali before his fight with Joe Frazier'

The UK Jewish Chronicle[1]

In 2014 a statue was erected at door 18 in the grounds of the great Portuguese soccer club Benfica. The sculpture was created by the Hungarian, Lászlo

Szátmari, to celebrate the 110th birthday of Benfica. The work depicts a man holding a large trophy in each arm. The man is the incomparable Béla Guttmann— a Hungarian national soccer player, Olympian, concentration camp survivor, and, many say, the greatest ever soccer coach.

David Bolchover wrote the compelling story of Guttmann's life.[2] **Béla Guttmann** (1899-1981) first played for Hungary in a match against Germany in June 1921. He scored one of Hungary's three goals in its victory over Germany. Six of the 11 players were Jewish. Bolchover makes the point that it is testament to the Jewish dominance of soccer in Hungary that even the extreme bigotry then prevalent could not stop these Jewish players being chosen to represent Hungary. In 1922 Guttmann left Hungary for Vienna in order to escape the anti-Semitic Horthy regime, which from 1921 to 1922, committed many atrocities against Jews. He was, however, recalled to represent Hungary in the 1924 Olympics in Paris.

In Vienna, Guttmann joined the Jewish club Hakoah Vienna. He was one of the all-conquering Hakoah team that won the Austrian Championship in 1925. He subsequently went on the hugely successful tour of America with the Hakoah team, and stayed on in the USA playing professional soccer.

In 1932 Guttmann retired from competitive soccer to

embark on an illustrious coaching career. The many countries in which he lived and coached, before and after the Holocaust, are a measure of his volatile temperament and his success as a coach. His career took him to 14 countries—Hungary, Austria, the USA, Yugoslavia, Holland, Romania, Italy, Argentina, Cyprus, Brazil, Portugal, Uruguay, Switzerland and Greece—some of which he lived in more than once. Unbelievably, Guttmann returned to Vienna in August 1938, not long after the Nazis were welcomed into Austria. Shortly after the Anschluss the Nazis shut down the Hakoah club. Aware that he was in serious danger, Guttmann now left for Hungary, which had not yet been taken over by Germany. There he coached Újpest—a town close to Budapest—to take the prestigious Mitropa Cup in the 1938/39 season.

In May 1939 the second Jewish Law was passed in Hungary. The restrictions on Jews were harsh and life for Jews became increasingly intolerable.

In 1944 every Jewish man in Hungary between 18 and 48 was instructed to report to a labour camp. Guttmann defied the order and hid in an attic with assistance from the non-Jewish brother of his girlfriend. Guttmann, however, had several close shaves with the Nazis and Bolchover believes that he finally chose to report to a labour camp thinking that it might be a way of survival.

In an interview with the sports journalist, Tibor Hámori, Guttmann described his time doing slave labour. If the sergeant was in a good mood they were made to carry tarred stones to his bunker while shouting 'we are shit, we are shit'. This was intolerable to the proud Guttmann who asked of himself: 'Was I a footballer from the national team, was I a successful coach? Was I a man? And how much more humiliation my friend!'[3] In 1944 while preparations were being made to transport those in the labour camp to almost certain death in concentration camps, Guttmann escaped. He managed to survive the Holocaust, but his father and sister perished in Auschwitz.

The war over, Guttmann's soccer coaching skills were in demand, and he coached in various countries. It was, however, his stint with the great Portuguese side, Benfica, for which he will forever be remembered. Guttmann coached Benfica to victory in the European Cup in 1961 and 1962—hence the two trophies in Szátmari's sculpture of Guttmann. It was the great Eusebio da Silva Ferreira who, with the score at three-all in the 1962 European Cup final, powered the ball into the net twice, destroying the hopes of Real Madrid and allowing Benfica to take the European Cup 5-3.

Soon after this coaching success Guttmann's relationship with Benfica soured—the parties fell out over Guttmann's demand for a pay rise. Guttmann resigned in a huff and is alleged to have cursed the club, saying a hundred years would pass before Benfica would again win the European Cup. More than fifty years have elapsed since Guttmann left Benfica and Benfica is yet to win the Cup again.

Neither curses nor prayers decide the outcome of sporting contests. Yet before the 1990 European Cup final, with Benfica due to play AC Milan, Eusébio, a devout Catholic, visited Guttmann's grave in the Jewish section of Vienna's Central Cemetery. Here he prayed that the Guttmann curse be lifted.

There is a corollary to the 'curse'—teams opposing Benfica are known to drink a toast to Guttmann and his curse.

The statue of Guttmann tells only a small part of Guttmann's story. David Bolchover tells the rest. In particular, Bolchover provides an insight into the character of this traumatised and complicated man. Bolchover surmises that Guttmann's character was fashioned by his life experiences. He summarises Guttmann as 'bullish, argumentative, out-spoken, distrustful, itinerant, iconoclastic, and impulsive— the archetypal outsider who knows the establishment would never accept him but scorned their judgement and ploughed his own furrow nevertheless'.[4] On at least one occasion Guttmann sought out an opposition player and punched him in the face because his religion had been insulted. In short, Guttmann could be the man who inspired Paul Anka's song, *I did it my way.*

In the soccer-mad country of Portugal, descendants of those who murdered thousands of Portuguese Jews during the Inquisition now file past the statue of Bella Guttmann. How many of them know the story behind the statue?

Guttmann's beloved Viennese Hakoah sports club was formed in 1909 by the world-renowned operatic lyricist **Fritz Löhner** and his friend **Ignaz Körner**.[5] The club was founded to counter the persistent stereotype of Jews as physical weaklings—mere intellectuals.

The Hakoah club also competed in fencing, hockey, wrestling, swimming and athletics, but it was in soccer that it had its greatest triumphs. In 1922 Hakoah finished second in the Austrian league. International Jewish stars such as **Max Gold**, **Max Grünwald** and **József Eisenhoffer** paved the way for Hakoah to become one of the best known soccer clubs in Europe. In 1923 the club went on tour to England and beat West Ham United 5-0, only months after West Ham had reached the FA Cup finals. This made Hakoah the first foreign team to defeat an English club in England.

This is what the West Ham captain, George Kay, said to the Hakoah players: 'You are the best team I have ever seen, and believe me, I have seen hundreds of football games'.[6]

From 1924 to 1926 Hakoah reigned as Austrian champions. They won the 1924/25 title in dramatic fashion. Contact with an opposing player resulted in the goalkeeper, **Alexander Fabian**, breaking his arm. Substitutes were not permitted in those times, so with his arm in a sling, Fabian swapped positions with one of the forwards and within a few minutes scored the goal that gave Hakoah the match and the title.

In 1924 Hakoah became the first club to defeat the all-conquering Slavia Prague team on home soil in more than 10 years. In 1926 Hakoah toured the USA, drawing record-breaking crowds to its matches.

In 1938, immediately after the unification of Germany and Austria, the Nazis suspended Hakoah from football, seized the club grounds for the German army and confiscated the club's assets.[7] Had the Hakoah club been too successful in fulfilling its aims? Were the Jews, described by Nazi propaganda as being no good at sport, in reality too good at sport? The worst was yet to come. The Nazis now set about murdering the Hakoah athletes and administrators.[8]

Max Scheuer, who had represented Austria and

captained Hakoah against West Ham, fled Austria but was captured in Vichy France and sent to Auschwitz where he perished.

Hakoah's left winger, **Otto Fischer**, represented Austria on seven occasions. He too was murdered by the Nazis. Other Hakoah players killed by the Nazis were **Oskar Grasgrün, Ernst Horowitz, Josef Kolisch, Erwin Pollak**, and **Ali Schönfeld**.

Friedrich Donnenfeld escaped to France where he joined the French resistance.

More Hakoah soccer stars would have been murdered had the rising anti-Semitic sentiment in Europe not persuaded several Hakoah players to remain in the USA following their 1926 tour.

The founder of the Hakoah club, the lawyer, writer, renowned librettist, and war veteran, Fritz Löhner, was sent to Dachau and later to Buchenwald. Here he wrote *Das Buchenwald,* the song that became the prisoners' anthem.

'O Buchenwald, we don't complain and wail and whatever our future may be,

we still will say Yes to life,

for some day the day will come when we are free.'

That day never came for Löhner. Ill and weak, Löhner, an officer and four-year veteran of the Austro-Hungarian army in World War One, was beaten to death for 'not working hard enough'. Löhner was but one of 300,000 Jewish men who served in the Austro-Hungarian army in the First World War.

Fittingly, David Bolchover describes the story of the Viennese Hakoah soccer team as 'the most romantic, gripping, heroic and tragic tale of any football team in history'.[9]

The devastation of Jewish soccer stars did not stop with the murders of the seven Hakoah club players. A further 11 international players representing Hungary, Poland and Germany, were murdered by the Nazis.[10] Most were Hungarian Jews. This is unsurprising because between the two World Wars Jewish Hungarians dominated Hungarian soccer. On many occasions more than half of the Hungarian team consisted of Jewish players. At least 11 of the squad of 23 players representing Hungary in the 1924 Olympics were Jewish, although at that time Jews comprised only 5% of Hungary's population.

On 6 April 1924 Hungary thrashed Italy 6-1 in Budapest. Six of the Hungarian side were Jewish, including the entire forward line of **József Braun, Rudolf Jeny, József Eisenhofer, Georgy Molnar** and **Zoltán Opata**. Molnar scored a hat-trick while Braun netted twice. Just as Einstein was not your run of the mill scientist, the Jewish Hungarian soccer stars were not run of the mill international soccer players. Amongst the Jewish soccer stars known to have been killed by the Nazis was **József Braun**, who played for Hungary on 28 occasions, scoring 11 goals. He played on the right wing and had pinpoint crossing ability. He is regarded as one of the greatest players ever to have represented Hungary. He died in a slave labour camp in 1943 aged forty-two.

Ferenc Weisz played 17 times for Hungary. Weisz, and his wife, were amongst the 437,402 Jews sent from Hungary to Auschwitz in 54 days in 1945. Both perished.

Mid-fielder **Antal Vágó** played 17 matches for Hungary. He is believed to be amongst the thousands of Budapest Jews who were lined up along the banks of the Danube and ordered to take off their shoes, before being shot into the river by fascist Arrow Cross militiamen. Today a monument stands on the bank of the Danube River in honour of those killed. The sculpture titled 'Shoes on the Danube Bank' consists of sixty pairs of shoes made of iron.

Henrik Nádler was another mid-fielder killed by the Nazis. Nadler played seven matches for Hungary in the mid-1920s. He was killed in 1944.

Imre Taussig represented Hungary five times as a right winger. In March 1945 he was murdered, aged 50, while working as a slave labourer in Austria.

Árpád Weisz played six times for Hungary on the left wing. Weisz subsequently enjoyed a stellar coaching career leading the club Internazionale to win the Italian Championships, and repeated the success twice more at Bologna. In October 1942 his wife and two children were gassed on arrival at Auschwitz. Weisz worked there for another 16 months as a slave labourer before he too was murdered.

Scoring a hat trick in an international soccer match happens for most players only in their wildest dreams. Could it be possible to do this three times? Jewish German, Gottfried Fuchs, did just that, scoring ten goals against Russia in the 1912 Olympics.

Gottfried Fuchs, Julius Hirsch and Fritz Förderer formed the legendary attacking trio of the German soccer club, Karlsruher KFV. Fuchs was considered the best centre forward in the world between 1911 and 1913. During these years he played for Germany on six occasions, scoring 14 goals.

Both Fuchs and Hirsch represented Germany in the 1912 Olympics. The team did not win a medal but Fuchs scored 10 goals in a 16-0 drubbing of Russia, making him the top goal scorer of the tournament.

Fuchs's ten goals in an International also equalled Sophus Nielsen's world record. The record stood for 89 years until Archie Thompson of Australia scored 13 goals in a 31-0 defeat of American Samoa in 2001.

During the First World War Fuchs was awarded the Iron Cross fighting for Germany as an artillery officer.

In 1935 this military officer and Olympian was barred from his local tennis club. Fuchs escaped the Holocaust by fleeing to France and then to England. In 1940 he made it to Canada. The German Football Association erased all references to Fuchs from their records between 1933 and 1945. Revisionism cannot, however, alter facts. As Jawaharlal Nehru stated, 'Facts are facts and will not disappear on account of your likes'. Nehru could have added 'or dislikes'.

In 1972 the former German international and national soccer coach, Sepp Herberger, suggested that the German Football Association invite Fuchs as a guest to an International against Russia in honour of the 60th anniversary of Fuchs playing for Germany. Herberger may have been trying to atone for his past membership of the Nazi Party. The Association denied the request, saying that they were reluctant to create a precedent. The reason for the denial was, however, baseless—Fuchs was the sole surviving former Jewish German international. Fuchs never got to know that Herberger's suggestion had been refused. He passed away a month before the decision was made.

Fuchs was finally recognised by the German Football Association in 2012 when the association sponsored the Julius Hirsch Prize for victims of the Nazi regime. In 2013 the Karlsruhe city council named the square next to the former KFV stadium 'Gottfried-Fuchs-Square' in Fuchs's memory.[11]

Julius Hirsch scored four goals against the Netherlands in 1912, becoming the first German to score four goals in a single match. Nicknamed 'Juller', Hirsch was known for his attacking style and his powerful kick. He retired in 1923 but stayed on with KFV as coach of the youth team. On 10 April 1933, with no forewarning, Hirsch read in the morning paper, *Sportbereicht Stuttgart*, the following resolution of the main German soccer clubs: 'The undersigned clubs... gladly and definitively place themselves at the disposal of the national government's efforts in the field of physical training and are prepared to make every effort to cooperate. In the interest of this cooperation, they are willing to effect consequences in any way, particularly as regards to the issue of the removal of Jews from sports clubs'.

Hirsch immediately resigned from the KFV club and in a letter to the club wrote: '...in this bully of a German nation, which is so hated today, there are still decent people and perhaps even more German Jews whose national loyalty is both evident in the way they think and proven by their deeds and the lifeblood they have shed'. Hirsch then detailed his four year service during World War One as well as that of his three brothers Leopold, Max and Rudolf. All four brothers were awarded the Iron Cross for courage. Leopold was killed on the Western Front. Of all his achievements it was his service in fighting for his country that gave Hirsch the most pride. The values of patriotism had been passed down to the Hirsch boys by their father who was a veteran of the Franco-Prussian war which resulted in the creation of the German Empire. The Hirsch family were no oddity. 100,000 German Jews placed their lives on the line for Germany in World War One. Twelve-thousand of those lives were lost.

Loyalty to one's country and heartfelt letters were, however, of no relevance to Nazis. Hirsch fled to Paris but was ultimately deported to Auschwitz. He was never heard of again. Hirsch was belatedly honoured by the German Football Federation. Since 2005 the 'Julius- Hirsch-Prize' has been awarded to groups and individuals in German soccer who represent the sanctity of human dignity and oppose anti-Semitism, racism and the exclusion of people while promoting diversity in the face of discrimination and xenophobia.

Fritz Förderer, the third of KFV's legendary attacking trio, abandoned his Jewish soccer mates to throw his lot in with the Nazis. His playing days over, Förderer became involved in soccer coaching. One of the teams he coached was located in Buchenwald and consisted of players who were members of the Third SS Death-Head unit. The unit was responsible for killing 56,000 people. Förderer died in 1952.[12]

Five of Poland's Jewish national players were murdered by the Nazis.[13]

Leon Sperling played on the left wing for Poland. Sperling's dribbling skills were described as mesmerising. He was capped 16 times for Poland. Sperling is believed to have been shot dead by a German soldier in the city Lvov's ghetto. His team mate, the centre half **József Klotz**, scored Poland's first goal in international soccer against Sweden in 1922. He was killed in Warsaw in 1941.

Zygmunt Steuermann and **Zygmunt Krumholz** both played as forwards in the Polish team. Steuermann scored a hat trick in his debut match against Turkey in 1926 in Lvov. Both were murdered by the Nazis.

Eddie Hamel (1902-1943) was born in New York on Manhattan's Upper East Side. His parents emigrated from Holland to the USA in 1901. Shortly after Eddie was born the Hamel family returned to Holland.

Hamel became the first American to play for the Dutch team Ajax—the finest football club in Holland.

He played 125 games on the right wing for Ajax over nine years. Nicknamed belhamel—the instigator or ring-leader—Hamel was renowned for his speed, dribbling skills and cross passes. In short, he was every goalkeeper's nightmare. An elderly Ajax club supporter remembered Hamel and described him as an idol—much like David Beckham in recent years. Sports writer, Michael McKnight, describes how Hamel was idolised by soccer greats such as Ge van Dijk and Wim Anderiesen. Van Dijk was an Ajax star of the 1940s and 50s and said of Hamel that he was 'an icon. He was always such a gentleman. He never kicked opponents or anything like that. He was my role model. I wanted to be like Eddie Hamel'. Legend Wim Anderiesen described Hamel as part of the strongest line-up he ever played with.

His playing days over, Hamel became a successful coach. Yet the Hamel family's decision to return to Holland proved fateful. The Nazi invasion of Holland meant that Jews were banned from sporting clubs. Hamel was banned from coaching Alkmaar—the team he had inspired to win the league title. Instead of being able to grow old and enjoy looking back on his life and his successes on the football field, Hamel's life was cut short. He was detained by the Nazis and sent to Birkenau where he was forced to do hard labour. On contracting a mouth abscess he was sent to Auschwitz where he was put to death in the gas chambers.

Unbeknown to him, Hamel's wife and twin boys had already been murdered by the Nazis.[14]

The Danish brothers, Harald and Niels Bohr, played on the same soccer team, with Niels keeping goal. **Harald Bohr** (1887-1951) also played for Denmark, taking silver in the 1908 Olympics. In the semi-finals against France the Danish team set an Olympic record that still stands—they beat the French 17-1! Denmark lost to Great Britain in the finals.

No Olympic medallist can have contributed more to the field of mathematics than Harald Bohr. Bohr worked in mathematical analysis, especially the Dirichlet series, on which he wrote his doctorate. He collaborated with Edmund Landau in describing the Bohr-Landau theorem regarding the distribution of zeroes in zeta functions. He also founded the field of 'almost periodic functions'. It is said that when presenting his doctoral thesis there were more football fans than academics in the audience![15]

While **Niels Bohr** (1885-1962) was not as accomplished as Harald at soccer, he was an even more distinguished academic.

These are some of Niels Bohr's achievements. He won the Nobel Prize for physics in 1922 for his research into the structure of atoms and the radiation emitted from them. He described the model of the atom with electrons revolving in stable orbits about the nucleus. The element bohrium was named after him.

Some of his honours include the Hughes Medal (1921), the Matteucci Medal (1923), the Franklin Medal (1926), the Coplev Medal (1938), the Atoms for Peace Award (1857) and the Sonning Prize (1961).

The Bohr brothers were, however, more than athletes and academic geniuses. They were activists against injustice. Not your standard black armband athlete, they put their lives on the line in words and deeds. In the 1930s Harald Bohr was an open critic of the anti-Semitism infecting German mathematical circles. Bohr was outspoken about the murder of the Lutheran pastor and playwright, Kaj Munk. Munk was disgusted at Hitler's treatment of Jews and the way Mussolini conducted the war in Ethiopia. In an open letter to Mussolini, Munk criticised the persecution of Jews. The letter was published in 1938 on the front page of the Danish newspaper, *Jyllands-Posten*. Munk also wrote two plays critical of the Nazi regime.

On 4 January 1944 the Gestapo arrested Munk. His body was found the next day in a roadside ditch. The Danish resistance newspaper—*De frie Danske*—published the reactions of influential Danes who condemned Munk's murder. Harald Bohr was one of those listed.[16] Following Germany's occupation of Denmark, Bohr and his family fled to Sweden to escape the Nazis.

Niels Bohr was an internationally acclaimed scientist when, in 1922, he met Werner Heisenberg—a talented German science student. Bohr was sixteen years older than Heisenberg but the two men formed a close bond professionally and personally. The two became the founders of quantum mechanics. In 1932 Heisenberg also became a Nobel Laureate. In early 1933 Hitler assumed power, and soon afterwards the Nazis banned Jews from working for the German state. More than 100 Jewish scientists, including Einstein, were displaced.

Niels Bohr became instrumental in assisting escapees from Nazism. Amongst the refugees were many distinguished scientists, most of them Jewish. Bohr assisted the refugees in obtaining temporary jobs at the Rockefeller Foundation and then helped find them positions around the world. Many of these scientists collaborated in the race against Germany and Russia in developing the atom bomb. Three of them—James Franck, Felix Bloch and George de Hevesey—were awarded the Nobel Prize.

Heisenberg was not a Nazi, nor was he anti-Semitic, but he was a German nationalist who took part in the military drills of his reserve unit. Heisenberg upset many of his scientific colleagues by refusing to follow their example and leave Germany. Instead he became a principal scientist in Germany's secret nuclear program. The previous good friends were now alienated. In September 1941, however, the two men had a mysterious and secret rendezvous that changed the course of World War Two.[17] Heisenberg came to Copenhagen to attend a German-sponsored conference and arranged to meet with Bohr. Bohr chose not to attend, in protest against Germany's recent invasion and occupation of Denmark.

Heisenberg's main motive for the meeting, it seems, was to ask his mentor whether a scientist should help his country build an atomic weapon in wartime. The two met in an uneasy and suspicious atmosphere. Bohr was angry about Heisenberg's insensitivity to the Nazi occupation of Denmark and the Nazis' treatment of their scientific colleagues. Heisenberg, it seems, was at this time convinced of a German victory and believed that his colleagues should come to the best terms possible with the Nazi regime. Heisenberg presumed that Bohr would have knowledge of the Allies' progress in building a nuclear weapon and spoke obliquely about the nuclear program. Bohr asked if it was really possible to make such a weapon. The meeting concluded on a sour note and it is likely that both men misunderstood each other. Bohr came away with the impression that Heisenberg was trying to obtain intelligence about the Allied nuclear weapons program and that Heisenberg was helping develop the bomb for Hitler. Heisenberg subsequently claimed that his intention for the meeting was to persuade the physicists on opposing sides to tacitly refuse to do further work on nuclear fission. In an ironic quirk, Heisenberg was to owe his life to another Jewish athlete and intellectual—Moe Berg, a catcher in Major League Baseball in the USA (this is explained later in the section on baseball).

In the autumn of 1943 Bohr was warned that he was about to be arrested by the German occupying forces. He escaped with his family by boat to Sweden. Once in Stockholm Bohr was flown by a military plane to Scotland and then to London.[18]

He then went to America where he joined the Manhattan Project in building an atomic weapon.[19, 20] He convinced the scientists involved in the project that the Germans were involved in a similar nuclear program. Some say that Bohr's influence spurred on the Allies and absolved them of the guilt associated with constructing such a weapon. The Allies successfully detonated the world's first nuclear device on 16 July 1945 on the Alamogordo Bombing and Gunnery Range in New Mexico. The bomb was finally deployed over Nagasaki and Hiroshima, effectively ending the war. The German nuclear program was disbanded within a year of the secret meeting between Bohr and Heisenberg.

Niels Bohr's son, Aage, continued the family's academic tradition. He emulated his father in winning a Nobel Prize for physics in 1975. He too, played a role in the Manhattan Project. A second Olympian in the Bohr family was Ernest Bohr, brother of Aage. Ernest played field hockey for Denmark in the 1948 London Olympics.[21]

Can there ever be a family to match the athletic, academic and activist achievements of the Bohr family? My guess is not.

It took more than a century before women's soccer was included as an Olympic sport in 1996. Almost immediately a Jewish American stamped her authority on the game. **Sara Whalen** (1976-) won a silver medal at the Sydney 2000 Olympics for the USA. Norway took gold.

Whalen played for the University of Connecticut and had the versatility to play as a forward or defender. Whalen's greatest achievement in soccer was being one of the USA national team that won the 1999 FIFA Women's World Cup. The final—against China—was decided by penalty kicks after extra time failed to produce a winner. Brandi Chastain scored the winning goal for the USA. Whalen's celebratory hug of Chastain featured on the cover of *Time* magazine and has become an iconic sporting image.

Whalen was one of twenty players who founded the Women's United Soccer Association which was responsible for the first women's professional soccer league. After an injury terminated Whalen's soccer career she changed tack to become a clinical psychologist.[22]

One of the greatest soccer players of all time is **David Beckham** (1975-). Beckham has only one Jewish grandparent, but he identifies as being Jewish.[23] Having one Jewish grandparent would also have been enough for him to have fallen foul of Hitler's Nuremberg laws had he lived in Nazi Germany or in a Nazi-aligned country.

In case you ever wondered about the meaning of the Hebrew tattoo on Beckham's left arm, it says: 'I am my beloved's and my beloved is mine, who browses among the lilies'. His wife, Victoria, sports the same tattoo. The words are from the Old Testament's Songs of Solomon.

Finally, it is appropriate that Jewish athletes have distinguished themselves in soccer—the sport of the people. It is again the Hungarian Jews who stand out.

Despite the Nazi destruction of the Hungarian Jewish population, the surviving remnant of approximately 11,000 Jews continued to provide players for the Hungarian national team. **Sándor Gellér** and **Árpád Orbán** are two such men. Both are Olympic gold medallists.

SUMMARY

European Jews, especially those from Hungary, dominated soccer until Europe's Jewry was all but obliterated by the Nazis. One of the great Jewish Hungarian stars was Béla Guttmann. Amongst the teams Guttmann played for were Hungary and the Viennese Hakoah club. The Jewish Hakoah team became the first overseas side to defeat an English club in England.

Guttmann survived a slave labour camp to become acknowledged by many as the greatest coach of all time. His story is told in gripping detail in David Bolchover's book *The Greatest Comeback*.

Bolchover describes the story of the Hakoah soccer team as 'the most romantic, gripping, heroic and tragic tale of any football team in history'. The Nazis erased the great Hakoah club and many of its players. They also deleted the records of their great Jewish soccer Olympian and World War One officer, Gottfried Fuchs. Fuchs scored 10 goals for Germany in a 16-0 drubbing of Russia at the 1912 Olympics making him the top goal scorer of the tournament.

At least 12 international soccer players representing Hungary, Germany, Holland and Poland were killed by the Nazis.

It's almost certain that there will never again be a family to match the athletic, academic and activist achievements of the Bohr family.

It is fitting that in soccer—the sport of the people—

the myth that Jews are no good at sport is decisively debunked.

MEDAL COMPARISON

Jewish soccer players have won ten Olympic medals.

Australia is yet to win an Olympic medal in soccer.

JEWISH OLYMPIC MEDALLISTS—SOCCER

1900
Jean Bloch, France, Silver

1908
Charles Buchwald, Denmark, Silver
Harald Bohr, Denmark, Silver

1912
Charles Buchwald, Denmark, Silver

1952
Sándor Gellér, Hungary, Gold

1956
Boris Razinsky, Russia, Gold

1964
Árpád Orbán, Hungary, Gold

1976
Leonid Buryak, Russia, Bronze

1980
Yuri Gavrilov, Russia, Bronze

2000
Sara Whalen, USA, Silver

CHAPTER 9

TABLE TENNIS

'Air Stewardess: Would you like something to read? Passenger: Do you have anything light? Air Stewardess: How about this leaflet, 'Famous Jewish Sports Legends?'

Exchange in the movie Airport

A table tennis ball travels at up to 65mph—not nearly as fast as a tennis or cricket ball but in table tennis the opponents are separated by only a few metres. Should you aspire to play competition table tennis you will need the following: agility, speed, athleticism, steadfast concentration and lightning reflexes.

Table tennis has been included in the Olympics since 1988. No Jewish or Australian athlete has won an Olympic medal in table tennis. But that is where the similarity between the two groups ends.

Prior to the Nazi regime Jewish table tennis players

dominated the sport. We know this because the World Championships in Table Tennis was held yearly from 1926 to 1956 and every second year thereafter. At these Championships players compete in singles, doubles, mixed and team events. The total number of medals won by Jewish exponents of table tennis at the World Championships is a staggering figure in excess of three hundred. One hundred and thirty-six of the medals were gold and were won by twenty-four Jewish athletes (nine of whom were Hungarian) between 1926 and 1956.[1] No Australian has won a World Championships medal.

The Hungarian world champions, **Victor Barna, Laszlo Bellak** and **Miklós Szabados**, were known as the three musketeers. **Victor Barna** (1911-1972) is considered to be the greatest table tennis player of all time.[2] Named 'Győző Braun', he was born in Budapest but changed his name because of anti-Semitism. Barna won 41 World Championships medals between 1929 and 1954. Twenty-one of the medals were gold, of which five were for singles. He won four of his singles titles in consecutive years between 1932 and 1935. At the start of World War Two Barna was in America. He left for England where he joined a British army commando unit.[3] Following the war the Barnas settled in London.

Barna represented England in table tennis from 1939 to 1954 (excluding the war years). He was inducted into the International Table Tennis Foundation Hall of Fame in 1993. His record tally of 41 World Championships medals is likely to stand forever.

Barna's younger brother Tibor was murdered by Hungarian fascists. Broken-hearted, Barna once said: 'Imagine, he won the Hungarian title, he followed in my footsteps, he had a great future in table tennis, and they killed him. I wish the people could have saved him, and not my trophies'. (His neighbours hid his trophy collection during the Nazi takeover and returned it to him at the end of the war.)[4] Barna subsequently wrote timeless books on table tennis.

Barna's haul of 41 World Championships medals dwarfed that of **Laszlo 'Laci' Bellak** (1911-2006), who nevertheless won 22 World Championships medals (seven gold). Bellack was known as the 'clown prince' of table tennis. The crowds loved Bellack's antics. He could play using the edge of the bat, playing with three or four balls in play at a time, and on occasion would blow the ball back to his opponent. He was also able to play alone, running around the table fast enough to return his own shots. There are several good stories told about the joker Bellack. Bellack's good friend, **Sándor Glancz** (1908-1974), who won fourteen World Championships medals, shared these two: The three musketeers, Victor Barna, Miklós Szabados and Laci Bellack, while walking the streets of Budapest, were arguing as to who was the best player. Finally Bellack said 'Look, I'm sick of your arguing. Why don't we ask the first stranger and let him decide?' So he stopped the first stranger and pointing at Barna and Szabados asked him if he knew either of the two gentlemen. The stranger replied: 'No Mr. Bellack, I don't'.

Glancz related how he shared a room with Bellack when they were playing in the World Championships in Stockholm in 1928. Glancz woke in the middle of the night to hear Bellack talking in his sleep. 'Captain,' he said, 'who is the greatest player you ever had on your team?' After a pause, Bellack said, 'Thank you, captain'.[5]

Bellack moved to the USA at the outbreak of World War Two. He enrolled in the USA Army and served in India and Burma, attaining the rank of sergeant. He was decorated on three occasions. Bellack was inducted into the International Table Tennis Foundation Hall of Fame in 1993.[6]

Miklós Szabados (1912–1962) won 24 World Championships medals (15 golds, of which one was for singles). In 1933 Szabados fled Hungary for Paris, and then on to London. In 1937 he and a fellow Hungarian, **István Kelen** (1912-2003), went on a tour of the Far East, South America and Australia, playing exhibition table tennis. Kelen won 15 World Championships medals, seven of them gold. He was also a journalist and playwright. Both players made Australia their final home. Szabados won several Australian titles and became a table tennis coach. He was inducted into the International Table Tennis Foundation Hall of Fame in 1993. Two of his pupils, Michael Wilcox and Cliff McDonald, won Australian singles titles.

The Romanian **Angelica Rozeanu** (1921-2006) is considered one of the best female table tennis players of all time. She was the Romanian women's champion but, along with other Romanian Jewish athletes, was barred from competing once the Nazis took control of Romania. Rozeanu was banned from 1940-1944. Following the war she became the first Romanian woman to win a world title in any sport. She won 30 World Championships medals (17 gold, of which six were singles titles won in consecutive years from 1950). In 1955 she won the World Championships singles title for a final time. It was also the last time a non-Asian woman won the event.

Romania subsequently honoured the athlete they had spurned. In 1954 Rozeanu received Romania's highest sporting award, the Romanian title of Merited Master of Sport. She was also awarded four Order of Work Honours. She was president of the Romanian Table Tennis Commission from 1950 until 1960, when she immigrated to Israel.[7] Rozeanu was inducted into the International Table Tennis Foundation Hall of Fame in 1995. Israel awarded her the Knesset medal in 1977.

Alojzy Ehrlich (1914-1992) was voted Poland's eighth most popular athlete in 1934 and was regarded as one of the best ever Polish table tennis players. Ehrlich won six World Championships medals. On three occasions he won silver in the World Championships singles event—twice losing to **Richard Bergmann**. Ehrlich was a 'chiseller'. In table tennis parlance a chiseller is a player who resolutely defends, forever pushing the ball back, never attacking, but waiting for their opponent to make an error. Ehrlich took chiselling to an unheard of degree. At the 1936 Prague World Championships, using an oversize bat, he played **Paneth Farkas** (1917-2009), tirelessly pushing back ball after ball. Unbelievably, it took two hours and twelve minutes to complete the first point, during which time the ball crossed the net more than 12,000 times. When Ehrlich's right arm tired he would switch to playing left handed. The umpire had to be replaced after 85 minutes because his neck locked. Twenty minutes into the second point Farkas had had enough and 'sent the ball and bat together sailing wildly over [Ehrlich's] head [and]…ran screaming from the court'. After this match the International Table Tennis Federation changed the rules by putting a time limit on contests. Should a match not be completed within the time limit then whoever was ahead was declared the winner.

Ehrlich was sent to Auschwitz during World War Two. He spent four years there. His life was saved by a guard who recognised him as a famous table tennis player and pulled him out of the line on the way to the gas chamber. Ehrlich survived the war and subsequently won table tennis championships in Ireland, France, the Netherlands and Germany.[8]

Shimcha Finkelstein (1917-1987), **Samuel Schief** and **Alojzy Ehrlich** were Polish singles champions. Together they won a bronze medal in the World Championships team event for Poland in 1936. Finkelstein and Schief fled the Nazi occupation of Poland for Palestine. Following the war they teamed up again, but now represented Israel in the World Championships. Finkelstein won Israel's first ever championship in table tennis.

Jewish Austrian table tennis champions included **Erwin Kohn, Paul Flussmann** and **Richard Bergmann. Erwin Kohn** (1911–1994) was 16 when he became the Austrian national champion. Between 1932 and 1936 he won eight World Championships medals (one gold). He fled to England in 1938 and subsequently immigrated to Argentina where he continued to pursue a successful table tennis career.[9]

Paul Flussmann won eight World Championships medals between 1926 and 1933.

Richard Bergmann (1920-1970) was described as the greatest defensive player in the history of table tennis. Bergmann played for Austria from 1936 to 1938. In 1937 and 1938 Bergmann won the World Championships singles title for Austria. When the Nazis invaded Austria Bergmann fled to England. He played for England from 1939 to 1955, winning the World Championships for England in 1948 and 1950. He won 22 World Championships medals (seven gold). In the mid-1950s Bergmann became the first table tennis player to turn professional. He was inducted into The International Table Tennis Foundation Hall of Fame in 1993.[10]

Ruth Aarons (1918-1980), was a feisty Jewish American champion who beat Nazi Germany's Astrid Krebsach to win the 1936 World Championships women's title. Aarons famously refused to shake Krebsach's hand, saying: 'I am Jewish'.

A year later Aarons defended her title against the Austrian, Gertrude Pritzi, in Vienna. Pritzi probably realised that she had little chance of winning and resorted to the blocking tactic of pushing the ball back. The judges invoked the new time-limit rule and declared the match over. The Americans expected Aarons to be announced the winner. Instead, both women were disqualified and the women's title left vacant. Was this because after Richard Bergmann won the men's title it would have been too much to have a

Jewish athlete also take the women's title?

This moment of sporting bastardry remained largely forgotten and unchallenged for decades. The injustice was, however, too much for one man. Steve Isaacson never won a World Championships title but was handy enough with the table tennis bat to be ranked in the top 10 in the USA. In 2001 Isaacson lobbied the International Table Tennis Foundation to have the judges' 1937 decision reversed. He was to some extent successful. Aarons and Pritzi were declared co-champions of the 1937 Women's World Championships. The USA Table Tennis Association presented Isaacson with the President's Award for his role in reversing this injustice. The Austrians remained silent. Isaacson describes his achievement as the 'big thrill of his life'.[11]

Altogether, Aarons won five World Championships medals (three golds—two for singles). She remains the only American—man or woman—to have won a singles title in the World Table Tennis Championships.

A table tennis enthusiast, Anita Currey, wrote of Aarons: 'She is about 5ft 2in…weighs approximately 100 pounds and dances around the table like Bill Robinson, the tap dancer, and finally hits the ball like a baseball player'.[12] See Aarons in action by searching 'Sensational Table Tennis (1941)' on YouTube.

After retiring from table tennis Aarons found equal success in managing show business celebrities. Amongst her clients were names such as Jack, David and Shaun Cassidy, Susan Dey, Janis Paige, Shirley Jones, Claibe Richardson and Celeste Holm.

Aarons died in 1980, denied the satisfaction of knowing that she had been reinstated as co-winner of the 1937 women's World Table Tennis Championships.

Czech table tennis champions interned by the Nazis were **Gertrude Kleinová** (1918-1975) and **Pavel Lowy**. Kleinová was a member of the Czech team that won the World Championships in 1935 and in 1936. She won a further World Championships gold in the mixed event in 1936. Kleinová, her husband, and **Eric Vogel**, her coach, were sent to the Theresienstadt concentration camp and from there to Auschwitz. Kleinová and Vogel survived but Kleinová's husband perished. Kleinová and Vogel subsequently married and immigrated to the USA in 1946. She died of cancer in 1975.[13]

Pavel Lowy won a bronze medal in the World Championships in 1937. He is presumed to have perished in a concentration camp. There is no record of him surviving the war.

Ivan Andreadis (1924-1992), a Czech of Greek descent, won 26 World Championships medals (nine gold) between 1947 and 1957. He was interned during World War Two in Kleinstein.[14] He was inducted into the International Table Tennis Hall of Fame in 1995.

I have described the brilliant Hungarians Victor Barna, Laszlo Bellak, Miklós Szabados and István Kelen. They were amongst a great depth of talent in Jewish Hungarian table tennis players prior to the Holocaust. Some of these players were:

Anna Sipos (1908-1988), who won 21 medals in World Championships between 1929 and 1935 (eleven gold of which two were for singles). She was inducted into the International Table Tennis Foundation Hall of Fame in 1993.

Zoltán Mechlovits (1891–1951) who won 11 World Championships medals between 1926 and 1929 (six gold, one of which was for singles).

Sándor Glancz (1908-1974), who was born in Budapest and died in New York, won 14 World Championships medals (four gold) between 1928 and 1934.

Dora Beregi, who fled from Hungary to England and later settled in Australia, won six World Championships medals (two gold). Her first medal was won representing Hungary in 1938. Between

1948 and 1950 she won five World Championships medals playing for England.

Tibor Házi (1912-1999), who was born Tibor Hoffmann. Hazi won nine World Championships medals (three gold) between 1932 and 1938. Házi married fellow international table tennis player **Magda Gál** (1907-1990), who won 20 World Championships medals between 1929 and 1936. They fled Hungary for the USA in 1939.

Daniel Pecsi who was a Hungarian won four World Championships medals (three gold) between 1926 and 1928.

Several Jewish Americans besides Ruth Aarons excelled at table tennis. **Martin 'Marty' Reisman** (1930-2012) won five World Championships medals between 1948 and 1952. In the 1948 World Championships his 115 mph forehand was named the 'Atomic Blast'. One of Reisman's tricks was to stand a cigarette at one end of the table and break it in two with a ball served from the other end.[15] Reisman made use of his skills as a hustler playing for bets and prizes in New York. In an interview with Trevis Gleason, the comedian Jonathan Katz recalled that as a youth Reisman beat him at table tennis playing with the flat end of a chess piece.[16] Reisman's autobiography, *The Money Player, The Confessions of America's Greatest Table Tennis Player and Hustler* was published in 1974. He is immortalised in the movie *Fact or Fiction: The Life and times Of A Ping-Pong Hustler.*

Leah Thall-Neuberger (1915-1993), dubbed Miss Ping, won six World Championships medals (one gold) representing the USA between 1947 and 1956. In 1951 Thall-Neuberger was the USA's top female table tennis player and was ranked third in the world. In 1971 she was the only American included in Canada's historic 'ping-pong diplomacy' tour of the People's Republic of China. She became the first American citizen in decades to visit China and speak face to face with Chinese premier Chou En-Lai. Their conversation belonged to a chain of events that brought to an end the cold war between the USA and China.[17] In 1941 Leah's sister, **Thelma Thall 'Tybie' Somner** (1924-), knocked on doors until she found a job in a collection agency. She was instructed to start typing envelopes. Fifteen minutes later someone rushed over and told Somner to fill in a job application form. One of the questions enquired as to which church she belonged. Somner answered that she belonged to a synagogue. She was told: 'Stop typing. We're not allowed to hire Jews'. Somner went on to win several USA tournaments as well as four World Championships medals. Her philosophy was: 'You don't have to be the best to beat the best'. She also said that what distinguishes winners from losers is the head and the heart. 'I really think attitude is more important than talent. I'm loaded with attitude'. In 1980 she was inducted into the USA Table Tennis Hall of Fame. In 2005 she was awarded the Lifetime Achievement Award by *USA Table Tennis*.[18]

Solomon Joseph Schiff (1917–2012) won three World Championships medals (two gold) between 1937 and 1938.

Hyman Lurie (1918-1982) represented England and won three medals at the World Championships between 1938 and 1939.

SUMMARY AND MEDAL COMPARISON

No Jewish or Australian athlete has won Olympic medals in table tennis. This is where the similarity between the two groups ends. Jewish athletes have won a mind boggling 308 medals in the World Championships in Table Tennis (WCTT). Most of these medals were won prior to the Holocaust. There is no telling how many Olympic medals Jewish athletes would have won had table tennis been an Olympic sport prior to World War Two and if Europe's Jewry had not been exterminated by the Nazis.

In Austria in 1937 the reigning world champion Ruth Aarons was denied gold in the World Championships. Her achievement was recognised decades later. Aarons remains the only American to have ever won a World Championships title in singles.

Victor Barna and childhood friend Laszlo Bellak were the world's best. They both fled Hungary to fight with the Allies.

One of the best female table tennis players of all time, Romanian Angelica Rozeanu won the 1955 World Championships singles title. She remains the last non-Asian woman to win the event.

No Australian has won a medal in the Table Tennis World Championships.

CHAPTER 10

BASKETBALL

Jews succeed in basketball because 'the game places a premium on an alert, scheming mind, flashy trickiness, artful dodging and general smart aleckness'.

Farewell to Sport[1]

In his essay: '*How Stereotypes Explain Everything And Nothing At All*', Gene Demby describes how in the first half of the 20th century the Ivy League Universities went about reducing the numbers of their Jewish students, who, on academic merit, filled up to 40% of places at these universities. They did this by enforcing quotas or introducing admission procedures requiring letters of recommendation, personal interviews, personal essays and lists of extra-curricular activities. Selection could now be on the basis of 'character'. 'Character' meant 'not being Jewish'. The system was effective and the number of Jewish students in these universities plunged. There was, however, a problem no-one anticipated. In the decades prior to World War Two Jewish athletes dominated basketball. By refusing to admit Jewish students the Ivy League Universities were hamstringing their basketball teams.

Denby gives the example of the star Yale player **Sam Pite**. Pite left the Yale team on account of his treatment by a bigoted coach. The Yale Bulldogs then finished the 1922 season in last place. To add salt to their wounds the Bulldogs were trounced by an amateur Jewish club.

The result? Angry alumni demanded that the university stop discriminating against Jewish applicants. A new coach was engaged, Pite returned, and the Yale Bulldogs won the title the following season.[2] The irony, not mentioned by Denby, is that these renowned places of learning were ready to compromise their academic standards by excluding Jewish students, but not their sporting standards. David Oshinsky, in his book *Polio,* describes how, due to the quotas on Jewish students, medical scientist **Jonas Salk** and hundreds like him did not apply to study at Ivy League universities. Salk first studied at the City College of New York (CCNY). Competition to get into CCNY was intense but the rules were applied fairly. No-one was advantaged by their pedigree. After completing his Bachelor of Science degree Salk then enrolled at New York University (NYU) to study medicine. This university, unlike Ivy

League universities such as Yale, Harvard, and Princeton, did not discriminate against Jewish students.[3] Fellow Jewish medical scientist **Albert Sabin** also completed his medical degree at NYU.[4]

Salk and Sabin went on separately to develop vaccines that virtually rid the world of polio. Ivy League University administrators would have queued to obtain their polio immunisation—developed by men unwelcome on their campuses. Had Salk or Sabin been champion basketball players things may have been different.

Sports journalist and novelist Paul Gallico resorted to a tacky stereotype in order to explain the successes of Jewish basketball players. Gallico said that basketball sat well with the temperament of Jews because 'the game places a premium on an alert, scheming mind, flashy trickiness, artful dodging, and general smart aleckness'. He added that because they were rather short they had better balance and speed.[5] Gallico was not alone in his views.

When those who see the world through the lens of a stereotype make observations that fit with their rigid and simplistic views, the stereotype is reinforced. When their observations run counter to their stereotype, these observations are ignored.

If you do an internet search of 'List of Jews in Sport'

you will find a very long list of top Jewish basketball players. Consider a few of these artful dodgers who succeeded in the USA National Basketball Association (NBA) despite their height!

Art Heyman (1941-2012) 6ft 5in—three NBA seasons.[6]

Amare'e Studemire (1982-) 6ft 10in—fourteen NBA seasons.[7]

Dolph Schayes (1928-2015) 6ft 8in—sixteen NBA seasons. On 11 January 1958, Schayes became the highest scorer in NBA history, his points total of 11,770 eclipsing that of the great George Mikan.[8]

Danny Schayes (1959-) 6ft 11in—son of Dolph Schayes—eighteen NBA seasons.[9]

Jordan Farmar (1986-) 6ft 2in—ten NBA seasons.[10]

Omri Casspi (1988-) 6ft 9in—ten NBA seasons.[11]

Rudy LaRusso (1937-2004) 6ft 7in—ten NBA seasons (four times an NBA All Star[12]).

Harry Boykoff 6ft 10in—two NBA seasons.[13]

Neal Walk (1948-2015) 6ft 10in—eight NBA seasons.[14]

Ernie Grunfeld (1955-) 6ft 6in—nine NBA seasons

(Olympic gold in 1976.)[15]

Two Jewish basketball players stood on the podium at Hitler's 1936 Olympic Games. **Samuel Balter** (1909-1998) was in the American team that took gold and **Irving Meretsky** (1912-1906) was in the Canadian team that took silver.[16] Balter was reluctant to attend Hitler's Games but did so after being reassured by Avery Brundage that there would be no Nazi propaganda. Brundage was wrong. According to Balter, magazines blaming everything on the Jews and depicting them as hook-nosed caricatures were sold on most street corners. Balter subsequently became a radio and television sports broadcaster. He acted as a radio announcer in movies, the best known being *The Champion*, starring Kirk Douglas.[17]

The Long Island basketball team would almost certainly have competed at the 1936 Olympics, but four of its members—**Jules Bender, Benjamin Kramer, Leo Merson** and **William Schwarz**—were Jewish and wanted to boycott the Games. They were supported by their Irish-American and Italian-American teammates and the team declared itself unavailable.

Two women deserve special mention—Sue Bird and Nancy Lieberman.

Sue Bird (1980-) 5ft 9in won four Olympic golds, in 2004, 2008, 2012 and 2016, playing basketball for the

USA. Bird is one of 11 women to have won an Olympic gold medal, a Women's National Basketball Association (WNBA) Championships and a National Collegiate Athletics Association (NCAA) Championships.

Bird won four golds in the International Basketball Federation (FIBA) World Cup —in 2002, 2010, 2014 and 2018—and a bronze in 2006. Bird is the only player—male or female—to win four World Cup gold medals. She is also the world's only player to have won as many as nine medals in the Olympics and in World Cups.[18]

At college, Bird played against Notre Dame in a match described as 'the best women's basketball game ever played'. Bird's shot at the buzzer gave the match to the University of Connecticut. The match and Bird were memorialised in the book *Bird at the Buzzer*.

The evergreen Bird, now 39, is not ready to retire and intends to try for another gold at the 2021 Olympics.[19]

Nancy Lieberman (1958-) 5ft 10in was regarded as one of the greatest players in American basketball. In an interview, Lieberman describes how she was with her mother at a fundraiser in New York when they were introduced to Muhammad Ali. Lieberman relates how she experienced difficulty breathing in the presence of the great man. Not so her mother, who said to the champion: 'Nancy said she's the greatest of all time'.

Ali replied: 'Listen here, lady, there's one greatest of all time and that's me'. Ali then turned to the very nervous 16 year old and said: 'Kid, your mother says you're really good'. Unable to look Ali in the eye, but keeping her composure, Lieberman said: 'Yeah, yes, Mr. Muhammad, I'm the greatest basketball player of all time'. Ali laughed, saying he hadn't realised there were two of him and gave Lieberman a big hug.[20] Yet Lieberman was right in a way. You would have to be at least one of the greatest basketball players to earn the nickname 'Lady Magic' after the legend Earvin 'Magic' Johnson.

Lieberman won silver in the 1976 Olympics and was picked for the USA team for the 1980 Games. The team did not compete due to the American boycott of the 1980 Games. Lieberman also took gold in the 1979 World Championships. In 2018 she became the first woman to coach a men's professional basketball team. She was inducted into the Basketball Hall of Fame in 1996.[21]

The 6ft 9in Uruguyan, **Oscar Moglia** (1935-1989), won bronze in the 1956 Olympics in Melbourne.

SUMMARY

Top American universities went to extreme lengths to exclude Jewish students from their campuses. Ivy League universities consequently lost out on academics such as Salk and Sabin who gave the world the polio vaccine. Ironically, these centres of learning bent their own rules when it came to Jewish basketball players.

The problems with stereotypes are illustrated using Paul Gallico's offensive description of Jewish basketballers.

Jewish basketballers, Samuel Balter and Irving Maretsky, stood on the podium at Hitler's 1936 Games.

Two Jewish women stand out, Sue Bird and Nancy Lieberman. Bird won four Olympic golds and is the only basketballer—man or woman—ever to win four World Cup gold medals. Nancy Lieberman won silver at the 1976 Olympics. She was nicknamed 'Lady Magic' after the legend Earvin 'Magic' Johnson. As a feisty 16 year old Lieberman squared up to Muhammad Ali telling him she was the greatest basketball player of all time.

MEDAL COMPARISON

Jewish basketball players have won twelve Olympic medals—seven gold, three silver and two bronze.

Australians have won five Olympic medals—three silver and two bronze. All five were won by the women's team. The total number of medals won by individual Australians is therefore 60 (a basketball side consists of five players on court with seven on the bench). No Australian has won an Olympic gold medal in basketball.

Sue Bird's haul of four Olympic gold basketball medals has only been bettered by one other woman—fellow American Teresa Edwards. Edwards has won five Olympic medals—four golds and a bronze.

JEWISH OLYMPIC MEDALLISTS—BASKETBALL

1936
Samuel Balter, USA, Gold
Irving Meretsky, Canada, Silver

1952
Alexandr Moiseyev, Sov. Union, Silver

1956
Oscar Moglia, Uruguay, Bronze

1960
Moysés Blás, Brazil, Bronze

1964
Lawrence Brown, USA, Gold

1976
Ernest Grunfeld, USA, Gold
Nancy Lieberman, USA, Silver

2000
Sue Bird, USA, Gold

2008
Sue Bird, USA, Gold

2012
Sue Bird, USA, Gold

2016
Sue Bird, USA, Gold

CHAPTER 11

TENNIS

'My attitude to sport is very simple – it's something that Jews just don't do'

Howard Jacobson—author[1]

The population of Chile is about 19 million.[2] Of this number about 18,000 are Jewish (0.09%).[3] **Nicolás Massú** (1976-) is one of the 18,000. In the Olympics of 2004 everything came together for Massú. The nail-biting doubles final was described as 'one of the most amazing tennis matches ever played' by tennis writer, Mark 'Scoop' Malinowski.

Malinowski describes how Massú and Fernando Gonzales saved four consecutive Olympic Gold match points (6-2 down in the fourth set tiebreaker) before overcoming Germany's Nicolas Kiefer and Raymond Schüttler.[4] The victory marked a milestone for Chile. Chile has competed in almost all the Olympics Games since the modern Games began in 1896. It took until 2004, however, for Massú and Gonzales to win Chile its first gold medal. Better still, Massú went on to win the singles, so doubling Chile's gold medal tally. Chile's total number of individual Olympic gold medals remains three as of 2020. On the way to the title, Massú defeated Gustavo Kuerten, Carlos Moya and Mardy Fish. Massú remains the only male player to have won both singles and doubles events in tennis at the Olympics.

Massú's life was also touched by the Holocaust. His Hungarian grandfather, Ladislao Fried Klein, managed to evade extermination by the Nazis during World War Two. Klein's wife survived Auschwitz whereas his parents and siblings did not. The number engraved on his grandfather's forearm was also engraved into the soul of Massú. He never gave up. He said: 'If my grandfather fought to survive [the Holocaust], why won't I be able to fight in a court to win a tennis match?' His fighting spirit earned him the moniker 'El Vampiro' (the vampire).[5]

Chile as a country has won 13 Olympic medals. As individuals Chileans have won three gold medals. Two of the golds belong to Nicolás Massú.[6]

Germany's best tennis player from 1928 to 1932 was **Dr. Daniel Prenn** (1904-1991). The Prenn family were amongst the five million Russians who fled to

Germany in order to escape the anti-Semitic pogroms that followed the 1917 Russian Revolution. Prenn became a clay court specialist, making use of a wide variety of strokes to exhaust his opponents. Prenn played 13 Davis Cup ties for Germany and was ranked six in the world.

In 1933 the Nazi government banned Prenn from competing for Germany, stating that 'non-Aryan players can no longer take part in international matches [and] that the player Dr. Daniel Prenn (a Jew) will not be selected for the Davis Cup in 1933'. The great tennis champions Fred Perry and Bunny Austin wrote to the *London Times* in protest. They stated: 'Sir we have read with considerable dismay the official statement which has appeared in the press that Dr. D.D. Prenn is not to represent Germany in the Davis Cup on the grounds that he is of Jewish origin. We cannot but recall the scene, when less than 12 months ago, Dr. Prenn before a large crowd at Berlin won for Germany against Great Britain the semi-final of the European Zone of the Davis Cup, and was carried from the arena amidst spontaneous and tremendous enthusiasm. We view with great misgivings any action which may well undermine all that is most valuable in international competition'.[7]

Simon Marks (of the Marks and Spencer department store) came to the rescue, arranging for Prenn and his wife to immigrate to England. Here Prenn became a successful businessman. He died in 1991.

In 1925 the Jewish tennis players **Ilse Friedleben** and **Nelly Neppach** were co-ranked No.1 in Germany. **Friedleben** (1893-1963) won the German Open six times in the years 1920-1926. She was only defeated once—losing to Neppach in the German Open Finals in 1925. Ilse's sister Toni was also one of Germany's top players and reached a ranking of four in Germany, while another sister, Anna, was ranked seven. Friedleben also won the championships of Switzerland, Denmark, Hungary and Sweden. Friedleben's final success was at the German Closed Championships in 1932, where she won the singles title. Once the Nazis came to power and began expelling Jews from sporting clubs, Friedleben fled Germany for Switzerland. She died in London in 1963.

Nelly Neppach's greatest victory was beating Ilse Friedleben in the finals of the German Championships in 1925. That same year she won eight of the nine possible German Championships. Neppach was forced out of sport by the Nazis in the 1930s and, faced with increasing persecution, she took her own life in 1933 at the age of 34. [8] Germany belatedly commemorated her life by placing a stolperstein (a small concrete cube inscribed with the name and life dates of victims of Nazi persecution or murder) near her former home in Berlin in October 2015.[9]

Another Jewish winner of the German Open was **Ladislav Hecht** (1909-2004). Hecht was ranked sixth in the world and was described in the *New York Times* as perhaps the best player on the European circuit immediately prior to World War Two. He defeated several of the world's best players including Bobby Riggs, Fred Perry and Jack Crawford. He captained Czechoslovakia's Davis Cup Team, representing his country from 1930-1939. He was a finalist in the Italian Open on two occasions. In 1939 he won the tennis championships at the first Maccabiah Games in Palestine.

After Germany annexed part of Czechoslovakia in 1938 an aide to Hitler invited Hecht to play Davis Cup competition for Germany. The aide was not aware that Hecht was Jewish. Hecht refused the invitation and fled the Nazi occupation of Czechoslovakia for the USA. Here he worked in a munitions factory for the duration of the war. Following the war he resumed playing tennis. He was by now too old to regain his former glory but nevertheless rose to be the number one player in the eastern USA.

The city of Bratislova honoured the Slovakian national hero by naming its new sporting stadium after Hecht in 1966. Hecht declined an invitation to attend the opening ceremony. According to his grandson Hecht considered such honours to be of no importance.[10]

The bigotry that bedevils the sport of tennis is well illustrated by the lives of the redoubtable **Angela Buxton** (1934-2020) and Althea Gibson. Buxton rose to number five in the world. As a promising youngster she had several lessons with a coach called Bill Blake. Buxton had completed membership application forms to London's Cumberland Tennis Club and kept asking Blake about her membership. Eventually Blake replied. 'Look Angela', he said, 'please don't ask me—you're not going to be able to join the club'. Buxton asked why not. 'Am I not good enough?' Blake replied: 'No, because you're Jewish'. Undeterred by the churlish bigots at the club, Buxton dealt with the situation as only she could. In her words: 'I made a point of going back to win their bloody tournament—twice, just to rub their noses in it—and they never gave me a cup of tea. Not even that'.[11] Several clubs refused membership to the future Wimbledon finalist yet Buxton would take home the silverware from those same club's tournaments. (Many tennis clubs have tournaments that are open to non-members).

Buxton said that 'in tennis if you win, you win and they can't deny you of that'. Buxton recalled club membership application forms asking for name, address and religion. As soon as you put 'Jewish' the answer was 'no'.[12]

While Buxton was discriminated against on account of her religion, Althea Gibson, an African-American, was discriminated against because of her colour. Both consequently had trouble finding doubles partners. The two outsiders, however, took refuge in each other, becoming the world's best doubles pairing. In 1956 they won the French, Queens and Wimbledon doubles titles. Buxton and Gibson's triumph at Wimbledon was reported by one British newspaper under the heading 'Minorities Win'. It was 'in very small type' according to Buxton, 'lest anyone should see it'. Buxton reached the finals of the Wimbledon singles in the same year, becoming the first British woman to reach the Wimbledon finals in 17 years.[13] She was also a semi-finalist at the French Open. From 1954-1956 Buxton represented Great Britain in the Wightman Cup.

Buxton was, however, never permitted to join the inappropriately named All England Lawn Tennis Club which hosts the Wimbledon tournament. In 2004 Buxton remarked that she had applied to become a member in 1956, soon after winning the Wimbledon doubles title with Althea Gibson. She has been on the waiting list ever since! Buxton added that her Grand Slam partner Althea Gibson would be on the same waiting list were she still alive.[14]

In his book, *Too Soon to Panic,* tennis Springbok Gordon Forbes describes the International Tennis Club founded in England in 1924. The club mushroomed and by 1995 there were 28 branches of the club throughout the world. The club seal displays four Latin words—'Benevolentia' (goodwill), 'Aequitas' (sportsmanship), 'Virtus' (courage and bravery), and 'Amicitia' (friendship). These virtues epitomise the essence of sporting competition. The All England Lawn Tennis Club displayed none of them in its treatment of Angela Buxton.

In case you're wondering whether any Jewish tennis players have won a Grand Slam singles title, the answer is 'yes'. **Helen Jacobs** won the US Open four times, Wimbledon once and the French Open twice; **Zsuzsa Körmöczy** won the French Open; **Dick Savitt** won Wimbledon and the Australian Open; **Vic Seixas** won Wimbledon and the US Open; and **Brian Teacher** won the Australian Open. That's thirteen Grand Slam Singles titles—and many more have been won by Jewish players in doubles and mixed doubles.

SUMMARY

Chile has competed in all the modern Olympics between 1896 and 2016. The population of Chile is ~19 million. Chile has won three gold Olympic medals. Two of them were won by Nicolás Massú. Massú is one of 18,000 Chilean Jews.

Germany persecuted its great Jewish players.

Angela Buxton and Althea Gibson responded to bigotry by joining forces to become the world's greatest double pairing.

MEDAL COMPARISON

Jewish tennis players have won 10 Olympic medals—three gold—one of which was in singles.

Australia has won six Olympic medals in tennis—one gold, one silver and four bronze.

As individuals Australians have won the same number of medals (10) as Jewish Olympians. No Australian has won gold in a singles event.

JEWISH OLYMPIC MEDALLISTS—TENNIS

1900
Hedwiga Rosenbaumova, Boh. Bronze; singles.
Hedwiga Rosenbaumova, Boh. Bronze; mixed

1912
Felix Pipes, Aust-Hun. Silver; doubles

1924
Umberto De Morpugno, Ita. Bronze; singles

1968 Demonstration Event
Julie Heldman, USA, Gold; mixed
Julie Heldman, USA, Silver; doubles
Julie Heldman, USA, Bronze; singles

1988
Brad Gilbert, USA, Bronze; singles

2004
Nicolás Massú, Chi. Gold; singles
Nicolás Massú, Chi. Gold; doubles

CHAPTER 12

FIELD HOCKEY

'[Boxing] is the one sport in Britain and the United States at which Jews have excelled'

Hollywood's Stereotype of the Wimpy Jew Refuses to Die[1]

Hans Schlesinger (1908-2005)—the goalkeeper who went from defence to attack. Schlesinger was regarded as Germany's number one goalkeeper and a certainty to keep goal for the 1936 Olympics. In 1935, however, the coach of the Frankfurt hockey club told Schlesinger that he could no longer compete because new restrictive laws had been enacted against Jews— the Nuremberg laws.

When he was informed that a Jew could be imprisoned for kissing an 'Aryan', Schlesinger decided to immigrate to the USA. He was able to get a job at the investment bank Bear Stearns as a messenger, and saved enough money to bring his family to the USA. The family were forced to leave their assets behind.

Schlesinger changed his name to the more American-sounding John Slade, and in 1942 he enlisted in the USA army. In 1945 Slade was in charge of a company of soldiers who came across a Bavarian castle in which 200 SS soldiers were hiding. Slade marched up to the door, demanding their surrender. They did so without resistance and Slade was awarded a Bronze Star for courage. Slade's fluent German made him invaluable in interrogating captured Nazi officers, one of whom, General Jurgen Stroop, had ordered the destruction of the Warsaw ghetto in which 400,000 Jews were imprisoned and starving.

In 1948, aged 40, Slade tried out for the USA hockey team bound for the London Olympics. He was chosen along with another German Jewish immigrant, **Claus Gerson**. The team failed to win a medal but to Slade this was unimportant. 'Here I was a Jewish refugee and I played on the American team,' he said. 'It meant more to me than if I had won a medal for the German team in 1936'.[2]

Carina Benninga (1962-) first represented the Netherlands in the 1983 World Championships in Kuala Lumpur. Her international playing career spanned nine years, ending in 1992. She played 158 international matches and captained the Dutch team from 1989 to 1992. The Dutch side won the World Championships in 1983 and 1990. Described as a dynamic midfield player, Benninga scored 25 goals in international matches. She won a gold medal at the 1984 Olympics and a bronze at the 1988 Games. At the 1992 Olympics she became the first woman to carry the flag for the Netherlands at the opening ceremony. In 1994 she was knighted by the Queen of Holland.[3]

In correspondence with Paul Yogi Mayer, Carina Benninga described what happened to her family during the Holocaust. Her maternal grandfather managed to get to Britain where he joined the Underground Resistance. Her grandmother and her grandmother's three children were arrested by the Germans in 1940 or 1941. One of the children was Benninga's mother. She managed to survive four years in Bergen-Belsen but was very ill and died some years later. Benninga's father was younger than her mother and he survived by being hidden behind a closet on a farm.[4]

Carina Benninga lives in Amsterdam and has two children. Benninga's elder brother **Marc Benninga** (1961-) also played hockey for the Netherlands. Along with his sister he won a bronze medal at the 1988 Olympics.

Giselle Kañevsky (1985-) has played as a defender for Argentina since 2006. She won a bronze medal at the 2008 Olympics and was a member of the Argentinian team that won the World Cup in 2010 in Rosario.

The South African hockey team captained by **Neville**

Berman in the 1970s is arguably as iconic as the Springbok cricket team captained by **Ali Bacher** in 1969/70.

Three other Jewish South Africans played hockey for South Africa at the same time—**Steve Jaspan, Brian Sher** and **Ponky Firer**. Berman (right striker), Jaspan (left wing) and Sher (centre forward) played alongside each other in a formidable line of forwards during the Springbok tour of Europe in 1975. Berman's team beat the world's best in winning the Eight Nations tournament in 1974.

Had South Africa not been banned from the Olympics during this period, it is likely that South African Jewish hockey players would have won medals in at least the 1972 and 1976 Games.

Finally, I need to mention **Randolph Lipscher** (1960-), who played on the USA national team from 1982 to 1984. He represented the USA at the 1984 Olympics as goalkeeper. The team failed to win a medal, but Lipscher was considered to be one of the world's best goalkeepers.

SUMMARY

Between them, sister and brother, Carina and Marc Benninga won three Olympic medals in hockey.

Their paternal grandfather served in the Dutch

resistance. On the maternal side, family members survived the Bergen-Belsen concentration camp.

Had Hans Schlesinger not been Jewish he would almost certainly have kept goal for Germany in Hitler's Games. Instead he fled Nazi Germany for America. He served in the USA military and was pivotal in the surrender of 200 SS men hiding in a Bavarian castle. He finally fulfilled his dream of playing hockey in the Olympics by representing the USA in the London 1948 Games.

The South African Jewish hockey players of the 1970s were amongst the world's best. They were unable to compete at the Olympic Games because of sporting sanctions against South Africa.

MEDAL COMPARISON

Jewish athletes have won four Olympic medals in hockey.

Australia as a country has won 12 medals in hockey—four gold, three silver and five bronze.

JEWISH OLYMPIC MEDALLISTS—HOCKEY

1984
Carina Benninga, Holland, Gold

1988
Carina Benninga, Holland, Bronze

Michael Meyerson

Marc Benninga, Holland, Bronze

2008
Giselle Kañevsky, Argentina, Bronze

CHAPTER 13

OTHER SPORTS

BASEBALL

Australia has won one medal in baseball, taking silver in the 2004 Athens Games. In the Australian team was a Jewish ex-South African, **Gavin Fingleson** (1976-). No other Jewish athlete has won an Olympic medal in baseball. This is because American Major League Baseball (MLB) players have not played at the Olympics. There have, however, been several professional Jewish baseball players who have ranked amongst the best in the world.

Amongst them are names like **Sandy Koufax, Hank Greenberg, Alex Bregman, Al Rosen, Lou Beudreau**, and **Shaun Green**. One of them is, however, worthy of special mention because, as with **Niels Bohr** (see chapter on soccer), his life intersected with that of Werner Heisenberg, the scientist in charge of Germany's nuclear program in World War Two. It was to this Jewish athlete—an unusually intellectually accomplished one, as we'll see—that Heisenberg owed his life. **Moe Berg** (1902-1972), played Major League Baseball (MLB) from 1926-1939. He was not the most gifted of baseballers although he stood out as a catcher. He is remembered more as the cleverest and most eccentric of professional baseballers. Berg graduated from Princeton University and Columbia Law School. As a star baseballer at Princeton he was invited to join a prestigious anti-Semitic dining club as long as he did not invite other Jews. He spoke a dozen languages including Latin, Spanish, Greek, German, Russian, Hebrew, Portuguese, Yiddish, French and English. His encyclopaedic knowledge made him a sensation in the quiz show *'Information, Please'*. He was equally at ease answering questions on subjects as diverse as astronomy and mythology. Tall and good looking Berg was described as the 'most mysterious, intellectual, bravest, sexiest, and in the end, perhaps the loneliest man of his time'.[1] He became a real life equivalent of James Bond.

Berg volunteered his services to the wartime intelligence agency, the Office of Strategic Services (OSS). He was tasked with going to Zurich to attend a lecture by Heisenberg. He was to assess whether Heisenberg was capable of producing a bomb. If so, he was to shoot him—in the lecture hall if necessary. As well as a pistol he had a cyanide tablet. The decision whether or not to kill Heisenberg was left to Berg alone. Heisenberg gave no indication that Germany was involved in a nuclear program during the lecture. Berg noted his own 'uncertainty principle' with respect to killing Heisenberg—an acknowledgement of Heisenberg's major contribution to quantum mechanics. Berg was then invited by Heisenberg's Swiss host, Paul Scherrer—an Office of Strategic Services source—to have dinner with Heisenberg later that week. During the dinner Heisenberg again revealed no detail about Germany's work on the bomb. Instead he lamented the inevitability of Germany losing the war. This probably confirmed for Berg that Heisenberg could not be part of a successful atomic project.[2] Berg chose not to kill Heisenberg and returned to the USA. Berg's decision was correct. Germany never did acquire a nuclear weapon.

In 1945 Berg was awarded the presidential Medal of Freedom—the USA's highest civilian honour. Berg turned down the medal, never saying why he declined the award. He revealed little of his life and if questioned would put a finger to his lips and say: 'Shhh! Spies and gentlemen don't talk'. He died in 1972. Even his death remains a mystery: it is not known where his remains were put to rest.[3] He lives on in the films: *'The Catcher was a Spy'* and *'The Spy Behind Home Plate'*.

For the first time, an Israeli team has qualified for the

Olympics in baseball and was due to compete in the 2020 Olympics in Japan. The event has been rescheduled for 2021 due to the Coronavirus.

RUGBY UNION

Rugby Union was played at the Olympics in 1900, 1908, 1920 and 1924. Australia has won a single Olympic medal in rugby union, beating Great Britain to take gold in 1908. Two Jewish brothers, **John 'Barney' Solomon** (1883-1952) and **Bert Solomon**, were in the British team that took silver.

John captained the British side but it was Bert who had the greater talent. Australia won the match 32-3 with Britain's only points coming from a try scored by Bert. Bert was regarded as the finest centre of the day and is credited for introducing the dummy pass into the game. It is said that no-one, before or since, has feinted a pass as well as he did. Wingers were known to have dived for the line convinced they were receiving a pass that was never sent and a referee once blew for a forward pass while the ball had not left Bert's hands.[4] Harry Houdini would have been proud.

On debut for England against Wales in 1910, Bert scored a spectacular 40m try and set up another.[5] He was instrumental in England defeating Wales for the first time in 12 years. Bert, however, turned down all further invitations to play for England, including an overseas tour with the British Lions. The reason? The modest Cornish miner felt ill at ease in the public school-dominated dressing room.[6] A contributing factor could have been that Bert loved nothing more than his pigeons. On occasion he refused to play for his club Redruth if his pigeons had not yet returned and he often had to be cajoled onto the field. Some said that his appearance could make a difference of 1,000 people at the gate. He was apparently offered 400 gold sovereigns to play rugby league in the North of England but even this offer he refused.[7] He died in 1961 aged 76.

RUGBY SEVENS

The Australian women's team won gold in 2016 in Rio.

No Jewish player has won an Olympic medal in sevens rugby.

SHOOTING

In shooting Jewish athletes have won 10 Olympic medals whereas Australia has won 11 medals. The Jewish athletes do, however, have a better spread of medals—six gold, three silver and one bronze.

Australia has won five gold, one silver and five bronze. Moreover, a Russian, **Yakov Zheleznyak** (1941-), set a new world record in the Running Game Target event at the 1972 Games.[8] No Australian has set a world record in shooting.

EQUESTRIAN

Jewish equestrians have won seven Olympic medals— one silver and six bronze.

Australian equestrians have won 12 Olympic medals, six of which are gold.

In the 2021 Olympics an Israeli equestrian team will be competing for the first time.

VOLLEYBALL

Jewish athletes have won 18 Olympic medals in volleyball—four gold.

Australia is yet to win a medal in this sport.

BEACH VOLLEYBALL

The Brazilian **Adriana Behar** (1969-) won silver at the 2000 and 2004 Olympics. Behar is regarded as one of the best volleyball players of her generation.

Australia has won Olympic bronze (1996) and gold (2000) medals in beach volleyball.

LACROSSE

Lacrosse has been played at only two Olympic Games: 1904 and 1908. **Philip Hess** and **Albert Lehman** won silver medals playing for the USA in 1904.

Australia was not represented at lacrosse in either of these Olympics.

CYCLING

Australia has won 51 Olympic medals in cycling—14 gold.

Jewish athletes are yet to win an Olympic medal in cycling.

DIVING, ARCHERY, SOFTBALL

No Jewish athletes have won Olympic medals in diving, archery and softball.

Australia has won 13 medals in diving, three in archery and four in softball.

JEWISH OLYMPIC MEDALLISTS—OTHER SPORTS BASEBALL

2004
Gavin Fingleson, Australia, Silver

RUGBY UNION

1908
John 'Barney' Solomon, Great Britain, Silver
Bert Solomon, Great Britain, Silver

SHOOTING

1908
Harry Simon, USA, Silver; rifle, free-standing 300m

1920
Morris Fisher, USA, Gold; free rifle, three positions
Morris Fisher, USA, Gold; free rifle, three positions team
Morris Fisher, USA, Gold; military rifle, team

1924
Morris Fisher, USA, Gold; free rifle, three positions
Morris Fisher, USA, Gold; free rifle, three positions team

1952
Lev Vainshtein, Sov. Union, Bronze; free rifle, three positions

1956
Allan Erdman, Sov. Union, Silver; free rifle, three positions

1972
Yakov Zheleznyak, Sov. Union, Gold; mixed running target
Boris Menik, Sov. Union, Silver; free rifle, three positions

EQUESTRIAN

1972
Neal Shapiro, USA, Silver; team jumping
Neal Shapiro, USA, Bronze; individual jumping

1976
Edith Master, USA, Bronze; team dressage

1992
Robert Dover, USA, Bronze; team dressage

1996
Robert Dover, USA, Bronze; team dressage

2000
Robert Dover, USA, Bronze; team dressage

2004
Robert Dover, USA, Bronze; team dressage

VOLLEYBALL

1964
Nelli Abramova, Sov. Union, Silver

Georgy Mondzolevski, Sov. Union, Gold
Yury Vengerovsky, Sov. Union, Gold

1968
Georgy Mondzolevski, Sov. Union, Gold
Yevgeny Lapinsky, Sov. Union, Gold

1972
Yevgeny Lapinsky, Sov. Union, Bronze
Vladimir Patkin, Sov. Union, Bronze
Yefim Chulak, Sov. Union, Bronze

1976
Vladimir Patkin, Sov. Union, Silver
Nataliya Kushnir, Sov. Union, Silver
Larisa Bergen, Sov. Union, Silver
Yefim Chulak, Sov. Union, Silver

1984
Bernard Rajzman, Brazil, Silver
Arie Selinger, USA, Silver

1988
Waldo Kantor, Argentina, Bronze

1992
Avital Selinger, USA, Silver
Dan Greenbaum, USA, Bronze

2008
Marcelo Elgarten, Brazil, Silver

BEACH VOLLEYBALL

2000
Adriana Behar, Brazil, Silver

2004
Adriana Behar, Brazil, Silver

LACROSSE

1908
Philip Hess, USA, Silver
Albert Lehman, USA, Silver

CONCLUSION

Jewish triathlon—gin rummy, then contract bridge, followed by a nap.

Haikus for Jews[1]

Jewish athletes have won approximately 525 medals at the Olympic Games. That medal count alone must put to rest the myth that Jews are no good at sport. It can, however, be difficult to change people's minds. It was Napoleon who said: 'It's easier to deceive than to undeceive'. This book is my attempt to undeceive people who hold the false belief that Jews are no good at sport. It's also a tribute to the Jewish athletes who deserve not to have their achievements diminished by tired clichés.

APPENDICES

JEWISH OLYMPIANS KILLED BY THE NAZIS

AGSTERIBBE, Estelle Dutch; gymnast; Gold at the 1912 Olympics

DE OLIVEIRA, Abraham Dutch; gymnast

FLATOW, Alfred German; gymnast; three Gold and one Silver at the 1896 Olympics

FLATOW, Gustav German; gymnast; two Gold at the 1896 Olympics

GARAY, János Hungarian; fencer; Silver and Bronze at the 1924 Olympics, Gold at the 1928 Olympics

GERDE, Oszkár Hungarian; fencer; Gold at the 1908 and 1912 Olympics

GOUDEKET, Isidore Dutch; gymnast

HERSCHMANN, Otto Austrian; swimmer and fencer; Silver at the 1896 Olympics (100m freestyle) and Silver at the 1912 Olympics (sabre).

JACOBS, Mozes Dutch; gymnast

KANTOR, Roman Polish; fencer

LEVY, Heinz Dutch; boxer

MÁNDI, Imre Hungarian; boxer

MELKMAN, Elias Dutch; gymnast

MOK, Abraham Dutch; gymnast

MUNK, József Hungarian; swimmer; Silver at the 1900 Olympics (4x200m relay)

NORDHEIM, Helene Dutch; gymnast; Gold at the 1912 Olympics

OKKER, Simon Dutch; fencer

PETSCHAUER, Attila Hungarian; fencer; Gold at the 1928 and 1932 Olympics, Silver at the 1928 Olympics

POLAK, Annie Dutch; gymnast; Gold at the 1912 Olympics

SIMONS, Judikje Dutch; gymnast; Gold at the 1912 Olympics

SLIER, Jonas Dutch; gymnast

SZRAJBMAN, Ilja Polish; swimmer

SZÉKELY, András Hungarian; swimmer; Bronze at the 1932 Olympics

VAN MOPPES, Jacob Dutch; wrestler

WIJNSCHENK, Israel Dutch; gymnast

ZACHÁR, Imre Hungarian; swimmer; Silver at the 1900 Olympics (4x200m relay)

JEWISH OLYMPIANS KILLED IN THE 1972 MUNICH MASSACRE

BERGER, David Israeli; weightlifting

FRIEDMAN, Ze'ev Israeli; weightlifting

HALFIN, Eliezer Israeli; wrestling

ROMANO, Yossef Israeli; weightlifting

SLAVIN, Mark Israeli; wrestling

ELITE JEWISH ATHLETES KILLED BY THE NAZIS

BARUCH, Hermann German; wrestling champion

BARUCH, Julius German; wrestling champion

EFRATI, Leone Italian; professional boxer

HENOCH, Lilli German; Germany's finest female athlete in the 1920s. She held world records in the shot put, discus and 4x100m relay

LOWY, Pavel Czech; table tennis champion—one of the Czech team that won the World Championships in 1935 and 1936

PEREZ, Victor Tunisian; boxer and world flyweight champion in 1931

SILBER, Klaus German; boxer

BRAUN, József played soccer for Hungary

FISCHER, Otto played soccer for Austria and the Vienna Hakoah Club

GRASGRÜN, Oscar played soccer for the Vienna Hakoah Club

HAMEL, Eddie played soccer for the Dutch club Ajax

HIRSCH, Julius played soccer for Germany

HOROWITZ, Ernst played soccer for the Vienna Hakoah Club

KLOTZ, József played soccer for Poland

KOLISCH, Josef played soccer for the Vienna Hakoah Club

KRUMHOLZ, Zygmunt played soccer for Poland

NÁDLER, Henrik played soccer for Hungary

POLLAK, Erwin played soccer for the Vienna Hakoah Club

SCHEUER, Max played soccer for Austria and the Vienna Hakoah Club

SCHÖNFELD, Ali played soccer for the Vienna Hakoah Club

SPERLING, Leon played soccer for Poland

STEUERMANN, Zygmunt played soccer for Poland

TAUSSIG, Imre played soccer for Hungary

VÁGÓ, Antal played soccer for Hungary

WEISZ, Árpád played soccer for Hungary

WEISZ, Ferenc played soccer for Hungary

JEWISH ATHLETES WHO SURVIVED INCARCERATION BY THE NAZIS

ANDREADIS, Ivan Czech; table tennis player; won 26 World Championships medals

AROUCH, Salomo Greek; boxer; middleweight champion of Greece and All Balkans

BRIL, Ben Dutch; boxer; flyweight champion

EHRLICH, Alojzy Polish; table tennis player; won six World Championships medals

EPSTEIN, Kurt Czech; water polo player; represented Czechoslavakia in water polo at the 1928 and 1936 Olympics

GUTTMANN, Béla Hungarian; soccer player; played for Hungary and the Vienna Hakoah Club, played in the 1924 Olympics

HAFT, Harry Polish; boxer; survived Nazi death camps to become a heavyweight professional boxer

HALBERSTADT, Hans German; épée fencing champion and Olympian

HELFGOTT, Ben Polish; weightlifter; competed at the 1956 and 1960 Olympics

KABOS, Endre Hungarian; fencer; won Gold and Bronze at the 1932 Olympics and two Golds at the 1936 Olympics

KELLNER (KÁRPÁTI), Károly Hungarian; wrestler; won Silver at the 1932 Olympics and Gold in the 1936 Olympics

KLEINOVA, Gertrude Czech table tennis champion

LADANY, Shaul Yugoslavian; race walker; competed in the 1958 and 1972 Olympics for Israel. Has held the world record for the 50 mile walk since 1972

LASKAU, Henry German; escaped a concentration camp to compete in race walking in the 1948, 1952 and 1956 Olympics for the USA. Held the one mile world record for 12 years

NAKACHE, Alfred French; swimmer; Competed in Hitler's Games. Set the world record for 200m breaststroke in July 1941. Survived Auschwitz to be one of the French team to break the world record for the 3x100m relay (three strokes) in 1946 and represented France in the 1948 Olympics

PUNKIN, Yakiv Russian; wrestler; won Gold at the 1952 Olympics

RAZON, Jacko Greek; boxer; middleweight champion of Greece

SHAPOW, Nathan Latvian; boxing champion

WEISZ, Richárd Hungarian; wrestler; won Gold at the 1908 Olympics

ELITE JEWISH ATHLETES BARRED FROM COMPETING

BERGMANN, Gretel German; high jump champion

FUCHS, Gottfried German; international and Olympic soccer player

GLICKMAN, Marty American; 4x100m relay runner excluded from competing in the 1936 Olympics by Nazi sympathiser Avery Brundage

JACOB, Martel German; javelin thrower

KELETI, Ágnes Hungarian; gymnast who won four medals at the 1952 Olympics

MAYER, Paul Yogi German; pentathlete

MEINSTEIN, Greta German; hurdler

MELLO, Ingeborg German; discus and shot put

NEPPACH, Nelly German; tennis champion

PRENN, Daniel German; Davis Cup tennis player. Ranked sixth in the world

ROZEANU, Angelica Romanian; table tennis player and world champion. Banned from competing from 1940-1944. In 1955 she became the last non-Asian woman to win the World Championships.

SCHLESINGER, Hans German; regarded as Germany's best field hockey goalkeeper in 1936

SEELIG, Erich German; middleweight boxing champion

STOLLER, Sam American; 4x100m relay runner excluded from competing in the 1936 Games by Nazi sympathiser Avery Brundage.

YOKL, Ernst German; 400m sprinter and 400m hurdler

JEWISH ATHLETES WHO BOYCOTTED HITLER'S GAMES

ALTMANN, Endre Romanian; fencer

BENDER, Jules American; basketballer

BRIL, Ben Dutch; boxing champion. Competed at the 1928 Olympics

CAHNERS, Norman American; 100 and 200m sprinter

COHEN, Harry Australian; boxer

DEUTSCH, Judith Austrian; swimmer

FISCHER, Frank Czech; water polo player

FRIESEL, Paul American; swimmer

GEVINSON, Louis American; boxer

GOLDNER, Lucie Austrian; swimmer

GREEN, Milton American; hurdler and world record holder

HIRSCHL, Nikolaus Austrian; heavyweight wrestling champion and 1932 Olympic medalist

JAEGER, Nat American; race walker

KIEL, Sid South African; hurdler; South Africa's only hope for a medal in track and field at the 1936 Olympics

KOFF, Sid American; high and broad jumper

KRAMER, Benjamin American; basketballer

KURLAND, Abraham Danish; wrestler; won Silver

at the 1932 Olympics and was a favourite for the 1936 Olympics in the lightweight division

LANGER, Ruth Austrian; swimmer

LUFTSPRING, Sammy Canadian; welterweight boxer; considered likely to win gold at the 1936 Games. Turned professional in 1936 and was ranked third in the world

MERSON, Leo American; basketballer

NEUGASS, Herman American; 100m sprinter

OBERLANDER, Fred Austrian; heavyweight wrestling champion

OSIIER, Ivan Danish; fencer; won Silver at the 1912 Olympics in individual épée

PERKINS, Pearl American; gymnast

POLACK, Julius Canadian; fencer; due to captain Canadian fencing team

SCHWARZ, William American; basketballer.

WOLFF, Albert French; fencer

YAKUBOWITZ, Benjamin Canadian; bantamweight boxing champion. Turned professional in 1937 and was ranked fourth in the world

ABOUT THE AUTHOR

Michael Meyerson has worked in South Africa, England and Australia in radiology for four decades. He has written several articles on scepticism, rationalism and sport. His articles have been published in The Skeptic, The Australian Rationalist, Free Inquiry, and The Australian. His interest in sport and sceptical mindset have come together in this book, which dispels the myth that Jews are no good at sport.

ACKNOWLEDGEMENTS

I'm indebted to:

My sister Denise, for her patience and invaluable advice. She rendered the manuscript concise by her constant repetition of the words—'Remember! less is more'.

Paul Taylor, an authority on the subject, for editing the book and his acute suggestions.

My great friend, Jon Cartoon, who read and re-read every chapter, endured almost daily calls, and retained the patience to provide great advice and encouragement. Jon's wife and ex-South African swimming champion, Carmel, for access to her treasure trove of scrapbooks.

Mark Toohey, who drew on his vast knowledge to alert me to Moe Berg.

My late mother Queenie who loved everything I wrote-well almost everything!

My partner, Susan, who considers sport of no great

import but nevertheless provided much needed support and was kind enough at least to find the book interesting!

Finally, Anne Brammage, Sam Katz and Steve Mayer thanks for reading and advising.

REFERENCES

Introduction

1 Shirley Povich, 'Berlin 1936: At the Olympics, Achievements of the Brave in a Year of Cowardice', *Washingtonpost.com*, 6 July 1996.

2 P. Adams, 'Jewels of the Diaspora', *Weekend Australian*, 4 October 2014.

3 Michael Meyerson, 'The hurdles', *The Skeptic*, Vol. 36, No. 1, March 2016, p.58.

4 P. Taylor, *Jews and the Olympic Games* (Sussex Academic Press, 2004) p. 152

5 NoelO, By Population Australia is on top of the medal tally, theroar.com.au, 7 August 2012.

Chapter One

CITIUS

1 N. MacMaster, *Racism in Europe: 1870-2000*, (Houndmills, Basingstoke, Hampshire and New York,

2001), p.212.

2 Harold Abrahams, Papers of, Archive Collection,<https://archiveshub.jisc.ac.uk/data/gb150-ath/ha>, accessed 16 May 2020.

3 B.Postal J.Silver and R. Silver, *Encyclopedia of Jews in sports,* (New York: Bloch Publishing Company, 1965), p. 460.

4 Tim Lane, 'It was 64 years ago today…', *The Sydney Morning Herald*, 29 July 2012.

5 David B. Green, 1924: Harold Abrahams Wins Olympic Gold, *Haaretz-Israel News*, 7 July 2013.

6 Harold Maurice Abrahams, managed by David Barry Kaplan, geni.com

7 B.Postal J.Silver and R. Silver, *Encyclopedia of Jews in sports,* (New York: Bloch Publishing Company, 1965), p. 460.

8 B.Postal J.Silver and R. Silver, *Encyclopedia of Jews in sports,* (New York: Bloch Publishing Company, 1965), p. 460.

9 M. Hannus, Elias Katz – Memory of a Forgotten Olympic Champion, *Journal of Olympic History*, Volume 10, (December 2001/January 2002), p.72.

10 Roger Robinson, The Mystery of the Flying Finn,

Runner's World, 10 July 2014.

11 Roger Robinson, The Mystery of the Flying Finn, *Runner's World*, 10 July 2014.

12 M. Hannus, Elias Katz – Memory of a Forgotten Olympic Champion, *Journal of Olympic History*, Volume 10, (December 2001/January 2002) pp.72-74.

13 M. Hannus, Elias Katz – Memory of a Forgotten Olympic Champion, *Journal of Olympic History*, Volume 10, (December 2001/January 2002) pp.72-74.

14 Shaul Adar, Forgotten Olympic track champion's legacy races on in Israel, *The Times of Israel*, 10 September 2019.

15 B.Postal J.Silver and R. Silver, *Encyclopedia of Jews in sports,* (New York: Bloch Publishing Company, 1965), p. 461.

16 P.Y.Mayer, *Jews And The Olympic Games*, (London and Portland, Vallentine Mitchell 2004), p. 38.

17 *Irena Szewinska-Kirszenstein*, (2008), ESPN Beijing 2008,
<http://www.espn.com/olympics/summer08/fanguide/athlete?athlete=13626>

18 *Hall of Fame Profile-Irena Szewinska (Poland) World Athletics*, Hall of Fame, (30 April 2012),

<https://www.worldathletics.org/news/news/hall-of-fame-profile-irena- szewinska-poland>.

19 Athletics: Irena Szewinska, greatest athlete of all time, *THE STRAITS TIMES* (10 June 2020).

20 Irena-Kirszenstein-Szewinska(1946-), <https://www.jewishvirtuallibrary.org/irena-kirszenstein-szewinska>, accessed 18 May 2020.

21 Harry Gordon, *Shirley de la Hunty (nee Strickland) AO MBE 1925-2004*, (2000) <www.athletics.com.au/hall-of-fame-director/shirley-strickland>, Athletics Australia.

22 *World Athletics, Hall Of Fame – Irena Szewinska (Poland)*, (30 April 2012), World Athletics, <www.worldathletics.org › news › news › hall-of-fame-p...>.

23 D. Wallechinsky and J. Loucky, *The Complete Book of the Olympics* (London, 2012), p.387.

24 Alex Suskind, Lucy Price, *The Hebrew Runner*, Forward, (9 December 2009) <https://forward.com/articles/120556/the-hebrew-runner/>.

25 T. Arbinder, 'City of Dreams: The 400-year Epic History of Immigrant New York', (New York: Houghton Mifflin Harcourt, 2016), p.292.

26 Frank Litsky, Abel Kiviat, Runner, Dies at 99; Held

World 1,500-Meter Record, *The New York Times*, 26 August 1991.

27 Sheldon Kirshner, Track and field star gets full biographical treatment, *The Canadian Jewish News,* 16 March 2011.

28 Paul Taylor, *Jews and the Olympic Games*, (Brighton and Portland: Sussex Academic Press (2004), p. 236.

29 *Hall Of Famer Bobbie Rosenveld*, Canada's Sports Hall of Fame, <https://www.sportshall.ca/hall-of-famers/hall-of-famers-search.html?proID=474&catID=all&lang=EN>, accessed 22 May 2020.

30 Malcolm Kelly, *Fanny "Bobbie" Rosenveld: An icon for all ages*, (21 June 2017), CBC Sports, <https://www.cbc.ca/sports/2.9056/canada-150-rosenfeld-1.4169819>, accessed 21 May 2020.

31 Danny Rosenberg, *Fanny "Bobbie"Rosenveld*, Jewish Women's Archive, <https://jwa.org/encyclopedia/article/rosenfeld-fanny>, accessed 22 May 2020.

32 Danny Rosenberg, *Fanny "Bobbie"Rosenveld*, Jewish Women's Archive, <https://jwa.org/encyclopedia/article/rosenfeld-fanny>, accessed 22 May 2020.

33 Danny Rosenberg, *Fanny "Bobbie"Rosenveld*, Jewish Women's Archive, <https://jwa.org/encyclopedia/article/rosenfeld-fanny>, accessed 22 May.

34 Teddy Smouha Bio, Stats, and Results, Olympics at Sports, <https://www.sports-reference.com/olympics/athletes/sm/teddy-smouha-1.html>, accessed 21 May 2020.

35 *Maria Leontyavna Itkina*, Prabook, <https://prabook.com/web/maria.itkina/722218>, accessed 21 May 2020.

36 *Maria Leontyavna Itkina*, International Jewish Sports Hall of Fame, <http://www.jewishsports.net/BioPages/MariaLeontyavnaItkina.htm>, accessed 25 April 2020.

37 Paul Taylor, *Jews and the Olympic Games*, (Brighton and Portland: Sussex Academic Press (2004), p. 89.

38 Peter Richman, *Marty Glickman, Jesse Owens and a Forgotten Story of the 1936 Berlin Olympics,* (23 August 2013), Bleacher Report, <https://bleacherreport.com/articles/1746428-marty-glickman-jesse-owens-and-a- forgotten-story-of-the-1936-berlin-olympics#:~:text=Glickman%20was%>.

39 Olympedia – Avery Brundage, <http://www.olympedia.org/athletes/78168>, accessed 25

May 2020.

40 A. Rippon, *Hitler's Olympics: The Story of the 1936 Nazi Games*, (Barnsley, South Yorkshire, Pen and Sword MILITARY, 2006), p174.

41 Mistake of 1936 Olympic Games Not Forgotten, *Los Angeles Times*, 29 March 1988.

42 Gerald Eskanazi, The Olympic Flame Burns Bright for Marty Glickman, a Sprinter Banned for Being Jewish, *Observer,* 13 August 2016.

43 David B. Green, *1917: A Jewish sports legend is born*, *Jewish World - Haaretz.com*, 14 August 2013, <https://www.haaretz.com/jewish/.premium-1917-jewish-sports-legend-is-born-1.5320715>.

44 *The Nazi Olympics Berlin 1936 | American Boycotters – Milton Green*, United States Holocust Memorial Museum, <https://www.ushmm.org/exhibition/olympics/?content=american_boycotters_milton_green&lang=en accessed, 25 May 2020>.

45 Jewish Virtual Library, *Syd Koff (1912-1999),* <https://www.jewishvirtuallibrary.org/syd-koff>, accessed 26 May 2020.

46 Paul Taylor, *Jews and the Olympic Games*, (Brighton and Portland: Sussex Academic Press (2004), p. 249.

47 Peter Finney, Ex-Tulane sprinter Herman Neugass remembered for stance 75 years ago, The Times-Picayune, 19 August 2011.

48 James Ring Adams, The Jim Thorpe Backlash: The Olympic Medals Debacle And the Demise of Carlisle, NMAI Magazine, (Summer 2012/ Vol. 13 No. 2).

49 Michael Meyerson, *Sid Kiel — a brilliant athlete from Yesteryear*, Cape Jewish Chronicle, September 2004.

50 Maurice Silbert, *Sid Kiel (18/07/1916-19/07/2007)*, *SAMJ Forum*, October 2007, Vol. 97, No. 10.

51 Frank Litsky, Dr. Ernst F. Jokl, a Pioneer In Sports Medicine, Dies at 90, *The New York Times*, 21 December 1997.

52 Floris Van Der Merwe, *Ernst Franz Jokl as the Father of Physical Education in South Africa*, LA 84 Digital Library, <https://digital.la84.org/digital/collection/p17103coll10/id/11190/>, accessed 27 May 2020.

53 *Henry 'Mr. Walking' Laskau (1916-2000)*, Find A Grave, <https://www.findagrave.com/memorial/169486763/henry-laskau>, accessed 23 October 2019.

54 Frank Litsky, Henry Laskau, Race Walker, is Dead at 83, *The New York Times*, 9 May 2000.

55 I. Deitch, An Israeli athlete was mutilated during 1972 Munich Olympics massacre, *Associated Press, ABS-CBN Sports,* 3 December 2015, <https://sports.abs-cbn.com/generalsports/news/2015/12/03/an-israeli-athlete-mutilated-1972-munich- massacre-6877>.

56 Maayan Jaffe-Hoffman, '*After decades of IOC silence, slain Israeli Olympians headed for recognition*', J-Wire, (28 May 2015), <https://www.jwire.com.au/after- decades-of-ioc-silence-slain-israeli-olympians-headed-for-recognition/>, accessed 8 July 2020.

57 Haaretz Sports Staff, Sports Shorts, <https://www.haaretz.com/1.4973729> accessed 14 August 2020.

58 *Gerald Ashworth,* International Jewish Sports Hall of Fame, <http://www.jewishsports.net/BioPages/GeraldAshworth.htm>, accessed 29 May 2020.

59 Gal Tziperman Lotan, No.5 Esther Roth-Sachamorov, *The Jerusalem Post*, 2 May 2008.

60 The Olympic Boycott, 1980, U.S. Department of State Archive, <https://2001-2009.state.gov/r/pa/ho/time/qfp/104481.htm>, accessed 29 May 2020.

61 *ZhannaPintusevich*, International Jewish Sports Hall of Fame,

<http://www.jewishsports.net/BioPages/ZhannaPintusevich>, accessed 29 May 2020.

62 Creator Of 'The Clear' Imprisoned, (4 August 2006), CBS News, <https://www.cbsnews.com/news/creator-of-the-clear-imprisoned/>, accessed 28 May 2020.

63 Zhanna Pintusevich Block, Alchetron, accessed 29 May 2020.

64 Simon Turnbull, London Eye: Heard about the Olympic 100m final no one won? The Independent, 23 December 2011.

65 Simon Turnbull, London Eye: Heard about the Olympic 100m final no one won? The Independent, 23 December 2011.

66 Meet Joanna Zeiger, Olympian and 2008 Ironman 70.3 World Champion, (29 November 2018), RIPPLE, <https://stillwaterbrands.life/blog/2018/11/29/meet-joanna-zeiger-olympian-and-2008-ironman-703-world-champion>.

ALTIUS

67 Vic Ahladeff, Gretel Bergmann, the world-class Jewish athlete Nazi Germany couldn't hold down, *The Sydney Morning Herald*, 11 April 2015.

68 D. Wallechinsky and J. Loucky, *The Complete Book of*

the Olympics (London, 2012), p.367.

69 Vic Ahladeff, Gretel Bergmann, the world-class Jewish athlete Nazi Germany couldn't hold down, *The Sydney Morning Herald*, 11 April 2015.

70 Evan Grossman, Margaret Lambert, German high-jump champ banned by Nazis for being Jewish, subject of new Olympic documentary, *New York Daily News*, 9 November 2017.

71 Karen Rosen, *Berlin Olympics Movie Blends Fact, Fiction*, 30 January 2010, Around The Rings, <http://wwwaroundtherings.com/site/A_34152_Berlin-Olympics- Movie-Fact-Fiction/292/Articles>, accessed 30 January 2020.

72 Obituary: Margaret Bergmann Lambert–The Great Jewish Hope, *The Irish Times*, 27 July 2017.

73 Dave Hunter, Dwight Stones: The Conscience Of Track & Field, High Jump Legend, TV Commentator Calls It As He Sees It, (15 December 2016), *RunBlogRun*, <http://www.runblogrun.com/2016/12/dwight-stones-the-conscience-of-track-field- high-jump-legend-tv-commentator-calls-it-as-he-sees-it.html>.

74 B.Postal J.Silver and R. Silver, *Encyclopedia of Jews in sports,* (New York: Bloch Publishing Company, 1965), p. 480.

75 B.Postal J.Silver and R. Silver, *Encyclopedia of Jews in sports,* (New York: Bloch Publishing Company, 1965), p. 481.

76 *The Story of Central New York's Most Decorated Olympian, Myer Prinstein*, Onandaga Historical Association, <https://www.cnyhistory.org/2014/12/myer-prinstein/>, accessed 25 June 2020.

FORTIUS

77 Amit Naor, The Exceptional Lilli Henoch: The Sad Story of a Champion Athlete, (7 April 2020), The Librarians, <https://blog.nli.org.il/en/lbh-lilli-henoch/>

78 P.Y.Mayer, *Jews And The Olympic Games*, (London and Portland, Vallentine Mitchell 2004), pp. 61-62.

79 Paul Taylor, *Jews and the Olympic Games*, (Brighton and Portland: Sussex Academic Press (2004), p. 249.

80 B.Postal J.Silver and R. Silver, *Encyclopedia of Jews in sports,* (New York: Bloch Publishing Company, 1965), p. 487.

81 P.Y.Mayer, *Jews And The Olympic Games*, (London and Portland, Vallentine Mitchell 2004), p. 83.

82 Dr. Gabe Mirkin, *Micheline Ostermeyer, Olympian and Concert Pianist,* (2 December 2018), DrMirkin.com, <https://www.drmirkin.com/histories-and-

mysteries/micheline-ostermeyer-olympian-and-concert-pianist.html>, accessed 25 June 2020.

83 *Three medals for Micheline Ostermeyer*, (10 August 1948), Athletics-Olympic News, <https://www.olympic.org/news/micheline-ostermeyer-athletics>.

84 *Olympic countdown: 57 Days*, BBC SPORT, Updated 16 June 2004, <http://news.bbc.co.uk/sport2/hi/olympics_2004/3810499.stm>

85 *Tamara Press*, Encyclopaedia Britannica, <https://www.britannica.com/biography/Tamara-Press>, accessed 30 May 2020.

86 D. Wallechinsky and J. Loucky, *The Complete Book of the Olympics* (London, 2012), p. 400 and 383.

87 Lisa Schweiger, *Tamara and Irina Press,* sex verification in sports, 8 June 2013, <http://genderverification.blogspot.com/2013/06/tamara-and-irina-press.html> accessed 31 May 2020.

88 J. Siegman, *Jewish Sports Legends,* (Brassey's Washington, London 2nd Edition, 1977) p.155.

89 P.Y.Mayer, *Jews And The Olympic Games*, (London and Portland, Vallentine Mitchell 2004), p.167.

90 Jews in Sports: Jewish Olympic Medallists (1896-Present), Jewish Virtual Library, <https://www.jewishvirtuallibrary.org/jewish-olympic-medalists-1896-present>, accessed 28 June 2020.

91 James Fuchs – Obituary - CT |GreenwichTime, <https://www.legacy.com/obituaries/greenwichtime/obituary.aspx?n=james-e-fuchs&pid=146004104&fhid=2058>, accessed 3 June 2020.

92 A. Goldman, *Stars of David*, (Johannesburg: Electric Printing Works, 1963), p. 184.

93 Helene Elliott, Parry O'Brien, 75; champion revolutionized shotput throw, *Los Angeles Times*, 23 April 2007.

94 A. Goldman, *Stars of David*, (Johannesburg: Electric Printing Works, 1963), pp.134-135.

95 Greg Sullivan, Boris Djerassi recalls Olympic experience, *The Herald News*, 28 July 2012.

96 D. Wallechinsky and J. Loucky, *The Complete Book of the Olympics* (London, 2012), p.255.

97 *History of US Nationals Results: Discus Throw – Men*, Track & Field News, <https://trackandfieldnews.com/history-of-us-nationals-results-discus-throw-men/>, accessed 1 June 2020.

98 A. Goldman, *Stars of David*, (Johannesburg: Electric Printing Works, 1963), pp.184.

99 A. Goldman, *Stars of David*, (Johannesburg: Electric Printing Works, 1963), pp.184.

100 Paid Notice: Deaths FRANK, Victor H. *The New York Times*, 9 April 2010, <https://archive.nytimes.com/query.nytimes.com/gst/fullpage-9A0DE0D71F3AF93AA35757C0A9669D8B63.html>, accessed 28 June 2020.

Chapter Two

1 The words of Jewish comedian, Jackie Mason, in a show he gave in Israel in 1996.

2 William F. Reed, 'Swimming Isn't Everything, Winning Is', Sports Illustrated Vault, 9 March 1970.

3 J. Siegman, *Jewish Sports Legends* (Washington, London: Brassey's Inc. 1997), p.135.

4 Keena Rothhammer (USA), International Swimming Hall of Fame, <https://ishof.org/keena-rothhammer-(usa).html>, accessed 9 May 2020.

5 Andy Bull, Holocaust survivor to Olympic gold: the remarkable life of Eva Szekely, *The Guardian,* 4 March 2020.

6 Daniel E. Slotnik, Eva Szekely Dies at 92; Survived Holocaust to Win Olympic Gold, *The New York Times,* 6 March 2020.

7 Andy Bull, Holocaust survivor to Olympic gold: the remarkable life of Eva Szekely, *The Guardian,* 4 March 2020.

8 Andrea Gyarmati (HUN), International Swimming Hall of Fame, <https://ishof.org/andrea- gyarmati-(hun).html>, accessed 9 May 2020.

9 Olivier Poirier-Leroy: *Jason Lezak and the Greatest Relay Leg of All-Time,* <https://www.yourswimlog.com/jason-lezak-and-the-greatest-relay-leg-of-all-time/>, YourSwimBook, accessed 1 July 2019.

10 Olivier Poirier-Leroy: *Jason Lezak and the Greatest Relay Leg of All-Time,* <https://www.yourswimlog.com/jason-lezak-and-the-greatest-relay-leg-of-all-time/>, YourSwimBook, accessed 10 May 2020.

11 Dan Hicks and Rowdy Gaines: *Verbal Performances of Jason Lezak's 4x100 Olympic Freestyle Relay Leg,* <https://www.americanrhetoric.com/speeches/jasonlezakolympicfreestylerelayvictory.htm>, accessed 4 July2020.

12 Olivier Pourier-Leroy: *Jason Lezak and Unleashing Your Competitive Fire*, YourSwimBook, <https://www.yourswimlog.com/jason-lezak-competitive-

fire/>, accessed 10 May 2020.

13 Karen Rosen, *The Greatest Split Ever: Jason Lezak Recalls His Iconic 4x100 Free Leg 10 Years Later*: (6 March 2018), Team USA, <https://www.teamusa.org/News/2018/March/06/The-Greatest-Split-Ever-Jason-Lezak- Recalls-His-Iconic-4x100-Free-Leg-10-Years-Later>, accessed 10 May 2020.

14 *Garrett Weber-Gale Bio*: SwimSwam, <https://swimswam.com/bio/garrett-weber-gale,%20Garrett%20Weber-Gale%20Bio>, accessed 10 May 2020.

15 2008 Beijing Summer Olympics – Ben Wildman-Tobriner Profile & Bio, Photos & Videos NBC Olympics.

16 *Hajos turns tragedy into glory in the water* – Olympic News, <https://www.olympic.org/news/hajos-turns-tragedy-into-glory-in-the-water>, accessed 10 May 2020.

17 SR/OLYMPIC SPORTS, <www.sports-reference.com/olympics/athletes/ha/henrik-hajos, <https://www.sports-reference.com/olympics.html>, accessed 23 April 2020

18 Meg Keller-Marvin: *Alfred Nakache, Auschwitz Survivor and Olympian, To Be Inducted into the International Swimming Hall of Fame*: (11 February 2019), Swimming World, <https://www.swimmingworldmagazine.com/news/alfred-

nakache-auschwitz-survivor- olympian-inducted-international-swimming-hall-fame/>, accessed 4 July 2020.

19 B.Postal J.Silver and R. Silver, *Encyclopedia of Jews in sports,* (New York: Bloch Publishing Company, 1965), p 421.

20 Mary Cronk Farrell: *Girls Give Up Olympic Dreams to Boycott Nazis*: (8 May 2016), <http://www.marycronkfarrell.net/blog/girls-give-up-olympic-dreams-to-boycott-nazis>, accessed 17 July 2019.

21 Haaretz Staff, *Swimming With a Strength of Mind and Body*, 29 April 2003, *Haaretz – Israel News*, <https://www.haaretz.com/1.4746341>, accessed 13 July 2019.

22 John Levi, *Swim champion, anti-Nazi hero 1918-2000*, *Sydney Morning Herald*, 26 September 2000, <https://lists.h-net.org/cgi-bin/logbrowse.pl?trx=vx&list=h-antisemitism&month=0010&=&msg=5417iPRTM3fww0oT3DtpNA&user=&pw=>, Daniel Leeson, Humanities and Social Sciences Net Online, 11 October 2000.

23 Frank Litsky, Ruth Langer Lawrence, 77, Who Boycotted '36 Olympics, *New York Times*, 6 June 1999.

24 Haaretz Staff, *Swimming With a Strength of Mind and Body*, 29 April 2003, *Haaretz – Israel News*,

<https://www.haaretz.com/1.4746341>, accessed 13 July 2019.

25 B.Postal J.Silver and R. Silver, *Encyclopedia of Jews in sports,* (New York: Bloch Publishing Company, 1965), p 422.

26 B.Postal J.Silver and R. Silver, *Encyclopedia of Jews in sports,* (New York: Bloch Publishing Company, 1965), p 424.

27 P.Y.Mayer, *Jews And The Olympic Games*, (London and Portland, Vallentine Mitchell, 2004), p. 50.

28 D. Wallechinsky and J. Loucky, *The Complete Book of the Olympics* (London, 2012), p. 1050.

29 *Andras Szekely, 1909-1943*: Our 6 Million, <http://www.shemvener.org.il/en/deceased/andras-szekely/>, accessed 13 May 2020.

30 D. Wallechinsky and J. Loucky, *The Complete Book of the Olympics* (London, 2012), p. 1049.

31 Kay Schaffer and Sidonie Smith, *The Olympics at the Millennium: Power, Politics and the Games*, (New Brunswick: Rutgers University Press, 2000), p.61.

32 Gerard Blitz (Bel), International Swimming Hall of Fame, <https://ishof.org/gerard- blitz.html>, accessed 29 April 2020.

33 Otto Wahle (AUT-USA), International Swimming Hall of Fame, <https://ishof.org/otto- wahle.html>, accessed 29 April 2020.

34 Payton Titus: *Dara Torres The Comeback Queen*: (23 July 2018), Swimming World, accessed 8 July 2019.

35 Philip Hersh: *"Pretty Super" Ledecky Gets Silver Surprise In 400 Free Relay*: (6 August 2016), Team USA, <https://www.teamusa.org/News/2016/August/06/Ledecky-Pretty-Super- As-Swift-Prelim-Anchor-In-4-x-100-Free-Relay>, accessed 13 May 2020.

36 Dylan Lee, Local professor honored for storied swimming past, *Enterprise, Yolo County News,* accessed 14 May 2020.

37 B.P. Robert Stephen Silverman, The Big Book Of Jewish Sports Heroes, (New York: S.P.I. Books, 2002), p. 155.

38 Dylan Lee, Local professor honored for storied swimming past, *Enterprise, Yolo County News,* accessed 14 May 2020.

39 Arun Janardhan: How Olympic swimmer Anthony Ervin rose, fell and rose again: (22 November 2017), Livemint,

<https://www.livemint.com/Leisure/2AcOVUByQMbV291R1pMSSJ/How-Olympic- swimmer-Anthony-Ervin-

rose-fell-and-rose-again.html www.livemint.com>, accessed 13 May 2020.

40 Lenny Krayzelburg (1975-), Jewish Virtual Library, <https://www.jewishvirtuallibrary.org/lenny-krayzelburg>, accessed 13 May 2020.

41 Lenny Krayzelburg (USA), International Swimming Hall of Fame, <https://ishof.org/lenny-krayzelburg-(usa).html>, accessed 13 May 2020.

42 Tiffany Cohen (USA), International Swimming Hall of Fame, <https://ishof.org/tiffany- cohen.html>, accessed 15 May 2020.

43 Wallace Wolf, International Jewish Sports Hall of Fame, <http://www.jewishsports.net/BioPages/Wallace-Wolf.htm>, accessed 15 May 2020.

44 Karen and Sarah Josephson(USA), International Swimming Hall of Fame, <https://ishof.org/karen-and-sarah-josephson-(usa).html>, accessed 22 July 2019.

45 Dennis Hands, *Pretoria News,* February 1971.

46 Desiree Firer, Dr Carmel Goodman, *Soul Sport Magazine*, July 2019, p. 48.

47 Personal correspondence

48 Sarah Poewe (1983-), Jewish Virtual Library,

<https://www.jewishvirtuallibrary.org/sarah- poewe>, accessed 14 May 2020.

49 Jack Milner, Sarah seems to have found her Jewish mojo, *South African Jewish Report*, 29 July 2015.

50 Hannah Rubin: *Olympic Champ Rebecca Soni Has Jewish Roots:* (8 August 2012), Forward , <https://forward.com/news/breaking-news/160756/olympic-champ-rebecca-soni- has-jewish-roots/> accessed 15 May 2020.

51 Veronika Bondarenko: *The Secret Jewish History of Rio Gold Medalist Katie Ledecky*: (7 August 2016), Forward, <https://forward.com/news/breaking-news/346537/the-secret-jewish- history-of-rio-gold-medalist-katie-ledecky/>, accessed 4 July 2020.

Chapter Three

1 P. Adams, Jewels of the Diaspora, *Weekend Australian*, 4 October 2014.

2 J. Goodbody, *The Illustrated History of Gymnastics* (New York: Beaufort Books, 1983).

3 R. Wiedeman, A Full Revolution, *The New Yorker: The Sporting Scene,* 30 May 2016.

4 *Alfred Flatow*: International Jewish Sports Hall of Fame, <http://www.jewishsports.net/BioPages/AlfredFlatow.htm

>, accessed 15 May 2020.

5 *Gustav Flatow*: International Jewish Sports Hall of Fame, http://www.jewishsports.net/BioPages/GustavFlatow.htm, accessed 15 May 2020.

6 P. Taylor, *Jews and the Olympic Games* (Brighton and Portland: Sussex Academic Press, 2004), p. 108.

7 P. Y. Mayer, *Jews and the Olympic Games* (London and Portland:Vallentine Mitchell, 2004) p.238.

8 P. Y. Mayer, *Jews and the Olympic Games* (London and Portland:Vallentine Mitchell, 2004) p.129.

9 *Pearl Perkins Nightingale*: Philadelphia Jewish Sports Hall of Fame, <http://phillyjewishsports.org/2014/03/pearl-perkins-nightingale/>, accessed 4 July 2020.

10 S. Kordova, 'Not Always a Soft Landing', *Haaretz-Israel News*, 4 July 2005, <https://www.haaretz.com/1.4917831>.

11 P. Taylor, *Jews and the Olympic Games* (Brighton and Portland: Sussex Academic Press, 2004) pp. 195-197.

12 B. Postal J.Silver and R. Silver, *Encyclopedia of Jews in Sports,* (New York: Bloch Publishing Company, 1965), p 299.

13 *Agnes Kéleti (Klein)*: International Jewish Sports Hall of Fame, <http://www.jewishsports.net/BioPages/AgnesKéleti(Klein).htm>, accessed 4 July 2020.

14 Craig Harkins: *Aladar Gerevich Named 6th Greatest Olympian Ever*: (8 March 2016), <https://www.fencing.net/15654/aladar-gerevich-olympian/>, accessed 4 July 2020.

15 *Maria Gorokhovskaya (1921-)*: Jewish Virtual Library, <https://www.jewishvirtuallibrary.org/maria-gorokhovskaya>, accessed 4 July 2020.

16 *Maria Gorokhovskaya*: International Jewish Sports Hall of Fame, <http://www.jewishsports.net/BioPages/MariaGorokhovskaya.htm>, accessed 4 July 2020.

17 *Galina Urbanovich*: International Jewish Sports Hall of Fame, <http://www.jewishsports.net/BioPages/Galina-Urbanovich.htm>, accessed 4 July 2020.

18 *Yelena Shushunova*: International Jewish Sports Hall of Fame, <http://www.jewishsports.net/BioPages/YelenaShushunova.htm>, accessed 12 April 2020.

19 *Valentina and Mitch Gaylord*: Mitchel Gaylord Biography, <https://www.imdb.com/name/nm0310942/bio>,

accessed 4 July 2020.

20 *Aly Raisman*: Biography, 16 January 2020, <https://www.biography.com/athlete/aly-raisman>, accessed 12 April 2020.

21 *Raisman earns two medals at 2012 Olympics: Team USA's first ever gold medal on floor, bronze medal on beam*, USA Gymnastics, 8 July 2012, <https://usagym.org/pages/post.html?PostID=10574&prog=e>, accessed 4 July 2020.

22 D. Diamond, 'Formidable, Fierce and Feminine The Aly Raisman Story', Soul Sport, December 2018.

23 Nancy Armour: *'US gymnastics hopeful's steady work impresses Karolyi'*: The Christian Science Monitor, Associated Press, 12 June 2012, <https://www.csmonitor.com/World/Olympics/Latest-News-Wires/2012/0612/US- gymnastics-hopeful-s-steady-work-impresses-Karolyi>.

24 Lanford Beard: *Olympics: 20 Unforgettable Moments: Entertainment*: (27 July 2012, <https://ew.com/gallery/olympics-20-unforgettable-tv-moments/?slide=379285#379285>, accessed 4 July 2020.

25 *Phoebe Mills (USA)*: Internet Archive WaybackMachine, <http://www.intlgymnast.com/cuw/mills.html>, accessed 12 April 2020.

26 Nick Zaccardi: *'U.S. Olympic gymnast to be snowboarding judge at Sochi Olympics'*: (31 October 2013), NBC Sports, <https://olympics.nbcsports.com/2013/10/31/phoebe-mills- olympic-snowboarding-judge-gymnastics/>, accessed 5 July 2020.

Chapter Four

FENCING

1 Shirley Povich, Berlin 1936: At the Olympics, Achievements of the Brave in a Year of Cowardice, *Washingtonpost.com,* 6 July 1996.

2 R. Cohen, *By the Sword*, (New York: Random House, 2002), p.xxii.

3 R. Rockaway: *When Jews Ruled the Fencing World*: (29 January 2019), <https://www.tabletmag.com/sections/news/articles/when-jews-ruled-the-fencing-world>, accessed 6 July 2020.

4 Les Carpenter, Nazi Germany's Jewish Champion; the mystery of Helene Mayer endures, *The Guardian*, 28 July 2016.

5 R. Cohen, *By the Sword*, (New York: Random House 2002), p.359.

6 R. Rockaway: *When Jews Ruled the Fencing World*: (29

January 2019), <https://www.tabletmag.com/sections/news/articles/when-jews-ruled-the-fencing-world>, accessed 6 July 2020.

7 P. Taylor, *Jews and the Olympic Games,* (Brighton and Portland: Sussex Academic Press, 2004), p.35.

8 *Ilona Elek*: Jewish Women's Archives, <https://jwa.org/people/elek-ilona>, accessed 23 April 2020.

9 *Preis, Ellen (1912-)*: Encyclopedia.com, <https://www.encyclopedia.com/women/dictionaries-thesauruses-pictures-and-press- releases/preis-ellen-1912>, accessed 6 July 2020.

10 P. Taylor, *Jews and the Olympic Games*, (Brighton and Portland: Sussex Academic Press (2004), p.33.

11 M. Gilbert, *Letters To Aunty Fori*, (London: Phoenix (2003), p.234.

12 *Famous Hungarian Jewish Athletes*: European Maccabi Games, <https://emg2019.com/famous-hungarian-jewish-athletes>, accessed 23 April 2020.

13 P. Taylor, *Jews and the Olympic Games*, (Brighton and Portland: Sussex Academic Press (2004), pp.23, 32-33.

14 M. Gilbert, *Letters To Aunty Fori*, (London: Phoenix (2003), p.234.

15 *George Worth*: SR/OLYMPIC SPORTS: <https://www.sports- reference.com/olympics.html>, accessed 23 April 2020.

16 Kristallnacht (Night of Broken Glass) refers to the nights of 9-10 November 1938. On these nights, Nazis in Germany, torched synagogues, vandalized Jewish homes, schools and businesses and killed almost 100 Jews. History.com/topics/holocaust/ Kristallnacht.

17 Halberstadt Fencers' Club, Mission Statement, <https://www.halberstadtfc.com/coachbios- all>, accessed 23 April 2020.

18 National Post Staff, The man with the iron heart: Grave of leading Nazi Reinhard Heydrich dug up in Berlin, *National Post*, 16 December 2019.

19 R. Cohen, *By the Sword*, (New York: Random House, 2002), p.335.

20 George Eisen: *Olympic Moments*: (14 September 2000), <https://jewishjournal.com/culture/sports/3276/>, accessed 23 April 2020.

21 D. Wallechinsky and J. Loucky, *The Complete Book of the Olympics* (London, 2012), pp.997 and 676.

22 *Otto Herschmann*: International Jewish Sports Hall of Fame, <www.jewishsports.net/BioPages/OttoHerschmann.htm>,

accessed 23 April 2020.

23 P.Y. Mayer, *Jews and the Olympic Games*, (London and Portland: Vallentine Mitchell, 2004), p.129.

24 Louisville Athlete Wins Athlete of Year, Hoosier State Chronicles, Jewish Post, Indianapolis Marion County, 29 October 1948.

25 *Wolff, Albert*: Museum of American Fencing, <http://museumofamericanfencing.com/wp/wolff-albert-2/>, accessed 24 April 2020.

26 B.Postal J.Silver and R. Silver, *Encyclopedia of Jews in sports,* (New York: Bloch Publishing Company, 1965), p 201.

27 Glosniak, Quinn, "The 1936 Nazi Olympic Games; The First Truly Modern Olympiad" (2017), Claremont Colleges Library,

<https://scholarship.claremont.edu/cmc_theses/1707/>, accessed 6 July 2020.

28 P. Taylor, *Jews and the Olympic Games*, (Brighton and Portland: Sussex Academic Press (2004), p.249.

29 Roy Tomizawa: *The Incredible Fencer Ujlaky-rejto Ildiko: The Deaf Olympic Champion*: (26 January 2016), The Olympians,
<https://theolympians.co/2016/01/26/the-incredible-

fencer-ujlaky-rejto-ildiko-the-deaf-olympic-champion/>, accessed 6 July 2020.

30 Adam Julian: *Seattle's Derrick Coleman: another great deaf sportsperson*: (2 February 2014), <https://www.theroar.com.au/2014/02/03/seattles-derrick-coleman-another-of-the-great-deaf-sportspeople/>, accessed 6 July 2020.

31 *Edgar Seligman*: JM Jewish Lives Project, <https://www.jewishlivesproject.com/profiles/edgar-seligman>, accessed 6 July 2020.

32 W. Rubenstein, Herbert Seligman: *The Palgrove Dictionary of Anglo-Jewish History*, United Kingdom: Palgrave Macmillan, (2011).

33 *David Tyshler*: International Jewish Hall of Fame, <http://www.jewishsports.net/BioPages/David-Tyshler>, accessed 6 July 2020.

34 J. Siegman, Jewish Sports Legends (Washington and London: Brassey's Inc. 1997), p.73.

35 *Eduard Teodorovich Vinokurov*: Prabook, <https://prabook.com/web/eduard.vinokurov/1035903>, accessed 6 July 2020.

36 Lev Krichevsky: *Russian Jewish Olympic presence dwindles*: (25 July 2004), <https://www.jta.org/2004/07/25/lifestyle/russian-jewish-

olympic-presence-dwindles>, accessed 25 April 2020.

37 Lev Krichevsky: *Russian Jewish Olympic presence dwindles*: (25 July 2004), <https://www.jta.org/2004/07/25/lifestyle/russian-jewish-olympic-presence-dwindles>, accessed 25 April 2020.

38 *Ukraine's new Cabinet Minister: Minister of Youth and Sports Vadym Gutzeit*, <https://112.international/ukraine-top-news/ukraines-new-cabinet-minister-of-youth-and-sports-vadym-gutzeit-49194.html>, accessed 25 April 2020.

39 *Mark Midler*: SR/OLYMPICSPORTS: <https://www.sports-reference.com/olympics/athletes/mi/mark-midler-1.html>, accessed 25 April 2020.

40 Olympic fencing champion Sergei Sharikov dies in car crash, USA TODAY, *Moscow (AP),* 8 June 2015 <https://www.usatoday.com/story/sports/olympics/2015/06/08/olympic- fencing-champion-sergei-sharikov-dies-in-car-crash/28675603/>.

41 Harald D. Goldsmith, 73, Was Executive, Athlete, *The Vineyard Gazette*, Obituary, 19 July 2004.

42 R. Cohen, Albert Axelrod, *The Independent*, 9 March 2004.

43 *Armitage, Norman C*: Museum of American Fencing,

<http://museumofamericanfencing.com/wp/armitage-norman-c/>, accessed 6 July 2020.

44 *Tim Morehouse*: Jewish Virtual Library, <https://www.jewishvirtuallibrary.org/tim- morehouse> accessed 26 April 2020.

45 *Jay, Allan Louis Neville*: Jewish Virtual Library, <https://www.jewishvirtuallibrary.org/jay-allan-louis-neville>, accessed 26 April 2020.

46 Jeff Wallenfeldt: *James Wolfensohn*: Encyclopedia Britannica: <https://www.britannica.com/biography/James-Wolfensohn>, accessed 6 July 2020.

BOXING

47 Mark Gould, Boxing pioneer remembered at last, *The Guardian*, 3 September 2008.

48 Allen Bodner: *When Boxing Was a Jewish Sport*: My Jewish Learning, <https://www.myjewishlearning.com/article/boxing-a-jewish-sport/>, accessed 30 April 2020.

49 Abe Attell, featherweight; Monte Attell, Bantamweight; Max Baer, Heavyweight; Benny Bass, featherweight; Fabine Benichou, Super bantamweight; Jack Kid Berg, junior welterweight; Jack Bernstein, Junior lightweight; Mushy Callahan, light welterweight; Robert

Cohen, bantamweight; Carolina Duer, Super flyweight and bantamweight; John 'Jackie' Fields, welterweight; Hagar Finer, WIBF Bantamweight; Yuri Foreman, super welterweight; Abe Goldstein, bantamweight; Roman Greenberg, IBO's Intercontinental heavyweight Champion; Alphonse Halimi, bantamweight; Harry Harris, bantamweight; Ben Jeby, middleweight, Solly Krieger, middleweight; Benny Leonard, lightweight; Battling Levinsky, light heavyweight; Harry Lewis, welterweight; Ted "Kid" Lewis, welterweight; Al McKoy, middleweight; Daniel Mendoza, heavyweight; Bob Olin, Light heavyweight; Victor Perez, flyweight; Charlie Phil Rosenberg, bantamweight; Dana Rosenblatt, middleweight; Maxie Rosenbloom, Light Heavyweight; Barney Ross, lightweight and junior lightweight; Mike Rossman, light heavyweight; Isadore Schwartz, flyweight; Al Singer, lightweight; Matt Wells, welterweight.

50 Dean Berks: *Max Baer, Clown Prince Who Could Have Been Heavyweight Royalty*, TOPCLASSBOXING, <https://topclassboxing.co.uk/historic/max-baer-clown-prince-who-could-have-been-heavyweight-royalty/>, accessed 30 April 2020.

51 *Max Baer*: International Boxing Hall Of Fame, <http://www.ibhof.com/pages/about/inductees/oldtimer/baer.html>, accessed 30 April 2020.

52 Jess Waid: *Max Baer*: (June 2015), <https://jesswaid.com/2015/06/>, accessed 7 July 2020.

53 Louis Bulow: *Max Schmeling*: Remember, <http://www.auschwitz.dk/schmeling.htm>, accessed 7 July 2.

54 *Eric Seelig*: New Jersey Boxing Hall of Fame, <http://www.njboxinghof.org/eric-seelig/>, accessed 30 April 2020.

55 Judische-sportstars, Between Success and Persecution, Exhibition at the Havenplatz in Bremenhaven, 16 October to 10 November 2019, <http://juedische-sportstars.de/index.php?id=170&L=2>, accessed 7 July 2020.

56 *Sammy Luftsprng*: Jewish Virtual Library, <https://www.jewishvirtuallibrary.org/luftspring-sammy>, accessed 2 May 2020.

57 Tom Hawthorn, The Canadian Boxers Who Thumbed Their Noses at Nazis, *The Tyee,* 26 July 2016.

58 *Sammy Luftspring*: Ontario Sports Hall of Fame, <https://www.oshof.ca/index.php/component/k2/item/90-sammy-luftspring>, accessed 2 May 2020.

59 Jack Milner, Jewish Boxers Supported 'People's Olympics', *South African Jewish Report*, 27 July 2016.

60 Kay Schaffer and Sidonie Smith, *The Olympics at the Millennium: Power, Politics and the Games*, (Rutgers University Press, 2000), p.104.

61 Anthony Hughes, Harry Cohen, Australian Jewry and the 1946 Berlin Olympics, Bridging three centuries, Fifth International Symposium for Olympic Research, pp. 215, 217.

62 *Imre Mandi*: SR/OLYMPIC SPORTS, <https://www.sports- reference.com/olympics.html>, accessed 23 April 2020.

63 Kay Schaffer and Sidonie Smith, *The Olympics at the Millennium: Power, Politics and the Games*, (Rutgers University Press, 2000), p.61.

64 *Heinz Levy*: Joods Monument: (1 March 2006), <https://www.joodsmonument.nl/en/page/227063/heinz-levy>, accessed 7 July 2020.

65 Jarrett Zook: *Tunisia's Finest: Victor Perez*: (26 November 2015), <http://www.boxing.com/tunisias_finest_victor_perez.html>, accessed 7 July 2020.

66 *Bril, Barend "Ben"*: World War II Graves, WW2 Gravestones, <https://ww2gravestone.com/people/bril-barend-ben/>, accessed 7 July 2020.

67 Ben Bril: BoxRec: Boxing's Official Record Keeper, <https://boxrec.com/en/referee/404029>, accessed 7 July 2020.

68 Mike Silver, Stars in the Ring: Jewish Champions in

the Golden Age of Boxing, (Rowman and Littlefield, 2016), p.99.

69 Matt Schudel, Salamo Arouch; boxer fought for his life at Auschwitz camp, *The San Diego Union-Tribune*, 3 May 2009.

70 Jacko Razon: Jewish Virtual Library, <https://www.jewishvirtuallibrary.org/razon-jacko>, accessed 3 May 2020.

71 Allon Sinai, Sinai Says: The lost legacy of slain Jewish-Italian boxer Leone Efrati, *Jerusalem Post*, 29 April 2017.

72 Robert Mladinich, Harry Haft, Auschwitz, and Rocky Marciano, *The Sweet Science,* 30 May 2006, <https://tss.ib.tv/boxing/boxing-articles-and-news-2006-videos-results-rankings- and-history/3855-harry-haft-auschwitz-and-rocky-marciano>

73 J. Bennett: *The Unspeakably Brutal Life of Harry Haft*: OZY (25 February 2020), <https://www.ozy.com/true-and-stories/the-unspeakably-brutal-life-of-harry-haft/274723/>, accessed 7 July 2020.

74 Ahron Bregman, Review: The Boxer's Story, *The Jewish Chronicle,* 9 November 2019.

75 Karen Price: *Boxer Joe Salas Won A Silver Medal, Blazed A Path For Latinos*: (26 September 2016), TeamUSA,

<https://www.teamusa.org/News/2016/September/26/Boxer- Joe-Salas-Won-A-Silver-Medal-Blazed-A-Path-For-Team-USA-Latinos>, accessed 7 July 2020.

76 Karen Price: *Boxer Joe Salas Won A Silver Medal, Blazed A Path For Latinos*: (26 September 2016), TeamUSA, <https://www.teamusa.org/News/2016/September/26/Boxer- Joe-Salas-Won-A-Silver-Medal-Blazed-A-Path-For-Team-USA-Latinos>, accessed 7 July 2020.

77 B.Postal J.Silver and R. Silver, *Encyclopedia of Jews in sports,* (New York: Bloch Publishing Company, 1965), p 460.

WRESTLING

78 *Fred Oberlander*: International Jewish Hall of fame, <http://www.jewishsports.net/BioPages/FredOberlander.htm>, 7 July 2020.

79 *Philip Oberlander*: <https://www.olympic.org/philip-oberlander>, accessed 7 July 2020.

80 Milt Sherman, Wrestling Greats-Nicholas 'Micky' Hirschl, *Wrestling USA Magazine*, (1 October 1985).

81 Paul Taylor, *Jews and the Olympic Games*, (Brighton and Portland: Sussex Academic Press (2004), p. 250.

82 Adam Ross: *The Gold Winning Jewish Wrestler Of The*

Nazi Games, (1 December 2018), The Jewish Website-aish.com, <https://www.aish.com/jw/s/The-Gold-Winning-Jewish- Wrestler-of-the-Nazi-Games.html>.

83 Arkady Boganov: *Through the concentration camp-to the Olympic gold*: (14 January 2012), Forum daily, <https://www.forumdaily.com/en/cherez-konclager-k-olimpijskomu- zolotu/>, accessed 4 May 2020.

84 B. Mallon, I. Buchanan, *The 1908 Olympic Games* (Jefferson, North Carolina and London, 2009), p.470.

85 P.Y.Mayer, *Jews And The Olympic Games*, (London and Portland, Vallentine Mitchell 2004), p. 129.

86 Uwe Lohalm: *The Jews in the Army—On the Origins and Pervasiveness of a Prejudice*: (22 September 2016), <https://jewish-history-online.net/article/lohalm-roth-jewish-census>, accessed 8 July 2020.

87 *World War 1-Jewish soldiers of the German Army*: IDF & Defense Establishment Archives, <http://www.archives.mod.gov.il/sites/English/Exhibitions/The_Jewish_Combatant_Collecti on/Pages/Jewish-soldiers-if-the-German-Army.aspx>, accessed 8 July 2020.

88 P.Y.Mayer, *Jews And The Olympic Games*, (London and Portland, Vallentine Mitchell 2004), pp. 54-55 and 124.

89 Richard Goldstein, 'Henry Wittenberg, Champion

Wrestler, Dies at 91', *New York Times*, 9 March 2010.

90 *Draw Paint Sculpt*: London atelier of representational art, <https://www.drawpaintsculpt.com/artist-biographies/rabin-sam>, accessed 21 April 2019.

91 Tom Morgan: *The Goldsmiths art teacher who won Olympic bronze*: (12 August 2016), Goldsmiths University of London, , <https://www.gold.ac.uk/news/samuel-rabin/#:~:text=A%20Goldsmiths%20art%20teacher%20who,Rabin%20is%20second%20fro m%20right.>, accessed 8 July 2020.

92 *Samuel Norton Gerson*: Penn University Archives and Records Center. <https://archives.upenn.edu/exhibits/penn-people/biography/samuel-norton-gerson>, accessed 5 May 2020.

JUDO

93 Yael Arad-Silver Medal-Barcelona 1992, <https://www.olympicsil.co.il/yael-arad/?lang=en>, accessed 5 May 2020.

94 Patrick Goodenough: *'Gut Infection' Denies Iranian Chance to Compete in Olympics Against Israeli*: (26 July 2012), CNS News, <https://cnsnews.com/news/article/gut-infection- denies-iranian-chance-compete-olympics-against-israeli>, accessed 30 December 2019.

95 Iranian forfeits judo match with Israeli, *The Sydney Morning Herald*, 16 August 2004.

96 Iran under scrutiny for political pull-out, *The Guardian*, 15 August 2014.

97 TOI staff, Israel's judo bronze medalist says he shrugged off Egyptian's snub, focused on winning, *The Times of Israel*, 13 August 2016.

98 Judo World Champ Finally Shares Secret of Her Infamous Choke, BJJEE, 31 January 2020.

99 Uri Talshir, Israeli Judo Champ Yarden Gerbi Announces Retirement, *Haaretz,* 3 October 2017.

Chapter Five

1 Shirley Povich, Berlin 1936: At the Olympics, Achievements of the Brave in a Year of Cowardice, *Washingtonpost.com,* 6 July 1996.

2 B.Postal, J. and R. Silver, *Encyclopedia of Jews in Sport,* (New York, Bloch Publishing Company, 1965), p. 509.

3 G. Eisen: Jewish Olympic Medalists, International Jewish Sports Hall of Fame, accessed 18 April 2020.

4 D. Wallechinsky and J. Loucky, *The Complete Book of The Olympics* (London: Aurum Press Ltd. 2012), p.1205.

5 P.Y.Mayer, *Jews And The Olympic Games*, (London and

Portland, Vallentine Mitchell 2004), pp. 54-55 and 124.

6 Michael Freedland, "I had to get on with living": How Ben Helfgott went from a concentration camp to Olympic weightlifting'. *The Guardian*, 8 May 2018.

7 Concentration camp survivor awarded knighthood for services to Holocaust *Remembrance and Education*: University of Southampton: (13 June 2018), <https://www.southampton.ac.uk/news/2018/06/ben-helfgott-kbe.page>, accessed 8 July2020.

8 Pesach Benson, *The Munich Massacre: The 1972 Slaughter of Israeli Athletes on German Soil,* (14 July 2019), Honest Reporting, <https://honestreporting.com/munich-massacre-1972- slaughter-israeli-athletes-german-soil/>, accessed 8 July 2020.

9 Pesach Benson, *The Munich Massacre: The 1972 Slaughter of Israeli Athletes on German Soil,* (14 July 2019), Honest Reporting, <https://honestreporting.com/munich-massacre- 1972-slaughter-israeli-athletes-german-soil/>, accessed 8 July 2020.

10 Liat Collins, Munich 11 athlete to be inducted into Sports Hall of Fame, *The Jerusalem Post*, 9 April 2013.

11 David Berger: National Park Service, <https://www.nps.gov/dabe/index.htm>, accessed 20/4/2020.

12 Phil Rossi, *Lifting Gold: "The World's Strongest Man'*, (19 March 2018), ART + marketing, <https://art+marketing.com/lifting-gold-the-worlds-strongest-man- 4a8f3ddbca44>, accessed 20 April 2020.

13 HickokSports.com-Biography-Isaac Berger, accessed 20 October 2019.

14 Isaac "Ike" Berger: International Jewish Sports Hall of Fame, <http://www.jewishsports.net/BioPages/IsaacBerger.htm>, accessed 20 October 2020.

15 One of the Strongest Jews in Olympic History is Selling His Gold Medal, *Haaretz*, 24 October 2017. <https://www.haaretz.com/jewish/one-of-the-strongest-jews-in-olympic- history-is-selling-his-gold-medal-1.5459962>.

16 Phil Rossi, *Lifting Gold: "The World's Strongest Man'*, (19 March 2018), ART + marketing, <https://art+marketing.com/lifting-gold-the-worlds-strongest-man- 4a8f3ddbca44>, accessed 20 April 2020.

17 Grigory Novak, SR/OLYMPIC SPORTS, <www.sports- reference.com.olympics/athletes/no/grigory-novak>, accessed 20April 2020.

18 B.Postal, J. and R. Silver, *Encyclopedia of Jews in Sport,* (New York, Bloch Publishing Company, 1965), p.510.

19 For 1948 Olympian, gold medal dream started in York, *York Daily Record,* 4 August 2012.

20 J. Siegman, *Jewish Sports Legends,* (Brassey's Washington, London 2nd Edition, 1977) p.163.

21 D. Wallechinsky and J. Loucky, *The Complete Book Of The Olympics* (London: Aurum Press Ltd. 2012), p.1231.

22 A. Goldman, Gary Gubner's Claim to be the Strongest Man in the World, *Stars Of David*, (Johannesburg: Electric Printing Works) pp. 134-135.

Chapter Six

ROWING

1 B.Postal, J. and R. Silver, *Encyclopedia of Jews in Sport,* (New York, Bloch Publishing Company, 1965), p. 405.

2 D. J. Brown, *The Boys In The Boat*, (London: Pan Books, 2013)

3 Stephen Sadis: *Washington's Jewish Sports Heroes: Bob Moch (1914-2005)*: (29 July 2014),HistoryLink.org. Accessed 31 March 2019, <https://www.historylink.org/File/10906>.

4 Nicola Pugh: *Scales tip against boat race favourites*, (20 March 2000), BBC NEWS, <http://news.bbc.co.uk/2/hi/sport/684197.stm>, accessed

10 July 2020.

5 Graham Morrison, Tall Story of British Olympic rowing hopeful, *The Jewish Chronicle,* 8 August 2008.

6 Forward Staff: *Jewish Athletes Reach for the Gold*: (31 July 2008), Forward, <https://forward.com/articles/13880/it-s-what-you-always-dream-about-as-a-kid-02273/>, accessed 9 July 2020.

7 Earth.usc.edu/~joshwest/website

8 Marcus Dysch, Oxford's new Boat Race cox, Zoe, *The Jewish Chronicle*, 22 March 2012.

9 New Zealand Jewish rower Nathan Cohen wins Olympic gold, *The Times of Israel*, 5 August 2012.

10 Andrew Alderson, Rowing: Retiring Sullivan fired up about his new job, *NZ Herald,* 5 June 2014.

11 *New Zealand sports awards puts rowing on a pedestal*: worldrowing: (15 February 2013), <http://www.worldrowing.com/news/new-zealand-sports-awards-puts-rowing-on-a- pedestal>, accessed 10 July 2020.

12 Nathan Cohen MNZM: <https://gg.govt.nz/images/nathan-cohen-mnzm>, accessed 7 May 2020.

13 Rowing champion Nathan Cohen on peculiar international honour: 'It's news to me': (17 December 2018): Stuff, https://www.stuff.co.nz/sport/other-sports/109411566/rowing- champion-nathan-cohen-on-peculiar-international-honour-its-news-to-me.

SAILING

14 Jews in the American Military, NMAJMH's Core Exhibit, <https://nmajmh.org/exhibitions/permanent-exhibitions/681-2/>, accessed 7 May 2020.

15 Michael Rugel: *Robert Halperin on D-Day*: (6 June 2017), National Museum of American Jewish History, <https://nmajmh.org/2017/06/robert-halperin-on-d-day/>, accessed 11 July 2020.

16 Kenan Heise, Robert Halperin, 77, War Hero, Executive, *Chicago Tribune*, 9 May 1985.

17 Michael Rugel: *Robert Halperin on D-Day*: (6 June 2017), National Museum of American Jewish History, <https://nmajmh.org/2017/06/robert-halperin-on-d-day/>, accessed 11 July 2020.

18 Kenan Heise, Robert Halperin, 77, War Hero, Executive, *Chicago Tribune*, 9 May 1985.

19 June Sandra Neal, Accuracy Gap of Olympic Proportions, *Hartford Courant*, 5 March 2006.

20 *Obituary: Valentin Mankin*: World Sailing: (3 June 2014), <https://www.sailing.org/news/18081.php#.Xwed7CgzaUk>, accessed 7 May 2020.

21 Keren Cook: *New Zealand sailor Jo Aleh inducted into Jewish Sport Hall of Fame*: (2 January 2017), J-Wire, <https://www.jwire.com.au/new-zealand-sailor-jo-aleh-inducted-into-jewish-sport-hall-of-fame/>, accessed 11 July 2020.

22 *New Year Honours List 2013*: Department of the Prime Minister and Cabinet (DPMC), (31 December 2012), <https://dpmc.govt.nz/publications/new-year-honours-list-2013>, accessed 7 May 2020.

PADDLING

23 Aaron Kalman, Surfing almost killed her. Now Lee Korzits hopes it will bring gold, *The Times of Israel*, 5 August 2012.

24 *Jess Fox becomes most awarded athlete at World Paddle Awards 2014-2018,* (23 March 2019), Paddle Australia, <https://paddle.org.au/2019/03/25/jessica-fox-becomes-the-most- awarded-athlete-at-the-world-paddle-awards-2014-2018/>, accessed 11 July 2020.

25 Dan Goldberg, Jewish Aussie 'Flying Fox' Wins Olympic Silver, *Haaretz*, 6 August 2012, <https://www.haaretz.com/jewish/aussie-flying-fox-wns-

olympic-silver-1.5277729>, accessed 25/February 2019.

Chapter Seven

1 A. Handler, *From The Ghetto To The Games Jewish Athletes In Hungary*, (New York, Columbia University Press, 1985) p.117.

2 P. Taylor, *Jews and the Olympic Games* (Brighton and Portland: Sussex Academic Press, 2004) p.143.

3 Wallechinsky and J. Loucky, *The Complete Book Of The Olympics* (London: Aurum Press Ltd., 2012), p.1180.

4 P. Taylor, *Jews and the Olympic Games* (Brighton and Portland: Sussex Academic Press, 2004) p.146.

5 P. Taylor, *Jews and the Olympic Games* (Brighton and Portland: Sussex Academic Press, 2004) p.95-96.

6 J. Siegman, *Jewish Sports Legends,* (Washington and London: Brassey's, 2nd Edition, 1977) p.160.

7 Gyorgy Brody, SR/OLYMPIC SPORTS, <https://www.sports-reference.com/olympics.html>, accessed 29 April 2020.

8 *Gerard Blitz (BEL),* International Swimming Hall of Fame, <https://ishof.org/gerard- blitz.html>, accessed 29 April 2020.

9 Joe Eskanazi, A Jew, a Czech, an officer and an Olympian &mdash no joke, *The Jewish News of Northern California*, 24 March 2006.

10 P. Y. Mayer, *Jews and the Olympic Games* (London and Portland: Vallentine Mitchell, 2004) p.104.

11 Kay Schaffer and Sidonie Smith, *The Olympics at the Millennium: Power, Politics and the Games*, (Rutgers University Press, 2000), p.57.

12 Gabe Friedman, 2016 Olympics: 7 Jewish American Olympians to watch in Rio, *Jewish Telegraphic Agency*, 31 July 2016.

Chapter Eight

1 A sporting rarity-The [UK] Jewish Chronicle, 7 January 2016.

2 D. Bolchover, *The Greatest Comeback,* (Great Britain: Biteback Publishing Ltd, 2017).

3 D. Bolchover, *The Greatest Comeback,* (Great Britain: Biteback Publishing Ltd, 2017) p98.

4 D. Bolchover, *The Greatest Comeback,* (Great Britain: Biteback Publishing Ltd, 2017) Introduction pp. xiii-xiv.

5 A. Philpott, 'Hakoah Wien: Football's Forgotten Pioneers', IBWM 18 July 2014, p.2.

6 David Bolchover, *The Greatest Comeback,* (Great Britain:Biteback Publishing Ltd, 2017) p33.

7 C. Heffernan, 'Football, Foreskins & the Fuhrer:Hakoah Wien', *Pundit Arena*, 20 October 2014, pp.3-4.

8 A. Philpott: '*Hakoah Wien: Football's Forgotten Pioneers'*, (18 July 2014), IBWM, p5, <http://inbedwithmaradona.com/journal/2014/7/17/hakoah-wien-footballs-forgotten- pioneers>, accessed 11 July2020.

9 D. Bolchover, *The Greatest Comeback,* (Great Britain: Biteback Publishing Ltd, 2017) p254.

10 David Bolchover, 'Remembering the cream of Jewish footballing talent killed in the Holocaust', *The Guardian*, 6 May 2019 pp.2-3.

11 L. Peiffer, Gottfried Fuchs, Between Success and Persecution, Exhibition at the Havenplatz in Bremerhaven, 16 October-10 November 2019.

12 B. Blickenststaff*: War, Auschwitz, and the Tragic Tale of Germany's Jewish Soccer Hero*: (13 April 2015), Vice, <https://www.vice.com/en_us/article/78yyz9/war-auschwitz-and-the-tragic-tale-of-germanys-jewish-soccer-hero>, accessed 11 July 2020.

13 David Bolchover, 'Remembering the cream of Jewish

footballing talent killed in the Holocaust', *The Guardian*, 6 May 2019 pp.2.

14 M. McKnight, Remember The Ringleader, *Sports Illustrated*, 12 February, 2019.

15 J.J. O'Connor and E.F. Robertson, Harald August Bohr, MT MacTutor, <https://mathshistory.st-andrews.ac.uk/Biographies/Bohr_Harald/>, accessed 14 April 2020.

16 World War II Danish Resistance: Kaj Munk (1898-1944): Children in History: (1 March 2018), <https://www.histclo.com/essay/war/ww2/cou/den/bio/w2db-munk.html>, accessed 14 April 2020.

17 Dr. Keith Huxen: *The Mysterious Meeting between Niels Bohr and Werner Heisenberg*: (15 September 2011): The National WWII Museum New Orleans, http://www.nww2m.com/2011/09/the-mysterious-meeting-between-niels-bohr-and-werner- heisenberg/, accessed 11 May 2020.

18 Finn Aaseraad, Niels Bohr, *Encyclopaedia Britannica*, (Encyclopaedia Britannica Inc., 14 November 2019), accessed 20 July 2020.

19 Zachary Solomon: *Niels Bohr, The Righteous Physicist*, (*12* August 2013), <https://www.jta.org/jewniverse/2013/neils-bohr-the-righteous-physicist>, accessed 14 April 2020.

20 Niels Bohr: Encyclopedia Britannica: (14 November 2019), <https://www.britannica.com/print/article/71670.>, accessed 14 April 2020.

21 The Nobel Prize: Niels Bohr Institute: (, 18 July 2012), <https://www.nbi.ku.dk/english/www/niels/bohr/nobelprisen>, accessed 10 July 2020.

22 Sara Whalen: People Pill: <https://peoplepill.com/people/sara-whalen/>, accessed 10 July 2020.

23 Sarah Ebner, Beckham shows united front as he reveals: 'I do see myself as Jewish', *Jewish Chronicle,* 16 June 2016.

Chapter Nine

1 B.Postal, J. and R. Silver, *Encyclopedia of Jews in Sport,* (New York, Bloch Publishing Company, 1965), pp. 439-440.

2 *Viktor Barna*: International Jewish Sports Hall of Fame, <http://www.jewishsports.net/BioPages/ViktorGyozoBarna.htm>, accessed 26 April 2020.

3 R. Slater, *Great Jews In Sports*, (New York: Jonathan David publishers, 1983) p.29.

4 Victor Barna: Prabook: <https://prabook.com/web/victor.barna/1346354>, accessed 26 April 2020.

5 Laszlo Bellak: Table Tennis: Team USA: <https://www.teamusa.org/USA-Table-Tennis/History/Hall-of-Fame/Profiles/Laszlo-Bellak>, accessed 26 April 2020.

6 Laszlo Bellak Explained: Everything Explained. Today: <http://everything.explained.today/Laszlo_Bellak/>, accessed 10 July 2020.

7 R. Slater, *Great Jews In Sports*, (New York: Jonathan David publishers, 1983) p.219-221.

8 They also serve, *The Observer,* 21 July 2002, accessed 25 April 2019.

9 Erwin Kohn: International Jewish Sports Hall of Fame, <http://www.jewishsports.net/BioPages/Erwin-Kohn>, accessed 26 April 2020.

10 *Richard Bergmann*: Encyclopedia.com: (29 July 2020), <https://www.encyclopedia.com/religion/encyclopedias-almanacs-transcripts-and- maps/bergmann-richard>, accessed 10 July 2020.

11 Pauline Dubkin Yearwood, 'Righting a wrong', *The Chicago Jewish News*, 8 March 2007.

12 Ruth Aarons: Table Tennis: Team USA: <https://www.teamusa.org/USA-Table-Tennis/History/Hall-of-Fame/Profiles/Ruth-Aarons>, accessed 10 July 2020.

13 Jacov Sobowitz: *Traute Kleinova*: *Jewish Women's Archive*, <https://jwa.org/encyclopedia/article/kleinova-traute>, accessed 27 April 2020.

14 Wieslaw Pieta, Aleksandra Pieta: Czech and Polish Table Tennis Players of Jewish Origin in International Competition (1926-1957), *Physical Culture And Sport Studies and Research*, 1 December 2011. <https://www.researchgate.net/publication/270257821_Czech_and_Polish_Table_Tennis_Players_of_Jewish_Origin_in_International_Competition_1926-1957>, accessed 10 July 2020.

15 Morris Kessler, The Greatest Sportsman You've Never Heard Of, *Esquire,* 8 August 2014.

16 Comedian Jonathan Katz on His Life with MS: Everyday Health, (27 March 2008), <www.everydayhealth.com/multiple-sclerosis/webcasts/comedian-jonathan-katz-on-his-life-with-ms.aspx>, accessed 10 July 2020.

17 Leah Thall-Neuberger ("Miss Ping"): International Jewish Sports Hall of Fame, <http://www.jewishsports.net/BioPages/LeahThall-

Neuberger>, accessed 26 April 2020.

18 Marilyn Hawkes, Table-tennis champ going strong at 89, *Jewish News*, 28 August 2013, <http://www.jewishaz.com/families_lifestyle/sports/table-tennis-champ-going-strong- at/article_6088fe98-0f6d-11e3-b3fa-0019bb30f31a.html>, accessed 10 July 2020.

Chapter Ten

1 P. Gallico, *Farewell to Sport*, (London: International Polygonics, 1990).

2 G. Demby: How Stereotypes Explain Everything And Nothing At All: NPR CODE SW!TCH, (8 April 2014).

3 D. M. Oshinsky, Polio: An American Story, (New York: Oxford University Press, 2005) pp. 96 and 98.

4 D. M. Oshinsky, Polio: An American Story, (New York: Oxford University Press, 2005) pp. 96 and 98.

5 G. Demby: How Stereotypes Explain Everything And Nothing At All: NPR CODE SW!TCH, (8 April 2014).

6 Art Heyman: Land of Basketball.com, <https://www.landofbasketball.com/nba_players/h/art_heyman.htm>, accessed 17 April 2020.

7 Amar'e Stoudemire: Land of Basketball.com, <https://www.landofbasketball.com/nba_players/s/amare_stoudemire.htm>, accessed 17 April 2020.

8 J. Siegman, *Jewish Sports Legends,* (Washington and London: Brassey's 2nd Edition, 1977) p.33.

9 Danny Schayes: Land of Basketball.com, <https://www.landofbasketball.com/nba_players/s/danny_schayes.htm>, accessed 17 April 2020.

10 Jordan Farmar; Land of Basketball.com, <https://www.landofbasketball.com/nba_players_stats/f/jordan_farmar.htm>, accessed 17 April 2020.

11 Omri Casspi: Land of Basketball.com, <https://www.landofbasketball.com/nba_players/c/omri_casspi.htm>, accessed 17 April 2020.

12 Rudy LaRusso, Land of Basketball.com, <https://www.landofbasketball.com/nba_players/l/rudy_larusso.htm>, accessed 17 April 2020.

13 Harry Boykoff, Land of Basketball.com, <https://www.landofbasketball.com/nba_players_stats/b/harry_boykoff.htm>, accessed 17 April 2020.

14 Neal Walk, Land of Basketball.com, <https://www.landofbasketball.com/nba_players/w/neal_walk.htm>, accessed 17 April 2020.

15 Ernie Grunfeld, Land of Basketball.com, <https://www.landofbasketball.com/nba_players_stats/g/ernie_grunfeld_tot.htm>, accessed 17 April 2020.

16 P.Y.Mayer, *Jews And The Olympic Games*, (London and Portland :Vallentine Mitchell, 2004), p.109.

17 C. Kahn: *My Jewish Grandpa's Triumph At Hitler's Olympics*: (8 August 2008), NPR, <https://www.npr.org/templates/story/story.php?storyId=93400660>, accessed 10 July 2020.

18 Sue Bird: USA basketball: (20 February 2020), <https://www.usab.com/suebird>, accessed 18 April 2020.

19 M. Voepel: *Storm's Sue Bird, 39, still eyeing Tokyo Olympics despite postponement*: (25 March 2020), <https://www.espn.com.au/olympics/basketball/story/_/id/28949831/storm-sue-bird-eyeing-tokyo-olympics-postponement>, accessed 10 July 2020.

20 Oral History Interview with Nancy Lieberman: Text: University of North Texas Libraries, UNT Digital Library: (8 Nov. 2012),

<https://digital.library.unt.edu/ark:/67531/metadc154712/citation/#top>, accessed 10 July 2020.

21 Nancy Lieberman: Big3: <https://big3.com/players/nancy-lieberman>, accessed 18 April 2020.

Chapter Eleven

1 Fiona Green, The king of ping.and prose! Howard

Jacobson on Jews and table tennis, *Jewish News*, 11 August 2016.

2 2020 World Population by Country: World Population Review: <https://worldpopulationreview.com/>, accessed 10 July 2020.

3 Chile: WJC: <https://www.worldjewishcongress.org/en/about/communities/CL>, accessed 10 July 2020.

4 S. Malinowski: *Nico Massu Remembers Making Tennis History in 2004*: (18 September 2017), TENNIS-PROSE.com, <http://www.tennis-prose.com/bios/nico-massu-remembers-making-tennis-history-in-2004/>, accessed 11 July 2020.

5 Leopoldo Iturra: *Massu; Spirit of a survivor (ATP World Tour-13 September 2012*: (13 September 2012), <http://nico-massu.over-blog.com/article-massu-spirit-of-a-survivor- 110063991.html>, accessed 22April 2020.

6 Chile-at the Olympics-facts and information, Olympian Database, <http://www.olympiandatabase.com/index.php?id=13356&L=1>, accessed 22 April 2020.

7 A. Lewin, Dr. Daniel Prenn: a tennis career cut short by Nazi Germany, *The Jewish Holocaust Centre's The Voice newsletter,* 14 October 2015.
<https://alewindotorg.wordpress.com/2015/10/14/dr-

daniel-prenn-a-tennis-career-cut-short- by-nazi-germany/>, accessed 10 July 2020.

8 Translated by Christian Eichler from the book 'Tennis in Deutschland. Von den Anfängen bis 2002. Zum100-jährigen Bestehen des Deutschen Tennis Bundes'. <https://www.tennisforum.com/threads/four-great-early-german-female-lawn-tennis- players.696890/>, accessed 22 April 2020.

9 'Nelly Nepach (geb. Bamberger)' Stolpersteine in Berlin. <https://www.stolpersteine- berlin.de/de/biografie/7539>, accessed 10 July 2020.

10 Frank Litsky, Ladislav Hecht, 94, a Tactician on the Tennis Courts in the 30's, *The New York Times*, 10 June 2004

11 Jon Henderson, Triumphing over prejudice, *The Guardian,* 8 July 2001.

12 Marissa Gottesman, Wimbledon champ recalls battling prejudice in 1950s, *Sun Sentinel,* January 28 2016.

13 Sally Jones, Angela Buxton and Althea Gibson's friendship was no ordinary bond, but their outsider statuses brought them together, *The Telegraph,* 20 June 2019.

14 TOI staff, Wimbledon champ says anti-Semitism led top UK club to snub her for decades, *Times of Israel,* 13 July 2019.

Chapter Twelve

1 Nathan Abrams, Hollywood's Stereotype of the Wimpy Jew Refuses to Die, *Jewish World, Haaretz-Israel News*, 24 July 2013.

2 John Slade (1908-2005): Jewish Virtual Library, <https://www.jewishvirtuallibrary.org/john-slade>, accessed 7 April 2019.

3 Carina Benninga: International Jewish Sports Hall of Fame, <http://www.jewishsports.net/BioPages/CarinaBenninga>, accessed 26 April 2020.

4 P. Y. Mayer, *Jews and the Olympic Games* (London and Portland: Vallentine Mitchell, 2004) p.180-181.

Chapter Thirteen

1 Jonathan Mark: *The Very Mysterious Moe Berg*: (28 May 2019): The New York Jewish Week, https://jewishweek.timesofisrael.com/the-very-mysterious-moe-berg/, accessed 25 July 2020.

2 Wiliam Tobey, 'Nuclear scientists as assassination targets', Bulletin of the Atomic Scientists, 1 January 2012, pp.63-64, https://journals.sagepub.com/doi/pdf/10.1177/0096340211433019, accessed 25 July 2020.

3 Manuel Roig-Franzia, The strange life and death of Moe Berg, the baseball catcher who became a spy, *The Washington Post*, 7 June 2019.

4 B. Levison, Rugby: An Anthology: The Brave, the Bruised and the Brilliant, (Robinson: London, 2015).

5 Bert Solomon (Redruth), Cornwall & England) Rugby Photograph: Sports Pages, <https://www.sportspages.com/product/bert_solomon_(redruth_cornwall_england)_29631>, accessed 8 May 2020.

6 Robert Kitson, Pride of Cornwall starting over, *The Guardian*, 9 November 2002.

7 B. Levison, Rugby: An Anthology: The Brave, the Bruised and the Brilliant, (Robinson: London, 2015).

8 P.Y.Mayer, *Jews And The Olympic Games*, (London and Portland, Vallentine Mitchell 2004), p.222.

Conclusion

1 David M. Bader, *Haikus for Jews*, New York: Harmony Books, 1999.

www.ingramcontent.com/pod-product-compliance
Lightning Source LLC
Chambersburg PA
CBHW051347290426
44108CB00015B/1917